Adventures of
MISSIONARY
HEROISM

Adventures of

MISSIONARY HEROISM

By John C. Lambert

*Edited by Joshua M. Wean
and Kevin Swanson*

First Master Books Printing: August 2017
Originally Published in 1912

Master Books® is a division of the New Leaf Publishing Group, Inc.

ISBN: 978-1-68344-080-2
ISBN: 978-1-61458-606-7 (digital)

Published in partnership with Generations
19039 Plaza Dr. Ste. 210
Parker, Colorado 80134
www.generations.org

Please consider requesting that a copy of this volume be purchased by your local library system.

Printed in the United States of America

Please visit our website for other great titles:
www.masterbooks.com

For information regarding author interviews,
please contact the publicity department at (870) 438-5288

CONTENTS

Foreword VII

Introduction. IX

Part I: Asia

1. In the Steppes and Deserts of Mongolia 3
2. In the Country of the Telugus 21
3. A Japanese Adventure 39
4. "From Far Formosa" 57
5. "The Savior of Liao-Yang" 75

Part II: Africa

6. "The Hero of Uganda" 93
7. The Lion-Hearted Bishop 111
8. Vortrekkers in Barotseland. 129
9. A Pioneer in Garenganze 141
10. A Tramp Through the Great Pygmy Forest. 159

Part III: America

11. Among the Indians and Eskimos of Hudson Bay 179
12. The "Praying Master" of the Redskins 195
13. In the Land of the Dakotas. 215
14. In the Forests of Guiana 231
15. The Sailor Missionary of Tierra del Fuego: Part I 247
16. The Schooner of Keppel Island: Part II 267

Part IV: South Pacific

17. The Martyr of Melanesia. 283
18. One of the Unreturning Brave 299
19. Among the Cannibal Islands 317
20. The Apostle of the New Hebrides 331
21. Kapiolani and the Goddess of the Volcano 349

LIST OF ILLUSTRATIONS

1. In a Mongol Encampment 15
2. Dr. Chamberlain Attacked by a Serpent 31
3. Attacked by a Spotted Tiger 35
4. Praying to Idols 43
5. Dr. Mackay and His Assistants as Dentists 63
6. Armed Head-Hunters in Formosa 71
11. A Visit From a Hippopotamus 118
12. Encounter with an Elephant and Rhinoceros 121
13. Hannington a Prisoner Shortly Before His Martyrdom ... 125
14. In the Footsteps of the Slave Traders 149
15. Arnot Defending His Food From Wild Beasts 153
16. A Visit From the Pygmies 170
17. Hunting Buffalo in Winter Time 204
18. Shoeing Dogs in Northern Canada 208
19. An Indian Hunting Buffalo on Horseback 226
20. A Titanic Combat 242
21. Types of Patagonian Women 257
22. A Native Cradle in Patagonia 257
23. Captain Gardiner in Peril 261
24. Bishop Patteson Defending Himself and
    His Men with a Rudder 295
25. A Native Village in New Guinea 307
26. A Critical Moment 311
27. New Guinea Lakatois Preparing to Sail 315
28. Dr. Paton's Life Saved by His Faithful Dogs 340
29. "You must kill me first!" 342
30. The Queen Defies the Goddess of the Volcano 358

FOREWORD

The 19th century has been called "The Greatest Century of Christian Missions." It was the century that the sheaves were gathered in, the captives were set free, the nations were discipled, the light of Christ scattered the darkness, and the Lord began restoring the years the locusts had eaten.

Until the end of the world and Jesus returns, these stories about the couragcous Gospel heralds of the 19th century must be told from one generation to the next. These are the greatest stories of faith in our age, to be appended on the Hebrews 11 list of the heroes of the faith. We republish this classic compendium of stories from John C. Lambert, who wrote virtually as an eyewitness to these accounts of pioneering missionaries serving in the greatest century of missions. Every Christian child growing up in Christian homes should know these stories by heart, and every family should pass this record in printed form on to the next generation.

Our hope is that our children will emulate the faith

of these saints who have gone before us. Today's heroism offered to our children for role models are too much limited to sports figures who are adept at throwing balls or actors who pretend to be very courageous in make-believe stories. Christian parents would much rather give their children real heroes who actually accomplished something of eternal substance for the sake of the Kingdom of God. They gave up their real lives in a real world. They faced real enemies for a real cause in order that real people might receive a real Gospel and be really blessed forever.

These stories do not speak only to a courageous, adventuresome spirit, but to faith in Jesus Christ and sacrificial love for Him. All of us are called to "deny ourselves, take up our cross daily, and follow" in the footsteps of the Lamb of Calvary. These missionaries give us tangible, real-life examples of how this is done.

Parents, as you read these stories to you children, be forewarned that you will probably break down in tears as you read some of these stories. The magnitude of the sacrifice and the authentic love of these great men and women of God will overwhelm you at points. But, what better message is there to communicate to your children?

—Kevin Swanson
2017

INTRODUCTION

In a "foreword" which he contributes to Dr. Jacob Chamberlain's attractive missionary book, *In the Tiger Jungle*, Dr. Francis E. Clark expresses the opinion that one need not patronize the sensational and unhealthy fiction to find stirring adventures and thrilling narrative, and then goes on to make the following statement:

"There is one source which furnishes stories of intense and dramatic interest, abounding in novel situations and spiced with abundant adventures; and this source is at the same time the purest and most invigorating fountain at which our youth can drink. To change the figure, this is a mine hitherto largely unworked; it contains rich nuggets of ore, which will well repay the prospector in this new field."

The field to which Dr. Clark refers is the history of Christian missions. His meaning is that the adventurous and stirring side of missionary experience needs to be brought out, and emphasis laid upon the fact that the romantic days of missions are by no means past. These are stories which are now among the classics of missionary adventure. Such are the expedition of Hans Egede to Greenland, the lonely journeys of David Brainerd among the Indian tribes of the North American forests, the voyage of John Williams from one coral island of the Pacific to another in the little ship which his own hands had built, the exploration of the Dark Continent by David Livingstone in the hope of emancipating the black man's soul.

But among missionary lives which are more recent or less known, there are many not less noble or less thrilling than those just referred to; and the chapters which follow are an attempt to make this plain. There is, of course, a deeper side to Christian missions—a side that is essential and invariable—while the elements of adventure and mystery are accidental and occasional. If in these pages the spiritual aspects of foreign mission work are but slightly touched upon, it is not because they are either forgotten or ignored, but simply because it was not part of the writer's present plan to deal with them. It is his hope, nevertheless, that some of those into whose hands this book may come will be induced by what they read to make fuller acquaintance with the lives and aims of our missionary heroes, and so will catch something of that spirit which led them to face innumerable dangers, toils, and trials among heathen and often savage peoples, whether in the frozen North or the burning South, whether in the hidden depths of some vast continent or among the scattered "islands of the ocean seas."

In the *Memoirs of Archbishop Temple* we find the future Primate of the Church of England, when but a youth of twenty, writing to tell his mother how his imagination had been stirred by the sight of Selwyn of New Zealand starting for the Pacific with a band of young men who had devoted themselves to the propagation of the Gospel among a benighted and barbarous people. "It is not mere momentary enthusiasm with me," he writes; "my heart beats whenever I think of it. I think it one of the noblest things England has done for a long time; almost the only thing really worthy of herself."

It is the author's earnest desire that the narratives which follow may help to kindle in some minds an enthusiasm for missions like that which characterized Frederick Temple to the very end of his long and strenuous life; or, better still, that they may even suggest to some who are looking forward to the future with a high ambition, and wondering how to make the most of life, whether there is any career which offers so many opportunities of romantic experience and heroic achievement as that of a Christian missionary.

—John C. Lambert
1912

Publisher's Note: This book is based on a 1912 edition of John C. Lambert's *The Romance of Missionary Heroism*, originally published by London-based Seeley, Service and Company, Limited. It is an exciting and inspiring account of courageous, God-fearing missionaries who brought the Gospel to remote, faraway places across the world during the 19th century. These men and women experienced incredible hardship and sacrifice as they served the Lord. In telling their uplifting stories and the historical details, we have preserved the original text as much as possible, with minimal changes.

However, this book is also a product of its time and place. It will not seem like a contemporary book because it is not one. The original style, formal tone, and British spellings and word usage remain intact. The text also depicts native cultures at a time when Westerners were often not well-informed about these people groups and often held misguided or unfounded assumptions about these people and cultures. As a result, at times the text may express attitudes that were very common in the early 1900s but are not considered acceptable now. We do want readers to be aware that these attitudes are expressed within the context of a historical presentation of a book from that time.

PART I

ASIA

IN THE STEPPES AND DESERTS OF MONGOLIA

C H A P T E R   O N E

FROM THE EDITORS: Great men do not arise by chance.
They often emerge from generations of faithful Christian
parents who laid the foundations and prepared the way
for future warriors of Christ. Such was the heritage of one
fearless missionary — James Gilmour. Born in Scotland on
June 12, 1843, the faithfulness of godly grandparents and
parents set the stage for his life's work. In his youth, his
mother's great joy was to gather her sons about her in the
evening and read to them about missionaries who carried
the precious Gospel of Jesus to foreign lands. His dedicated
father made family worship such a priority that neighbors
wanting to visit had to wait until this special evening hour
was concluded before bringing up their business.

After completing his primary education, Gilmour
attended Glasgow University and upon graduating offered
himself to the London Missionary Society for service on
a foreign field. He ended up in Mongolia, and as we shall
soon see, he met the challenge with great enthusiasm in a
land that was anything but welcoming. After several years

of service, a helpmeet was brought his way to join in his efforts, and he married Miss Emily Prankard in 1872. He wrote of her: "She is a jolly girl, as much, perhaps more, of a Christian and Christian missionary than I am." Together they continued to serve the cause of Christ in Mongolia and China for ten years until her illness-related death. Faithful to the end of his short time on earth, James Gilmour traveled, preached, and taught throughout Mongolia and parts of China until he contracted a malignant strain of typhus fever and died at age 48, on May 12, 1891. Upon hearing the news of his death, the fierce Mongol men who had been affected by his life broke down in tears when told, "their Gilmour was dead."

Throughout a history of over 2,000 years, Mongolia has been a largely nomadic and pagan country. First inhabited by the Huns before the time of Christ, and later by the Turks and Kirghiz tribes in the 7th-10th centuries, it was the home of the great Genghis Khan. The Khan formed a powerful empire that lasted for hundreds of years, stretching at times from the East China Sea to Western Europe. By the time James Gilmour began his missionary adventures, the Mongol people were a vast collection of tribes which had lost something of their former greatness.

Though just a short synopsis of the life and work of James Gilmour is presented here, you will soon discover the courage, ingenuity, energy, loyalty, passion, fervor, and at times eccentricities that made this man of God so remarkable. Although he labored for years with little fruit, God knows what effect his humble life of service had on countless men, women, and children, and their progeny.

The adventures of this man have given some biographers reason to call him "Robinson Crusoe turned missionary."

James Gilmour (1843–1891)

About the middle of the year 1870 there arrived in Peking (now Beijing) a young Scotchman, James Gilmour by name, who had been sent out to China by the London Missionary Society to begin work in the capital. Within a few weeks of his arrival, there took place at Tientsin, the port of Peking, that fanatical outbreak known as the Tientsin massacre, in which a Roman Catholic convent was destroyed and thirteen French people murdered. A widespread panic at once took hold of the capital. The European community felt that they were living on the edge of a volcano, for no one knew but that this massacre might be the prelude to a general outburst of anti-foreign hatred such as was witnessed later in connection with the Boxer Rebellion movement. All around Gilmour, his acquaintances were packing up their most precious belongings and holding themselves in readiness for a hurried flight to the south. It was at this moment that the newcomer resolved on a bold and original move. Instead of fleeing to the south in search of safety, he would turn his face northwards and see if an opening could be found for Christian work among the Mongols of the great Mongolian plains. He was utterly unacquainted both with the country and the language, but he had long felt a deep and romantic interest in that vast, lonely plateau which lies between China proper and Siberia. The suspension of work in Peking seemed to offer the very opportunity he wanted for pushing his way into Mongolia. And so as soon as the necessary preparations could be made, for Gilmour was never the man to let the grass grow beneath his feet, he left the capital behind with all its rumors and alarms. Before long the Great Wall was passed, which ever since the third century B.C. has defended China from Mongolia. And then, with two camels and a camel-cart, our intrepid traveler set his face towards the Desert of Gobi, which lies in the very heart of the Mongolian plain.

Mongolia, the home of the Mongols, has been described as a rough parallelogram, 1,800 miles from east to west, and 1,000 miles from north to south. It is a huge plateau lifted high above the sea, in part desert, in part a treeless expanse of grassy steppe, and in part covered by mountain ranges whose peaks rise up to the line of perpetual snow. The climate, hot and dry in summer and bitterly cold in winter, makes agriculture impossible except in some favored spots, and so by the force of his circumstances the Mongol is a nomad, dwelling in a tent, and pasturing his flocks and herds upon the grass of the steppe. For long centuries the people were a constant terror to the Chinese. Even the Great Wall proved an ineffectual barrier against them, and time and again they poured like a mighty flood over the rich lands of their more peace-loving neighbors to the south. But around the 1400's A.D., they converted from their earlier pagan faith to Buddhism in its corrupted form of Lamanism, and this change of faith has had a decidedly softening effect upon the national character. Much of this, no doubt, must be attributed to the custom that prevails among them of devoting one or more sons in every family to the priesthood. One result of this custom is, that the Mongol priests, or *lamas* as they are called, actually form the majority of the male population, and as the lamas are celibates in virtue of their office, another result has been a great reduction in the population, as compared with early days. It has been calculated that at the turn of the twentieth century there were not more than two million Mongols occupying this vast territory of 1,300,000 square miles. Mongolia is no longer entitled now to the name it once received of *officina gentium*, "the manufactory of nations." It does not now possess those surplus swarms of bold and warlike horsemen which it once sent out to overrun and conquer other lands. But, like all nomads, its people are still an active and hardy race. As horsemen, too, they still excel. From their very infancy both men and women are accustomed to the saddle, and even yet some of them could rival the feats of the horsemen of Genghis Khan, the greatest of all the Mongol conquerors of long ago. It was to this country and this interesting, but little known people, that James Gilmour devoted his life.

His first journey across the great plateau began at Kalgan, which lies to the northwest of Peking, just within the Great Wall, and terminated at Kiachta on the southern frontier of Siberia. He made this journey over plain and desert, which occupied only a month, in the company of a Russian official who knew no English, while he himself knew neither Russian nor Mongolian. He was glad, therefore, on reaching Kiachta to meet a fellow-countryman, one of the world's ubiquitous Scots, in the person of a trader named Grant. Grant was exceedingly kind to him, and took him into his own comfortable house. But finding that this contact with civilization was hindering him in his strenuous efforts to master the Mongolian language without delay, Gilmour formed a characteristic resolution. This was nothing else than to go out upon the plain and try to persuade some Mongolian to receive him as an inmate of his tent.

It was at night that this idea occurred to him, and the next morning he left Kiachta, taking nothing with him but his "Penang lawyer." This, it should be explained, is a heavy walking stick, so called because in Penang it is supposed to be useful in settling disputes. Gilmour had already discovered that in Mongolia it was not only useful, but altogether indispensable, as a protection against the ferocious assaults of the wolfish-looking dogs which inevitably rush at a traveler if he draws near to any encampment. One of the first incidents of the caravan journey from Kalgan had been the narrow escape of a Russian soldier from being torn down by a pack of Mongolian dogs. With a stout "limb of the law" in his fist, however, Gilmour feared nothing, but strode cheerfully over the plain, making for the first tent he saw on the horizon.

As he drew near he heard the sound of a monotonous voice engaged in some kind of chant, and when he entered found a lama at his prayers. The lama, hearing footsteps, looked round and pronounced the one word, "Sit!" and then continued his devotions. For another quarter of an hour he went on, taking no further notice of his visitor meanwhile. But suddenly his droning chant ceased, and he came forward and gave Gilmour a hospitable welcome. Gilmour opened his mind to him without delay, telling him that it was his desire to spend the winter in his tent and learn Mongolian from his instruction. The lama was surprised, but perfectly willing, and agreed to receive his visitor as a paying guest for an indefinite period at the modest rate of about a shilling a day (about $3.50 per day). And so within a few months of his departure from London we find Gilmour living the life of a nomad in the tent of a lama on the Mongolian plain.

Once the first novelty had worn off, he found the life somewhat monotonous. Dinner was the great event of the day, the more so as it is the only meal in which a Mongol indulges. The preparations for this repast were unvarying, as also was the subsequent menu. Towards the sunset the lama's servant, who was himself a lama, melted a block of ice in a huge pot, over a fire which filled the tent with smoke. Taking a hatchet, he next hewed a solid lump of mutton from a frozen carcass and put it into the water. As soon as it was boiled, he fished it out with the fire-tongs and laid it on a board before his master and Gilmour, who then attacked it with finger and knives. Forks were things unknown. When a Mongol eats he takes a piece of meat in his left hand, seizes it with his teeth, and then cuts off his mouthful close to his lips by a quick upward movement of his knife. The operation looks dangerous, but the flatness of the native nose makes it safe enough, though it would be very risky in the case of one who was otherwise endowed.

The Mongols always thought Gilmour's nose tremendous, and they excused him for cutting off his mouthfuls first, and appropriating them afterwards.

Meanwhile, as this first course was in progress, the servant had thrown some millet into the water used for boiling the meat, and when the diners had partaken sufficiently of the solid fare, this thin gruel was served up as a kind of soup. The mutton, Gilmour says, was tough; but he declares that seldom in his life did he taste any preparations of civilized cookery so delicious as this millet soup. He admits that he has no doubt that it was chiefly the desert hunger that made it seem so good.

Though he ate only once a day, the lama, like all Mongols, consumed vast quantities of tea. At dawn, and again at noon, the servant prepared a pail full of the cheering beverage, giving it always ten or fifteen minutes hard boiling, and seasoning it with fat and a little meal instead of milk. Gilmour accustomed himself to the ways of the tent. As a concession to his Scotch tastes, however, he was provided every morning with a cupful of meal made into something like porridge by the addition of boiling water. This the lama and his servant called "Scotland," and they were careful to set it aside regularly for the use of "Our Gilmour," to whom, Buddhist priests though they were, they soon became quite attached.

Before leaving the subject of meals, we may mention that on the last day of the year Mongols make up for their abstemiousness during the other 364 days by taking no fewer than seven dinners. When New Year's Eve arrived, the lama insisted that his visitor should do his duty like a Mongolian, and a yellow-coated old lama, who was present as a guest on the occasion, was told to keep count of his progress. Gilmour managed to put down three dinners and was just wondering what to do next when he discovered that his guardian lama had got drunk and lost count. In this case, although himself a strict teetotaler, he did not feel disposed to take too severe a view of the old gentleman's failing.

When the time came at last to re-cross the plains, Gilmour decided to make the homeward journey on horseback instead of by camel-cart. The one drawback was that he had never learned to ride. But as he had found that the best way to learn Mongolian was by being compelled to speak it, he considered that a ride of a good many hundred miles might be the best way of learning to sit on a horse. The plan proved a decided success. In Mongolia a man who cannot ride is looked upon as a curiosity, and when Gilmour first mounted everybody turned out to enjoy the sight of his awkwardness. But though he had one or two nasty falls from his horse stumbling into holes on treacherous bits of ground, such as are very frequent on the plains where the rats have excavated galleries underground, he soon learned to be quite at home on the back of his steed. When he rode at last once more through a gateway of the Great Wall, passing thus out of Mongolia into China again, he felt that after the training he had received on his way across the steppes and the desert, he would be ready henceforth to take to the saddle in any circumstance. Indeed, so sure of his seat had he become that we find him on a subsequent occasion, when he formed one of a company mounted for a journey on Chinese mules, which will not travel except in single file, riding with his face to the tail of his beast, so as to be better able to engage in conversation with the cavalier who came behind him.

This crossing and re-crossing of the Mongolian plain, and especially the winter he had spent in the lama's tent, had already given Gilmour a knowledge of the Mongolian language, and a familiarity with the habits and thoughts of the Mongols themselves, such as hardly any other Westerner could pretend to. Peking, when he returned to it, had settled down to something like its normal quiet, but he felt that the ordinary routine of work in the city was not the work to which he was specifically called. The desert air was in his blood now, and Mongolia was calling. Henceforth it was for the Mongols that he lived.

Year by year Gilmour fared forth into the Great Plain in prosecution of his chosen task. And although it was his custom to return to Peking for the winter, he still continued while there to devote himself to his Mongol flock. Between China and Mongolia a considerable trade is carried on, the Mongols bringing in hides, cheese, butter, and the other products of a pastoral territory, and carrying away in return vast quantities of cheap tea in the form of compressed bricks, these bricks being used in Gilmour's time not only for the preparation of the favorite beverage, but as a means of exchange in lieu of money. During the winter months large numbers of traders arrive in Peking from all parts of Mongolia, and many of them camp out in their tents in open spaces, just as they do when living on the plains. Gilmour frequented these encampments, and took every opportunity he could make or find of conversing about religious matters, and especially of seeking to commend "the Jesus-doctrine," as the Buddhists called it. One plan that he followed was to go about like a Chinese peddler, with two bags of books in the Mongolian language hanging from his shoulders. All were invited to buy, and in many cases this literature was taken up quite eagerly. Often a would-be purchaser demanded to have a book read aloud to him before he made up his mind about it, and this gave the peddler a welcome chance of reading from the Gospels to the crowd which gathered, and then of introducing a conversation, which sometimes passed into a discussion, about the merits of Jesus and Buddha. Sometimes those who were anxious to buy had no money, but were prepared to pay in kind. And so, not infrequently, Gilmour was to be seen at night making his way back to his lodgings in the city "with a miscellaneous collection of cheese, sour-curd, butter, millet-cake, and the sheep's fat, representing the produce of part of the day's sales."

Among the most remarkable of Gilmour's many journeys through Mongolia was one that he made in 1884, and made entirely on foot. He was a tremendous walker at times, more perhaps by reason of his unusual will power than because of exceptional physical strength, and is known to have covered 300 miles in seven and a half days—an average of forty miles a day. On the occasion of his long tramp over the plains and back, he had special reasons for adopting that method of locomotion.

One reason was that grass was so scarce during that year that it would hardly have been possible to get pasture for a camel or a horse. Another reason was that the love of simplicity and unconventionality, which was so marked a feature of his character, grew stronger and stronger, and also the desire to get as near as possible to the poorest and humblest of the people. At a later period we find him adopting in its entirety "not only the native dress, but practically the native food, and so far as a Christian man could, native habits of life." An idea of the length to which he carried the rule of plains living may be gathered from the fact that for some time his rate of expenditure was only threepence a day. His biographer, Mr. Lovett, gives us a graphic picture of him taking his bowl of porridge, native fashion, in the street, sitting down upon a low stool beside the boiler of the itinerant vendor from whom he had just purchased it. And the plainness of his garb at times may be judged of when we mention that in one village on the borders of China he was turned out of the two respectable inns which the place could boast, on the ground that he was a foot-traveler without cart or animal, who must be content to betake himself to the tavern for tramps.

It was in keeping with his tastes, therefore, as well as from necessity, that he once tramped through Mongolia with all his belongings on his back. His equipment when he set out consisted of a postman's brown bag on one side containing his kit and provisions; on the other an angler's waterproof bag with books, etc.; together with a Chinaman's sheepskin coat slung over his shoulder by means of a rough stick of the "Penang lawyer" type. In the course of this tramp, his formidable stick notwithstanding, he had sometimes to be rescued from the teeth of the dogs which flew, not unnaturally, at a character so suspicious

IN A MONGOL ENCAMPMENT

Mr. Gilmour always dressed in Chinese clothes, and when on tour generally had a post-man's bag strapped over one shoulder and a waterproof fishing-bag over the other, these two containing all his baggage.

looking. But he met with much hospitality from the people, both lamas and laymen, where he went; and returned to Kalgan without any serious mishap. From two dangers of the country he altogether escaped. One was the risk of being attacked by wolves, which are a perfect terror to the Chinese traveler over the plains, though the inhabitants themselves make light of them, and never hesitate when they catch sight of one to become the attacking party. The result of this is that a wolf is said to distinguish from afar between a Mongol and a Chinaman, slinking off as hastily as possible if it sees a wayfarer approaching in long skin robes, but anticipating a good dinner at the sight of another in blue jacket and trousers. Gilmour himself was of opinion that Mongolian wolves are not so dangerous as the Siberian ones. The reason he gives is that, unlike the Russians, the Mongols keep such poor sheepfolds that a wolf can help itself to a sheep whenever it likes, and so is seldom driven by hunger to attack a man. The other danger is from bandits. For there are parts of the Desert of Gobi, crossed as it is by the great trade routes between Siberia and China, which are quite as unpleasant to traverse as the ancient road between Jerusalem and Jericho. But Gilmour was probably never more secure against highway robbery than when he walked through Mongolia as a missionary tramp.

It is impossible to enter into the details of the strange and romantic experiences which befell this adventurous spirit in the course of his many wanderings. Now we find him spending the night in a lama's tent, most probably discussing sacred things with his host till far on towards morning over a glowing fire of *argol*, or dried cow's dung, the customary fuel of the plains. At another time he is careening across the desert on horseback as swiftly as his Mongol companions, for he was a man who never liked to be beaten. Now he is at a marriage feast, looking on with observant and humorous eyes at the rough but harmless merry-makings. Again, he is in the court of justice, where punishment is meted out on the spot upon the culprit's back, in the presence of a highly appreciative crowd. At one time, with a heart full of pity for a superstitious and deluded people, he is watching a Buddhist turning his praying-wheel with his own hand or hanging it up in front of his tent to be turned for him by the wind. At another, as he passes a criminal in an iron cage who is condemned to be starved to death, and is set day by day in front of an eating-house in a large trading settlement for the aggravation of his tortures (a common Mongol practice), he is reflecting on the defects of a false religion that can permit its followers to enjoy the public exhibition of a fellow-creature's dying pains. In his journeys he was constantly exposed to the bitter cold of a land where the thermometer falls in winter to thirty or forty degrees below zero, and all through the heat of summer huge lumps of ice remain frozen in the wells. Often he had to endure long spells of hunger and thirst when on the march. Worst of all, he had to share the filth and vermin of a Mongol tent as well as its hospitality. But these things he looked upon as all "in the day's work" and with the Apostle Paul, he counted them but loss for the sake of the high calling of Jesus Christ; and though he may sometime chronicle them in his diary as facts, he never makes them matter of complaint.

Among the most interesting incidents which he records are some in connection with his endeavors to bring relief to those whom he found in sickness and pain. Although not a doctor by profession, he had picked up some medical and surgical skill, and did not hesitate to use it on behalf of those for whom no better skill was available. In doing this he sometimes ran great risks, for with all their hospitality the Mongols are terribly suspicious, and ready to entertain the most extraordinary rumors about the designs of any stranger.

Once he persuaded a blind man to come with him to Peking, to have his eyes operated on for cataracts in the hospital there. The operation was unsuccessful, and the story was spread over a large region that Gilmour enticed people to Peking in order to steal "the jewels of their eyes" that he might preserve them in a bottle and sell them for hundreds of taels. In consequence of this he lived for months under what almost amounted to a sentence of death. Only by showing no consciousness of fear and by patiently living suspicion down, did he escape from being murdered.

Once he had undertaken to treat a soldier for a bullet wound received in an encounter with brigands, thinking that it was only a flesh wound he had to deal with. It turned out to be a difficult bone complication. Now Gilmour knew hardly anything of anatomy, and he had absolutely no books to consult. "What could I do," he says, "but pray?" And a strange thing happened. There tottered up to him through the crowd a live skeleton—a man whose bones literally stood out as distinctly as if he were a specimen in an anatomical museum, with only a yellow skin drawn loosely over them. The man came to beg for cough medicine, but

Gilmour was soon busy fingering a particular part of his skeleton, with so strange a smile on his face that he heard a bystander remark, "That smile means something." "So it did," Gilmour adds. "It meant among other things that I knew what to do with the wounded soldier's damaged bone; and in a short time his wound was in a fair way of healing."

James Gilmour's *Among the Mongols* (now out of print but available from rare book dealers) is a book to be read, not only for the adventures of its subject matter, but because of the author's remarkable gift for realistic statement—his power of making his reader see things in bodily presence just as his own eyes had seen them. In more ways than one he reminds us of Borrow, but especially in what Borrow himself described as "the art of telling a plain story." On the first appearance of *Among the Mongols* a very competent reviewer traced a striking resemblance.

"Robinson Crusoe," he said "has turned missionary, lived years in Mongolia, and written a book about it. That is this book." It was high praise, but it contained no small degree of truth. And to the advantage of Gilmour's book as compared to Defoe's, it must be remembered that everything that the former tells us is literally true.

NOTES AND AUTHORITIES: *Among the Mongols* by Rev. James Gilmour, M.A. and *James Gilmour of Mongolia* by Richard Lovett, M.A. (Religious Tract Society); *The Far East* by Archibald Little (The Clarendon Press).

IN THE COUNTRY
OF THE TELUGUS

C H A P T E R   T W O

FROM THE EDITORS: India — a land of jungles, a land of
mystery, a land of tigers and deadly serpents, an ancient
land once under the rule of King Darius and the Persians
with a history spanning 5,000 years — a land of millions of
souls in desperate need of Jesus Christ. Founded in ancient
times, then conquered by the Turks and Mongols, and
finally incorporated into the British Empire by the early 18th
century, India today has the second largest population on
earth. Today it is inhabited by Muslims, Hindus, Buddhists,
numerous pagan tribal groups, and by an estimated 27
million Christians. It is a land of great variety. Christians
ventured into India from the time of Jesus' death, when
His disciple Thomas first brought the light of the Gospel to
this dark land about 50 A.D. Then, from the 1500s until the
1900s American and British missionaries answered the call
of Christ to once again spread the Good News there.

    To this far off land came Dr. Jacob Chamberlain, a man
venturing to risk all for the sake of the Gospel of Christ;
willing not only to risk all, but ultimately, like so many

others, to give his all. Born April 13, 1835 in Connecticut, at an early age he felt the call of God to be a missionary. At first, his service on the field was delayed. That he might honor his father's wishes, he remained on the family farm and cared for his aging parents. After experiencing several narrow escapes from accidents at home, Jacob sensed God was preserving his life in order that he might go to India as a missionary. With his father's release and blessing from filial duties, he attended seminary at Case Western Reserve University, and then earned a medical degree from Cleveland Medical College in Cleveland, Ohio. He married Charlotte Close Birge in September of 1859.

The couple arrived on the mission field in India on April 12, 1860, where Dr. Chamberlain was assigned to work with the Telugu people at Madanapalle. Controlled by a keen interest to minister to both soul and body, Dr. Chamberlain would often see patients in the morning and evening and conduct short preaching tours in the middle of the day. From time to time he would also venture out to remote areas of the jungle to reach native groups and to explore lands never before reached by the Gospel.

During his many years in India, the Doctor worked on a Telugu translation of the Bible; he helped establish numerous Christian schools and dispensaries and later wrote several books on his experiences in India. On one missionary tour, he contracted a jungle fever that in time would ravage his body. By 1902 he was partially paralyzed, though he continued faithfully in his calling for six more years. Dr. Jacob Chamberlain died on March 2, 1908, after 48 years of service in India. It was to India he felt his calling in life; it was in India that he spent his life, and it was for countless Indian souls that he ultimately gave up his life.

Dr. Jacob Chamberlain (1835–1908)

Apart from the Tibeto-Burman tribes scattered along the skirts of the Himalayas, the peoples of India have been commonly divided by ethnologists into three great race groups—the aborigines (often called the Kolarians), the Dravidians, and the Aryans. The aborigines are now found chiefly in the jungles and mountains of the Central Provinces, into which they were driven at a very early period by the Dravidians, the first invaders of India. Mr. Kipling, who has done so much to make India more intelligible to the English, has not forgotten to give us pictures of the aboriginal peoples in his famous *Jungle Book*. In his *The Tomb of His Ancestors* again, we have a vivid sketch of the mountain Bhils, whose combination of superstition, courage, and loyalty reminds us of the Scottish Highlanders in the days of Prince Charlie.

These aborigines of the hills were long neglected by the Church, but much is now being done on their behalf. Doctor Shepherd, for example, a Scotch medical missionary, carried both the Gospel and the healing powers of modern science into the wild country of the Bhils and Rajputana, and could tell tales of his experiences among them as striking and thrilling as any that have come from the pen of Rudyard Kipling.

The Dravidians, who first overran India and drove the earlier inhabitants into the hills, were afterwards themselves supplanted to a large extent by the more powerful Aryans. These Aryans were members of that same original stock to which the nations of Europe trace their origin, for while one section of the race moved southwards upon India through the Himalayas from the great plains of Central Asia, another flowed to the west and took possession of Europe. Through the Aryan invasion of India the Dravidians were pushed for the most part into the southern portion of the vast peninsula, where they have formed ever since a numerous and powerful group. Five Dravidian peoples are usually distinguished, the Tamils and Telugus being the most important of the five. It is of work among the Telugus that we are to speak in the present chapter.

The country of the Telugus stretches northwards from Madras for some five hundred miles along the shores of the Bay of Bengal, while to the west it extends about halfway across the peninsula, and so includes large parts not only of the Presidency of Madras, but the kingdom of Mysore and the dominions of the Nizam of Hyderabad. It is a region which attracts those who go to India for sport and adventure, for its jungles still abound in tigers and other wild animals. From the point of view of Christian missions, it has this special interest, that there is no part of all Hindustan where the Gospel has been preached with more marked success in the 1900's, or where the people have been gathered more rapidly into the Christian Church. One of the most enterprising of modern Indian missionaries was Dr. Jacob Chamberlain, of the American

Reformed Church, who began his labors as a medical evangelist to the Telugus. He is the author of two books, *The Cobra's Den* and *In the Tiger Jungle*, which give graphic sketches of his experiences in city and village and jungle, on horseback and in bullock-cart, in the surgery with operating knife in hand, and at the busy fair when a crowd has gathered round and the knife that cures the body has been exchanged for the Book that saves the soul. Taking these two delightful volumes as our authorities, we shall first glance at Dr. Chamberlain in the midst of his medical and surgical work, and see how effective such work becomes in opening the way for Christian teaching. Then we shall follow him on one of his longer evangelistic tours through the Telugu country. Let us look in and find where Dr. Chamberlain begins his day and read about one of his missionary journeys.

All morning, ever since sunrise, the doctor has been busy with the patients who have come from far and near to be treated or prescribed for, until about a hundred persons are gathered in front of the little dispensary. The heat of the day is now coming on, but before dismissing them and distributing the medicines they have waited for, he takes down his Telugu Bible, reads and explains a chapter, and then kneels to ask a blessing upon all those who have need of healing.

It is now breakfast time, and after several hours of hard work the doctor is quite ready for a good meal. But just as he is about to go home for the purpose, he hears the familiar chant used by the natives when carrying a heavy burden, and looking out sees four men approaching, two in front and two behind, with a long bamboo pole on their shoulders and a blanket slung on it in hammock fashion with a sick man inside. Behind this primitive ambulance, two men are walking, one leading the other by the hand.

In a few minutes the sick man is laid in his blanket on the floor of the veranda, and the little company have told their tale. They have come from a village two days' journey off. They have heard of the foreign doctor that he can work wonderful cures. The young man in the blanket is dying; the old man led by the hand is his uncle, who has recently grown blind. Their friends have brought them to the Doctor Padre to see if he can make them well.

On examination Dr. Chamberlain finds that the young man's case is almost hopeless, but that there is just a chance of saving him by a serious surgical operation—and this he performs the same afternoon. At first the patient seems to be sinking under the shock, but he rallies by and by, and gradually comes back to health and strength again. The old man's blindness is a simpler case. An easy operation and careful treatment are all that are required. So when uncle and nephew have been in the hospital for a few weeks, the doctor is able to send them back to their village—the young man walking on his own feet, and the old man no longer needing to be led by the hand.

But here the story does not end. Every day while in hospital the two patients had heard the doctor read a chapter from the Gospel and make its meaning plain. And when the time for leaving came they begged for a copy of the history of Yesu Kristu, "the Divine Guru" so that they might let all their neighbors know of the glad news they had heard. They acknowledged that they could not read, for they were poor weavers who had never been to school. "But when the cloth merchant comes to buy our webs," they said, "we will gather the villagers, and put the book into his hand, and say, 'Read us this book, and then we will talk business.' And when the tax gatherer comes we will say, 'Read us this book, and then we will settle our taxes.' Let us have the book therefore, for we want all our village to know about the Divine Guru, Yesu Kristu."

They got the book and went away, and for three years Dr. Chamberlain heard nothing of them. But at last on a wide preaching tour he met them again. They had learned of his approach, and when he entered the village at sunrise the whole population was gathered under the "Council-Tree," while his two patients of three years ago came forward with smiling faces to greet him, and told him that through the reading of the Gospel everyone in the place had agreed to give up his idols if the Doctor Padre would send someone to teach them more about Jesus. Dr. Chamberlain discussed the matter fully with them, and when he saw that they were thoroughly in earnest, promised to send a teacher as soon as possible. But just before leaving to proceed on his journey he noticed, near at hand, the little village temple, with its stone idols standing on their platform at the farther end of the shrine.

"What are you going to do with these idols now?" he asked the people.

"The idols are nothing to us any longer," they replied; "we have renounced them all."

"But are you going to leave them standing there in the very heart of the village?"

"What would you have us do with them?" they asked.

"Well," said the doctor, wishing to test their sincerity, "I would like to take one of them away with me." He knew the superstitious dread which even converted natives are apt to entertain for the idols of their fathers, and the unwillingness they usually have to lay violent hands on them. He did not expect anything more than that they might permit him to remove one of the images for himself. But at this point Ramudu, the old man whose sight had been restored, stepped forward and said, "I'll bring out the chief Swami for you;" and going into the shrine he shook the biggest idol from the plaster from which it was fastened to the stone platform, and then handed it to the doctor, saying as he did so something like this:

"Well, old fellow, be off with you! We and our ancestors for a thousand years have feared and worshiped you. Now we have found a better God, and are done with you. Be off with you, and a good riddance to us. Jesus is now our God and Savior."

And so the ugly stone Swami that had lorded it so long over the consciences of these Telugu villagers was "dethroned," as Dr. Chamberlain puts it, "by the surgeon's knife," and passed in due course to a missionary museum in the United States. But Yesu Kristu, the Divine Guru, reigned in its stead.

But now let us follow the doctor in some of the more striking episodes of one of his earliest tours. It was a journey of 1,200 miles through the native kingdom of Hyderabad and on into Central India—a region where at that time no missionary had ever worked before. He rode all the way on a sturdy native pony, but was accompanied by four Indian assistants, with two bullock-carts full of Gospels and other Christian literature which he hoped to sell to the people at low prices.

One of the first and most dangerous adventures was in a walled city of Hyderabad. They had already disposed of a few Gospels and tracts when some Brahmin priests and Mohammedan fanatics raised the mob against them. It was done in this way. A number of the Gospels were bound in cloth boards of a buff color. The Mohammedan zealots spread a rumor that these books were bound in pigskin—a thing which no true disciple of Mahomet will touch. The Brahmans, on the other hand, told their followers that these yellow boards were made of calfskin—and to a Hindu the cow is a sacred animal. The crowd got thoroughly excited, and soon Dr. Chamberlain and his four helpers were standing in the market place with their backs to a wall, while a howling multitude surged in front, many of whom had already begun to tear up the cobblestones with which the street was paved in order to stone the intruders to death. The doctor saved the situation by getting permission to tell a wonderful story. Nothing catches an Indian crowd like the promise of a story. Their curiosity was aroused from the first, and soon their hearts were touched as they listened to a simple and graphic description of the death of Jesus on the cross. The stones dropped from the hands that clutched them, tears stood in many eyes, and when the speaker had finished, every copy of the Gospel which had been brought into the city from the little camp without the walls, was eagerly bought up by priests as well as people.

But dangers of this sort were rare. For the most part, both in town and country, the white traveler was welcomed courteously, and gladly listened to as he stood in the busy market place or sat beside the village elders on the stone seat beneath the "Council-tree," and explained the purpose of his coming. Dangers of another kind, however, were common enough, and Dr. Chamberlain tells of some narrow escapes from serpents, tigers, and the other perils of the Indian jungle.

They were passing through the great teak forest, where the trees towered one hundred and fifty feet above their heads, when they came in sight one day of a large village in a forest clearing. As they drew near, the elders of the place came out to salute them. The doctor asked if they could give him a suitable place to pitch his tent, but they did better than that, for they gave him the free use of a newly erected shed.

Somewhat tired out with a long forenoon's march, Dr. Chamberlain lay down to rest his limbs, and took up his Greek Testament meanwhile to read a chapter, holding the book over his face as he lay stretched out on his back. By and by he let his arm fall, and suddenly became aware that a huge serpent was coiled on one of the bamboo rafters just above him, and that it had gradually been letting itself down until some four feet of its body were hanging directly over his head, while its tongue was already forked out—a sure sign that it was just about ready to strike. He says that when studying the anatomy of the human frame he had sometimes wondered whether a person lying on his back could jump sideways, without first erecting himself, and

DR. CHAMBERLAIN ATTACKED BY A SERPENT

that he discovered on this occasion that, with a proper incentive, the thing could be done.

Bounding from his dangerous position, he ran to the door of the shed and took from the bullock-cart which was standing there a huge iron spit five or six feet long, which was made for roasting meat in a jungle camp. With this as a spear he attacked the serpent, and was successful at his first thrust in pinning it to the rafter round which it was coiled. Holding the spit firmly in its place to prevent the struggling animal from shaking it out, though he ran the utmost risk of being struck as it shot out its fanged mouth in its efforts to reach his hand, he called loudly to his servant to bring him a bamboo cane. The cane was quickly brought, and then, still holding the spit in position with one hand, he beat the brute about the head till life was extinct. When quite sure that it was dead, he drew the spit out of the rafter and held it at arm's length on a level with his shoulder, the transfixed reptile hanging from it. He found that both the head and the tail touched the ground, thus showing that the serpent was not less than ten feet long.

Just at that moment the village watchman looked in at the door, and then passed on quickly into the village. And immediately it flashed into the doctor's mind that he had got himself into trouble, for he knew that these people worship serpents as gods. They never dared to kill one, and if they saw a stranger trying to do so, would intercede for its life.

He was still considering what to do when he saw the chief men of the village advancing, and noticed, to his surprise, that they were carrying brass trays in their hands covered with sweetmeats, coconuts, and limes.

His surprise was greater still when, as they reached this doorway in which he stood to meet them, they bowed down before him to the ground and presented their simple offerings, hailing him at the same time as the deliverer of their village. That deadly serpent, they told him, had been the terror of the place for several years. It had killed a child and several of their cattle, but they had never ventured to attack it, for they knew that if any of them did so he would be accursed. The kindred of the dead serpent would wage war upon that man and his family, until every one of them was exterminated. But their visitor had killed it without their knowledge or consent, and so they were freed from the pest of their lives, and at the same time were absolutely guiltless of its blood. Their gratitude knew no bounds. They pressed upon the doctor the fattest sheep in their flocks. They sent the village crier with his tom-tom all round the place to summon the people to come and hear the words of "the serpent-destroyer." And when Dr. Chamberlain seized the opportunity to speak to them about "that old serpent called the devil," and One who came to bruise the serpent's head, they listened to him as he had rarely been listened to before.

While serpents were, and still are, the most frequent danger of the traveler in the jungle, tigers were very numerous in the Telugu country at this time. Dr. Chamberlain told stories both of the striped tiger, the royal tiger as it is commonly called, and the smaller spotted variety, which is marked like a leopard, but has a tiger's claws and cannot climb trees as a leopard can. On one occasion, when all alone and unarmed, he met a spotted tiger face to face on a narrow mountain path, but succeeded in putting the beast to flight by suddenly opening his big white umbrella and letting out a war-whoop which he had learned when a boy from a tribe of American Indians in Michigan. An experience with a tiger of the larger sort, however, though less dramatic, was probably a good deal more dangerous.

It was about three weeks after their narrow escape from stoning in that walled city of Hydria (Hyderabad), and they were still in the territories of the Nina, but about one hundred miles farther north and in the midst of hill and jungle. The native assistants with the servants and bullock-carts had made an earlier start, and the doctor was riding on to overtake them when he noticed in the path, and side by side with the fresh cart tracks, the footprints of a huge tiger and its cub. He had been warned before plunging into the forest that seven people had recently been killed in this very neighborhood by man-eating tigers; and it seemed evident that this tiger was following the carts with murderous intent. It is not the way of a tiger to attack a group of travelers. It watches and waits until one of them falls behind or gets detached from the rest, and then it makes its spring. Dr. Chamberlain realized the situation at once. The little caravan was safe so long as all kept together, but if any one lagged behind the others, or stopped to quench his thirst at the wayside stream, the tiger would be on him in a moment.

Pulling out a loaded fourteen-inch Navy revolver, the only weapon he carried with him in his expeditions through the jungle, and dashing his spurs into his pony, he

ATTACKED BY A SPOTTED TIGER

Dr. Chamberlain came face to face with a spotted tiger in a lonely mountain path,
he had no weapon, but emitting a war-whoop and suddenly putting up his umbrella,
he put the animal to flight.

galloped on through the forest to warn those ahead. As he flew onwards his eye was on the path, and always he saw the cart tracks and the footprints of the tiger side by side. A deadly fear took hold of him that he might be too late. But suddenly there came a turn in the road, and there, not far in front, were the two carts and their attendants moving slowly and peacefully forward. And now the doctor noticed that the tiger tracks were gone. He had seen them last at the very corner round which the carts came into sight. Hearing the sharp tattoo of the pony's hoofs coming up behind, the tiger must have leaped into the bushes at that very point. Probably it was only a few feet from the horseman as he whisked past. But either his sudden appearance on his galloping steed gave it a fright, or else his motion was too rapid to offer the chance of a successful spring.

Not the least of the difficulties of travel in the wild parts of India is caused by the tropical floods. On one occasion Dr. Chamberlain and his little band were swept bodily down a river, usually fordable, but swollen now by recent rains. For a moment or two the doctor and his pony were submerged, but ultimately the whole company managed to swim or scramble to safety to the opposite bank.

But it was a flood on the great Godavery river and its affluents that caused the worst predicament of all. By that time they had reached the extreme point of the expedition, up among the mountain Gonds, and had turned to the southeast to make the return journey by a different route. At a certain point they found that the steamer on which they had counted had broken down in attempting to stem the furious current, and that there was nothing for it but to march through seventy-five miles of a jungly, fever-haunted swamp in order to reach another steamer lower down. Bullock-carts were of no use, but by the aid of a hookam or firman from Nizam himself which the doctor had got hold of, he succeeded in obtaining a large body of bearers from a native deputy-governor. These men, however, though promised threefold wages, were most unwilling to accompany him, for with the country in flood the jungle becomes a place of special dangers; and it was only by much flourishing of the aforesaid Navy pistol, though without any intention of using it, that the doctor could make his men march at all or keep them from deserting.

But by and by an unforeseen trouble emerged. The constant dripping rain, the steamy heat, the jungle fever, the prowling tigers had all been taken into account. What had not been realized was the exceptional violence of the floods. And so one evening, when they came to a little tributary of the Godavery, which must be crossed if they were to reach a place of safety for the night, they found that the backwater of the main stream, rushing up this channel, had made a passage absolutely impossible.

For a time they were almost at their wit's end, for it would have been almost as much as their lives were worth to spend the night in the midst of the swamp, and it was too late now to get back to the place from which they had started that morning. But guidance came in answer to prayer. Dr. Chamberlain tells us that all at once he seemed to hear a voice saying, "Turn to the left to the Godavery, and you will find rescue." And though the native guides assured him that to do so would only be a foolish waste of time and strength, as the Godavery was now a swirling flood three miles across, and no boat or raft could possibly be got within a distance of many miles, he made his men turn sharp to the left and march in the direction of the Godavery bank. To his great delight, and to the astonishment of the natives, the first thing they saw as they emerged from the bushes was a large flat boat, just at their feet, fastened to a tree on the shore.

The boatmen told them that early that morning their cables had snapped, and they had been carried away by the flood from a mooring station higher upstream and on the British side of the river. To this precise spot they had been swept, they could not tell how. But to Dr. Chamberlain and his four native evangelists it seemed clear that God had sent this boat expressly for their deliverance. They pitched their tent on the broad deck and kindled a large fire on the shore to keep wild beasts away. And though the tigers scented them, and could be heard growling and snarling in the bushes that fringed the bank, the night was passed in comparative comfort and safety. Next day they floated down the stream towards the steamer that was to carry them southwards.

And so ended the more adventurous part of this long missionary journey through the country of the Telugus.

NOTES AND AUTHORITIES: The material for this chapter is derived from Dr. Chamberlain's two books already referred to, *The Cobra's Den* and *In the Tiger Jungle*, both published by Messrs. Oliphant, Anderson, and Ferrier.

A JAPANESE ADVENTURE

C H A P T E R   T H R E E

FROM THE EDITORS: Sometimes in the course of history, God will raise up a man who will change the destiny of his nation. To secular scholars and to most men of his day, this man might seem ordinary and simple and influential only in a small sphere. But from a heavenly perspective this man may well be a giant, a man destined by God from before time began to have a powerful impact on his generation so that the mercy and glory of God might be more evident. It is often only in looking back across time that we mortals can see the impact — the measure of a man's life.

One such man was Joseph Hardy Neesima. He was born Shimeta Neesima in Tokyo, Japan at a time when the samurai were still revered warriors. Class structure still determined a person's value and future, and Christians were still executed or exiled if they were found. The year was 1843. It was only ten years later when American Commodore Matthew Perry would arrive in Japan bringing the winds of change to a secret land. As a lad, Neesima showed early on a passion for liberty, a thirst for knowledge, and a longing to know the one True God. Through the providence of God he managed a daring escape from Japan, a crime punishable by death. On his voyage to America, he obtained a Chinese New Testament and discovered the answer to his quest to know God. He arrived in America on July 20, 1865, the year the Civil War ended. Destitute, but guided by a sovereign God who had a great plan for his life, he was taken in by a kind, godly couple who saw in Joseph a young man of great potential. Through their financing of his education, he graduated from Amherst College and entered Andover Theological Seminary.

Later, in 1872, he was offered the opportunity to serve a Japanese delegation to the United States and provided with a passport and invitation to return to his own native land. At this time, Neesima believed God had given him a vision for the formation of an educational program and college in Japan for the training of preachers and teachers in Christian doctrine. Upon his graduation from Andover Seminary, his commencement address was on "The Preaching of Christ in Japan." He pled for help from the American church to bring about this vision.

Back in Japan, Neesima received a permit to start a Christian school to educate young men. At first the danger was great, as Neesima essentially was challenging Buddhism and Shintoism, the national religions, with the saving grace of Jesus Christ. With dogged perseverance he graduated his first class of 15 students on June 12, 1879. Great things are often accomplished through small beginnings. Fifteen years later, over 900 students were participating in Doshisha College. Thousands of young people were being trained as Christian witnesses to reach Japan.

Joseph Hardy Neesima (1843—1890)

The sudden awakening of the Japanese people from their sleep of centuries, their transition in the course of a single generation from something like European medievalism to the most up-to-date modernity, may fairly be described as one of the greatest wonders of history. Wonderful, too, as every traveler tells us, are the sights of the country and the ways of the people wherever Old Japan survives—the houses, the gardens, the elaborate courtesies, the artistic costumes, and the combination of a frank naturalism with an artificiality, which has become a second nature.

In reading about Japan we sometimes feel as if we had to do not with the world of sober realities, but with a fascinating chapter out of a new volume of *Arabian Knights*. And yet even in a land in which wonders meet us on every side, the strange story of Joseph Neesima deserves to be called romantic.

He was born in 1843. This was ten years before that memorable Sabbath morning when Commodore Perry, of the U.S. Navy, with his fleet of "barbarian" ships steamed into the harbor of Uraga, in the Bay of Yedo, and extorted from the reluctant Japanese Government those treaties of friendship and commerce which broke down forever the walls of seclusion behind which Japan had hid herself from the eyes of the world. Neesima was a *samurai*, a member of the old fighting caste of feudal times, and so even as a boy wore a sword and was sworn to a life of fealty to the *daimio* or prince on whose estate he was born.

From the first, however, it was evident that this little serf had a mind and will of his own, and also a passionate longing for truth and freedom. He devoted all his spare time to study, often sitting up over his books until the morning cocks began to crow. Once the prince, his master, caught him running away from his ordinary duties to go to the house of a teacher whom he was in the habit of visiting by stealth. After giving the boy a severe flogging, he asked him where he was going. Neesima's answer will be best given in his own words at a time when he had learned only enough English to write it in the "pidgin" fashion. "'Why you run out from here?' the *daimio* said. Then I answered him, 'That I wish to learn foreign knowledge, because foreigners have got best knowledge, and I hope to understand very quickly.' Then he said, 'With what reason will you like foreign knowledge? Perhaps it will mistake yourself.' I said to him sooner, 'Why will it mistake myself? I guess every one must take some knowledge. If a man has not any knowledge, I will worth him as a dog or a pig.' Then he laughed, and said to me, 'You are a stable-boy.'"

Not less remarkable than this thirst for knowledge was the lad's consciousness of the rights of human beings, and passionate desire for fuller liberty:

"A day my comrade sent me an Atlas of United States, which was written in Chinese letter by some American

PRAYING TO IDOLS

A Japanese peasant girl saying her prayers to the stone images of Amida. The load on her back is firewood.

minister. I read it many times, and I was wondered so much as my brain would melted out of my head, because I liked it very much—picking one President, building free schools, poorhouses, house of correction, and machine-working, and so forth, and I though that a government of every country must be as President of United States. And I murmured myself that, O governor of Japan! Why you keep down us, as a dog or a pig? We are people of Japan; if you govern us, you must love us as your children."

But above all young Neesima felt a deep longing after God. When he was about fifteen years of age, to the great distress of his relatives, he refused to worship any longer the family gods which stood on a shelf in the house. He saw for himself that they were "only whittled things," and that they never touched the food and drink which he offered to them. Not long after this he got possession of an abridged Bible history in the Chinese language, with which he was well acquainted, and was immensely struck by the opening sentence, "In the beginning God created the heaven and the earth." Immediately he recognized the Creator's claim to be worshipped. To this Unknown God he began thereafter to pray, "Oh, if You have eyes, look upon me; if You have ears, listen for me."

Before long it became Neesima's constant desire to find his way to the port of Hakodate, as an open port, where he thought he might fall in with some Englishman or American from whom to obtain knowledge that he wanted. He made application to the *daimio* to be allowed to undertake the voyage, but got only a scolding and a beating for his pains. Yet he did not despair. In the quaint language of his earliest English style, "My stableness did not destroy by their expostulations." He waited patiently for four or five years, and at last, to his inexpressible joy, secured permission to go to Hakodate in a sailing-junk which belonged to his master. The junk was a coaster, and it was several weeks before he reached the haven of his hopes. Getting to Hakodate at last, it seemed for a time as if nothing but disappointment was in store for him there. He could find no one to teach him English, and meanwhile his little stock of money melted rapidly away. At length matters began to look brighter. He fell in with a Russian priest who gave him some employment, and he made the acquaintance of a young Japanese, Mr. Munokite, who was a clerk in an English store, and who not only taught him a little English, but helped to carry out a secret determination he had now formed of escaping to America at the earliest opportunity.

He had not come to this decision without long and anxious thought. It involved great sacrifices and no small danger. In those days a Japanese subject was forbidden to leave the country on pain of death. If caught in the act of attempting to do so, he forfeited his life; while if he made good his escape, this meant that he had banished himself for ever from the "Land of the Rising Sun."

It was painful for the youth to think of leaving his parents without even saying good-bye, and with no prospect of ever seeing them again, especially as he had been brought up under the influence of the Confucian doctrine of filial obedience. But he thought the matter out, and saw at last that in the search for truth and God it may be proper to set all other claims aside. "I discovered for the first time," he wrote afterwards, "that the doctrines of Confucius on the filial relations are narrow and fallacious. I felt that I must take my own course. I must serve my Heavenly Father more than my earthly parents."

And Neesima loved his country as well as his home, for patriotism is a sentiment which glows with extraordinary warmth in every Japanese heart. Moreover, he was something of a poet as well as a patriot, seeing his country in the glowing hues of a lively imagination. The verses he wrote far out on the China Sea, after he had made good his flight, show how his heart kept turning back to the dear land of flowers. "If a man be determined in his mind to run away a thousand miles," one of his poems says, "he expects to have to endure great sufferings, and why can he be anxious about his home? But how strange! In the night, when the spring wind is blowing, in a dream he sees flowers in the garden at home."

But we are anticipating somewhat, for the story of Neesima's adventurous flight has yet to be told. After endless difficulties, his friend Munokite secured leave for him to work his passage to Shanghai on an American schooner, the *Berlin*, under Captain Savory. He had, of course, to smuggle himself on board at his own risk, and to do so with the full knowledge that if detected by the harbor police he would be handed over to the executioner without delay. His plans had accordingly to be laid with the utmost caution. When night fell, he had a secret meeting in a private house with Munokite and two other young friends. They supped together, and passed round the *sake*-cup in token of love and faithfulness. At midnight the fugitive crept out of the house in the garb of a servant, carrying a bundle and following one of his friends who walked in front with a dignified air wearing two swords, as if he were the master. By back streets and dark lanes they found their way to the water's edge, where a small boat was already in waiting. Neesima was placed in the bottom of the boat and covered up with a tarpaulin as if he were a cargo of provisions; and then swiftly, but with muffled oars, the boatman pulled out to the schooner. A rope was thrown over the side, and the cargo suddenly becoming very much alive, scrambled on board and hurried below.

That night he never slept a wink, for he knew that the worst danger was yet to come. In those days every vessel leaving Hakodate harbor was keenly searched at the last moment to make sure that no Japanese subject was secreted anywhere on board. Early next morning the police boat was seen coming off to the schooner for this purpose; and Neesima felt that his hour of destiny was at hand. But Captain Savory had laid his plans carefully too, for he also was running a risk; and he hid his dangerous passenger in a part of the ship where the watchdogs of the port never thought of looking for him. The search was over at last; the anchor weighed; the sails spread to an offshore breeze. The *Berlin* forged her way through the shipping and out to the open sea. Neesima was now safe and free. It was on July 18, 1864, and the hero of our story was only 21 years of age.

After a very disagreeable passage to Shanghai and ten days of wretchedness and uncertainty in that busy port, where he could not get rid of the idea that even yet he might be betrayed and sent back to Japan, our adventurer found another American vessel, the *Wild Rover*, bound for Boston, and succeeded in persuading the captain to take him on board without wages as his own personal servant. The voyage was a tedious one, for the *Wild Rover* was a "tramp," which sailed here and there about the China Seas for eight months before turning homewards, and spent four months more on the ocean passage. While they were lying in Hong Kong harbor, Neesima discovered a Chinese New Testament in a shop, and felt that he must secure it at all costs. But he had not a copper of his own, and having promised to work his passage without wages, felt that he could not ask the captain for any money. At last he bethought himself of his sword, which, being a *samurai*, he had brought with him as a matter of course. Could he honorably part with this weapon which marked the dignity of his caste, and was to him like his shield to a young Spartan—an indispensable badge of his own self-respect? He was not long in deciding. The Japanese sword was soon in the hand of a dealer, and Neesima triumphantly bore his prize back to the ship. He read the book day and night, and found in it answers to some of the questions which had so long perplexed his mind.

When the *Wild Rover* reached Boston our hero's trials were by no means over. The Civil War had lately ended. Work was scarce; the price of everything was high. Nobody wanted this Japanese lad with his "pidgin" English and his demand to be sent to school. He began to fear that the hopes of years might only have been delusions after all. "I could not read book very cheerfully," he remarks, "and I'm only looking around myself a long time as a lunatic."

It is quite characteristic of his romantic experiences that his first real comfort came from a copy of *Robinson Crusoe* which he picked up for a few cents in a second hand bookstore. Possibly he felt that there were some analogies between his adventures and trials and those of the hero of Defoe's great novel, and that he was almost as friendless and solitary on the shores of this great continent as the shipwrecked mariner on that lonely island beach. But what appealed to him most of all were Crusoe's prayers. Hitherto he had cried to God as an unknown God, feeling all the while that perhaps God had no eyes to see him, no ears to listen for him. Now he learned from Crusoe's manner of praying that in all his troubles he must cry to God as a present, personal friend. And so day-by-day, in the full belief that God was listening, he uttered this prayer: "Please don't cast me away into miserable condition. Please let me reach my great aim."

Neesima's worst anxieties were nearly over now. His "great aim" was almost in sight. As soon as the *Wild Rover* reached Boston, the captain had gone off on a long visit to his friends, not thinking much about his Japanese cabin boy or expecting to see him again. But on his return to his ship some weeks after, he found "Joe," as the lad was called on shipboard, still hovering about the vessel as his one ark of refuge. This led him to speak to his owner, a Mr. Hardy, of the queer young Oriental he had brought to America, and Mr. Hardy, who was a large-hearted and generous Christian man, at once declared that he would make some provision for the poor fellow. His first idea was to employ him as a house servant; but when his wife and he met the youth and heard his wonderful story, they saw immediately that this was no ordinary immigrant of the stowaway order; and instead of making him a servant they took him into their family practically as an adopted son, and gave him a thorough education, first in an academy at Andover and afterwards at Amherst College. It was in token of this adoption, that when he was baptized as a member of the Christian Church, he took his full name of Joseph Hardy Neesima. On shipboard, as has been mentioned, he was called "Joe," the sailors having decided that he must have some short and handy name, and "Joe" suggesting itself as convenient. "Keep the name," Mr. Hardy said after hearing how it was given. For he felt that, like another Joseph, who went down to Egypt as a captive and became the savior of his brethren, Joseph Neesima, the Japanese runaway, might yet become a benefactor to his country. He lived long enough to see his hopes much more than realized.

After graduating honorably at Amherst College, Neesima entered himself a student at Andover Theological Seminary, with the view of being ordained as a fully qualified missionary to his own countrymen. Soon after this a pathway for his return to Japan opened up in a manner that was almost dramatic. Since his departure from Hakodate in 1864, the chariot wheels of progress had been moving rapidly in the land of his birth. Japan was beginning to deserve in a wider sense than before its name of "The Land of the Rising Sun." Instead of closing all her doors and windows and endeavoring to shut out the light at every chink, she was now eager to live and move in the full sunshine of Western knowledge. The great political and

social revolution had taken place. The Mikado had issued
that epoch-making proclamation in which he declared;
"The uncivilized customs of former times will be broken;
the impartiality and justice displayed in the workings
of nature adopted as a basis of action; and intellect and
learning will be sought for throughout the world in order to
establish the foundations of empire."

It was in pursuance of this new policy that there came
to Washington in the winter of 1871-72 a distinguished
embassy from the Imperial Court of Japan, which had for
its special commission to inspect and report upon the
workings of Western civilization. The embassy soon felt
the need of someone who could not only act as interpreter,
but also assist it in the task of examining the institutions,
and especially the educational institutions, of foreign lands.
For some time Mr. Mori, the Japanese Minister in the
United States, had had his eye on his young countryman
at Andover, and he now invited him to Washington
to be introduced to the embassy. So favorable was the
impression produced by his personal appearance, and so
evident was it that he was thoroughly conversant with the
principles and methods of Western culture, that he was
immediately requested to accompany the ambassadors in
the capacity of advisors, on their tour through the United
States and Europe; while overtures of the most flattering
kind were made to him, with brilliant prospects in the
political world whenever he returned to his native land.
But Neesima's mind was now fully made up regarding his
work in life. When he returned to Japan it would not be as
a politician, but as a Christian missionary. In the meantime,

however, he willingly put his services at the disposal of the Mikado's embassy, and thereby not only greatly enlarged his experience, but gained influential friends among the rising statesmen of Japan, friends who were afterwards of no small help to him in his efforts to promote among his countrymen the cause of a Christian civilization. The special task was assigned to him of drawing up a paper on "The Universal Education of Japan." He discharged the duty with such ability that his essay became the basis of the report subsequently made by the embassy on the subject of education. And this report, with certain modifications, was the foundation of the Japanese system of education as it has existed ever since.

After a year had been spent in this interesting way, Neesima returned to Andover, and on the completion of his theological course was ordained by the American Board of Missions as an evangelist to his fellow countrymen, his foster father, Mr. Hardy, undertaking to provide for his support. Ten years had now elapsed from the time he was smuggled out of Japan in the hold of a little schooner—a poor and unknown lad, and a criminal in the eyes of the law. He was about to return a highly cultured Christian gentlemen, with not a few influential friends on both sides of the Pacific. And he was returning with a purpose. He had found the Light he came to seek, but he was far from being satisfied with that. His aim now was to be a light-bringer to Japan. He was deeply conscious of the truth that:

> Heaven doth with us as we with torches do,
> Not light them for themselves.

"He was unwilling," says Dr. Davis, his colleague in after years and one of his biographers, "to go back with a full heart but with an empty hand." His purpose was to start a Christian College in which he could meet the craving of Young Japan for Western knowledge—the craving which he knew so well—while at the same time might surround the students with a Christian atmosphere, and train some of them to be preachers and teachers of Jesus Christ. But he could not start a college without means, and where means were to come from he did not know.

He spoke of his plans in the first place to various members of the American Board. But the Board's hands were full, and he met with no encouragement. Then he took counsel with himself. It had been arranged that before leaving America he should give an address at the annual public meeting of the Board, and he determined to utilize this opportunity. To the very best of his ability he prepared a speech. But when he stepped on the platform and faced the great audience, a fate befell him which has often come to public speakers at a critical moment in the beginning of their careers. His carefully arranged ideas all disappeared; his mind became a perfect blank; and everyone present thought he had completely broken down. But suddenly a thought flashed into his mind. Opening up an entirely fresh line of address, and for fifteen minutes, while the tears streamed down his cheeks, he pleaded the cause of his country with such overwhelming earnestness that at the end of his short speech, $5,000 were subscribed on the spot, and Neesima knew the foundation stone of a Christian College in Japan was already laid.

It was characteristic of our hero's indomitable courage that when he reached Japan he started his College, which he called the "Doshisha," or "Company of One Endeavor"—not in any city of the coast, where Western ideas had become familiar, but in Kyoto itself, the sacred city of the interior, a city of six thousand temples, and the very heart of the religious life of Old Japan. In this place, where Buddhism and Shintoism had flourished unchallenged for 1,000 years, Neesima was subjected for a time to the furious hatred of the native priests and even to the opposition of the magistrates. For the most part these men had no objections to Western education, but Christian education they would have liked to suppress. It was now that he realized the advantage of the friendship of the members of the embassy of 1871-72. Several of those gentlemen, including the present Marquis Ito, had become prominent members of the Japanese cabinet, and they did not a little to remove difficulties out of Neesima's way.

And so the Doshisha took root and flourished, until in the last year of its founders life, when he had been engaged in his work for fifteen years, the number of students in all departments, young women as well as young men, had risen to over 900. Neesima wore himself out by his labors, and died at the comparatively early age of 47, just when he had taken steps to broaden out the Doshisha College into the Doshisha University, and had secured large sums for this purpose, including a single gift of $100,000 from a gentleman in New England, and a collection of 31,000 yen subscribed at a dinner party in Tokyo in the house of Count Inouye, after those present had been addressed by Neesima himself, who was one of the guests.

Neesima's widow had fulfilled his last wish, spoken from the depths of a humble Christian heart: "Raise no monument after my death. It is enough, that on a wooden cross there stands the word, 'The grave of Joseph Neesima.'" But the Doshisha is Neesima's living monument to Japan. More than 5,000 students have passed through it, of whom in 1903 above 80 were preachers of the Gospel, 161 were teachers, 27 were government officials, and 16 were newspaper editors. By turning out a succession of highly educated men and women, trained under Christian influences, Neesima's college has contributed no small part in the creation of that New Japan which has so swiftly stepped in these late years into the foremost rank of the great company of nations.

NOTES AND AUTHORITIES: The chief authority for this chapter is *A Maker of New Japan. Joseph Hardy Neesima*, by Rev. J. D. Davis, D.D. (Fleming H. Revell Co.)

"FROM FAR FORMOSA"

C H A P T E R F O U R

"How dear is Formosa to my heart! On that island the best of my years have been spent.

How dear is Formosa to my heart! A lifetime of joy is centered here.

I love to look up to its lofty peaks, down into its yawning chasms, and away out on its surging seas. How willing I am to gaze upon these forever!

My heart's ties to Taiwan cannot be severed! To that island I devote my life.

My heart's ties to Taiwan cannot be severed! There I find my joy.

I should like to find a final resting place within sound of its surf and under the shade of its waving bamboo."

—"My Final Resting Place" by George Mackay

FROM THE EDITORS: Born in Ontario, Canada, the youngest of six children, George Leslie Mackay from an early age had a passion for Christ and missions. This passion would in time flower into a life dedicated to the people of Taiwan, or

Formosa as it used to be called. During the 19th century, a wave of Western missionaries streamed into China, Taiwan and other Asian countries. George Mackay was one of this number, arriving in Taiwan in March of 1872. His amazing linguistic gifts, his love for the people, and his active ministry life made a profound impact on the entire nation. Upon his departure for Canada years later, Christians and non-Christians alike filled the street to cheer for him. In the course of time, Mackay married a Taiwanese lady and raised a family on the island. He created a Taiwanese-English dictionary, and he ministered to the headhunters of the highlands as well as to the Chinese in the cities. He opened a medical clinic and applied his knowledge of dentistry to help heal the body while boldly preaching the Gospel of Jesus everywhere he went. He also taught and equipped a group of young men to continue the work.

George Mackay's ministry initially received great persecution to include the martyrdoms of many of his coworkers and converts, but he pressed on and persevered in faith. One might ask why he persevered through such hardship? Why pay the price and spend his life in such a place? The answer is found in his own words — love — the love of God poured out through Mackay's life; the overflowing love for the men and women of Formosa who were perishing, but to whom the Gospel had come so that they might have everlasting life.

Dr. George Leslie Mackay (1844—1901)

For the title of this chapter we have taken the name of a book by Dr. George Leslie Mackay, of the Canadian Presbyterian Church, whose acquaintance with Formosa (now known as Taiwan) and its people—the people of the mountains as well as the plains—is of an altogether unique kind. The title is appropriate, for though on the map Formosa is not more distant than China or Japan, it is much farther off than the moon to the vast majority of people, so far as any knowledge of its history was concerned at the turn of the 20th century. But it had early on attracted the attention of Mr. Mackay, a young Canadian of Highland Scottish decent. Sent out to China as a missionary by the Presbyterian Church of Canada, which gave him a pretty free hand in the selection of a definite sphere, he chose the northern part of Formosa—perfectly virgin soil so far as any Christian work was concerned. The evangelization of North Formosa was a hard and dangerous task to be attempted by a single man, but Mackay flung himself into it with all the enthusiasm of a Celt, as well as the steady devotion of a brave soldier of the Cross.

Formosa was a wild and lawless land, with its mixture of mutually hostile races, its debased Mongolian and savage Malayans, its men of the plains and men of the mountains, its corrupt officials in the towns and savage head-hunters in the hill forests. Mackay, however, went about fearlessly, with a dentist's forceps (a wonderful talisman) in one hand and a Bible in the other. At one time we find him sleeping contentedly in the filthy cabin of a

farmer on the swampy rice plains with a litter of pigs, it
might almost be said, for his bedfellows, the pig being a
highly domesticated animal in Formosa and treated by its
master as an Englishman treats his pet dog. Again, he is far
up amongst the mountains in the land of the headhunters,
where his sleeping apartment, which is also the sleeping
apartment of the whole family, is adorned with a row of
grinning skulls and queues that testify to the prowess of
his host in murdering Chinamen and other dwellers on the
plains. It was by a courage and persistence which nothing
could daunt that this young Scotch-Canadian won his way
in Formosa, until to those who are interested in the history
of missions, "Mackay of Formosa" seems as natural and
inevitable a title as "Mackay of Uganda" or "Chalmers of
New Guinea."

Apart from the Japanese settlers who have planted
themselves in the island since the war of 1895, the population
of Formosa is divided between the aborigines, who are of
a Malayan stock, and the Chinese, who in ever increasing
numbers have poured in from the adjacent mainland.
Though only half the size of Scotland, the island is dominated
by a range of mountains quite Alpine in their height, the
loftiest rising to between 14,000 and 15,000 feet above the
sea. Along the coast, however, there are fertile stretches,
perfectly flat, formed by the alluvial deposits washed down
in the course of ages. On the richer of these plains, as well
as on the lower reaches of the hills, the incoming Chinamen
settled, usually by no better title than the right of might.
"Rice farms and tea plantations took the place of forest tangle
and wild plateau; the rude hamlets of another race vanished;

towns and cities with their unmistakable marks of the 'Middle Kingdom' took their place; and the Chinese became a superior power in Formosa."

To the Chinese, of course, the original inhabitants without exception were "barbarians," but the Malayan population, though comprising a great many different tribes, may be roughly divided into well-defined sections. First there are those who have accepted Chinese authority, and in a modified form have adopted the Chinese civilization and religion. These go by the name of Pe-po-hoan, or "barbarians of the plain." Then there are those who have absolutely refused to acknowledge the Chinese invaders as the masters of Formosa, and, though driven into the mountains and forests, have retained their ancestral freedom. These are the much-dreaded Chhi-hoan or "raw barbarians," whose manner of life in many respects recalls that of their kinsmen the Hill Dyaks of Borneo. Among these mountain savages, as formerly among the Dyaks, headhunting is cultivated as a fine art. They hate the Chinese with a deadly hatred, and hardly less their own Pe-po-hoan kinsfolk who have yielded to the stranger and accepted his ways. Pe-po-hoan and Chinamen alike are considered as fair game, and their skulls are mingled indiscriminately in the ghastly collection, which is the chief glory of the mountain brave, as it forms the principal adornment of his dwelling.

Naturally it was among the Chinese in the towns that Mackay began his work. He was fortunate in gathering round him very early some earnest young men, who not only accepted Christianity for themselves, but became his disciples and followers with a view to teaching and helping others. These students, as they were called, accompanied him on all his tours, not only gaining valuable experience thereby, but being of real assistance in various ways. For instance, Mackay soon discovered that the people of Formosa, partly because of the prevalence of malarial fever, and partly because they are constantly chewing the betel nut, have very rotten teeth and suffer dreadfully from toothache. Though not a doctor, he knew a little of medicine and surgery, having attended classes in these subjects by way of preparing himself for his work abroad; but he found that nothing helped him so much in making his way among the people as his modest skill in dentistry. The priests and other enemies of Christianity might persuade the people that their fevers and other ailments had been cured not by the medicines of the "foreign devil," but by the intervention of their own gods. The power of the missionary, however, to give instantaneous relief to one in the agonies of toothache was unmistakable, and tooth-extraction worked wonders in breaking down prejudice and opposition. It was here that some of the students proved especially useful. They learned to draw teeth almost if not quite as well as Mackay himself, so that between them they were able to dispose of as many as 500 patients in an afternoon.

The usual custom of Mackay and his little band of students as they journeyed about the country was to take their stand in an open space, often on the stone steps of a temple, and after singing a hymn or two to attract attention, to proceed to the work of tooth-pulling, thereafter inviting the people to listen to their message. For the most part the

DR. MACKAY AND HIS ASSISTANTS AS DENTISTS

crowd was very willing to listen. Sudden relief from pain produces gratitude even towards a "foreign devil," and the innate Chinese suspicion of some black arts or other evil designs was always guarded against by scrupulously placing the tooth of each patient in the palm of his own hand. The people began to love Mackay, and this opened their hearts to his preaching. Men and women came to confess their faith, and in one large village which was the center of operations there were so many converts that a preaching hall had to be secured, which Sunday after Sunday was packed by an expectant crowd.

Opposition is often the best proof of success, and in Mackay's case it soon came in cruel and tragic forms. A cunning plot was laid between the priestly party and the civil officials to accuse a number of these Chinese Christians of conspiring to assassinate the mandarin. Six innocent men were seized and put in the stocks in the dungeons of the city of Bang-kah. Mock trials were held, in the course of which the prisoners were bambooed, made to kneel on red-hot chains, and tortured in various other ways. At last one morning two of the heroic band, a father and son, were taken out of their dungeon and dragged off to the place of execution. Both were beheaded, son first, then father. Then their heads, placed in baskets, were carried slowly back to Bang-kah with the notice fixed above them, Jip kon-e lang than ("Heads of the Christians"). All along the way the town crier summoned the multitude to witness the fate of those who followed the "barbarian." And when the walls of Bang-kah were reached the two heads were fastened above the city gate, just as the heads of criminals or martyrs used to be set above the Netherbow at Edinburgh or Temple Bar in London, for a terror and a warning to all who passed by. It was a cruel fate, and yet better than that of the remaining prisoners. Their lot was to be slowly starved or tortured to death in their filthy dungeons.

But in spite of these horrors—partly, we might say, because of them—the number of Christians in North Formosa steadily grew, until at length, as Dr. Mackay puts it, "Bank-kah itself was taken." Not that this important place, "the Gibraltar of heathendom" in the island, was transformed into a Christian city. But it ceased, at all events, to be fiercely anti-Christian, and came to honor the very man whom it had hustled, hooted at, pelted with mud and rotten eggs, and often plotted to kill. A striking proof of the change was given by and by when Mackay was about to return to Canada on a visit. The headmen of the city sent a deputation to ask him to allow them to show their appreciation of himself and his work by according him a public send off. He was not sure about it at first, not caring much for demonstrations of this kind, but on reflection concluded that it might be well, and might do good to the Christian cause, to allow them to have their own way. So he was carried through the streets of Bang-kah to the jetty in a silk-lined sedan chair, preceded by the officials of the place, and followed by three hundred soldiers and bands of civilians bearing flags and banners, to a musical accompaniment provided by no fewer than eight Chinese orchestras made up of cymbals, drums, gongs, pipes, guitars, mandolins, tambourines, and clarionets. Heathens and Christians alike cheered him as he boarded the steam launch which was to take him off from the shore, while the Christians who had stood firmly by him through turbulent times broke into a Chinese version of the old Scottish paraphrase, "I'm not ashamed to own my Lord."

But while Mackay found his base of operations among the Chinese in the north and west of Formosa, he did not forget the Malayan aborigines, whether those of the plains or those of the mountains. As soon as he had got a firm footing and gathered a band of competent helpers around him, he began to turn his attention to the Pe-po-hoan, the "barbarians of the plains," who cultivate their rice farms in the low-laying and malarial districts along the northeast coast. He had already experienced many of the drawbacks of Formosan travel. He had known what it was to be swept down the current in trying to ford dangerous streams, to push his way through jungles full of lurking serpents, to encounter hostile crowds in village or town who jeered at the "foreign devils," or regarded him, as the boy said of birds in his essay on the subject, as being "very useful to throw stones at." And night, when it came, he often found not less trying than day, possibly still more so. The filthy rest houses were not places of much rest to a white man. Pigs frisked out and in, and slept or grunted beneath the traveler's bed. The bed itself was a plank with brick legs, the mattress a dirty grass mat on which coolies had smoked opium for years. And when, overpowered by weariness he fell asleep, he was apt to be suddenly awakened by the attacks of what he humorously described as "three generations of crawling creatures."

Greater dangers and worse discomforts than these,

however, had now to be faced in carrying the Gospel to the country of the Pe-po-hoan. In the mountains over which it was necessary to pass in order to cross from the west coast to the east, Mackay and his students had to run the gauntlet of the stealthy headhunters. They had more than one narrow escape. Passing by the mouth of a gorge one day, they heard in the distance blood-curdling yells and screams, and presently a Chinese man came rushing up all out of breath and told them that he and four others had just been attacked by the savages, and that his companions were all speared and beheaded, while he had only managed to escape with his life. When the plains were reached the Pe-po-hoan did not prove at first a friendly or receptive people. From village after village they were turned away with reviling, the inhabitants often setting their wolfish dogs upon them. The weather was bad, and in that low-lying region the roads were soon turned into quagmires where the feet sank into eighteen inches of mud. When night fell a Chinese inn would have been welcome enough; but sometimes no better sleeping place could be had than the lee side of a dripping rice-stack.

But after a while things began to improve. Like Jesus in Galilee, Mackay found his first disciples in the Kap-tsu-lan plain among the fishermen—bold, hardy fellows, who live in scattered villages along that coast. Three of these fishers came to him one day and said, "You have been going through and through our plain, and none has received you. Come to our village, and we will listen to you." They led Mackay and his students to their village, gave them a good supper of rice and fish, and then one of them took a large conch shell, which in other days had served as a war-trumpet, and summoned the whole population to an assembly. Till the small hours of the morning Mackay was kept busy preaching, conversing, discussing, and answering questions. The very next day these people determined to have a church of their own in which to worship the true God. They sailed down the coast to the forest country farther south to cut logs of wood, and though they were attacked by the savages while doing so, and some of them wounded, they returned in due course with a load of timber. Bricks were made out of mud and rice-chaff, and a primitive little chapel was soon erected, in which every evening at the blowing of the conch the entire village met to hear the preacher. Mackay stayed two months in this place, and by that time it had become nominally Christian. Several times, he tells us, he dried his dripping clothes at night in front of a fire made of idolatrous paper, idols, and ancestral tablets which the people had given him to destroy. One reason for this rapid and wholesale conversion to Christianity no doubt lay in the fact that the Chinese idolatry, which these Pe-po-hoan fishermen had been induced to accept, never came very near to their hearts. Originally they or their fathers had been nature worshipers, as all the mountain savages still are, and many of them were inclined to look upon the rites and ceremonies to which they submitted as unwelcome reminders of their subjection to an alien race.

What took place in this one village was soon repeated in several others on the Kap-tsu-lan plain. Even in places where men, women, and children had rejected him at first and hurled "the contumelious stone" at his head, Mackay came to be welcomed by the people as their best friend. And by and by no fewer than nineteen chapels sprang up in that plain, the preachers and pastors in every case being native Christians, and several of them being drawn from among the Pe-po-hoan themselves.

But something must now be said about the Chhi-hoan or savage barbarians of the mountains. More than once in the course of his tours among the Pe-po-hoan Mackay narrowly escaped from the spears and knives of these warriors, who live by hunting wild animals in the primeval forest, but whose peculiar delight it is to hunt for human heads, and above all for the heads of the hated Chinese. On one occasion a party of Chinese traders with whom he was staying in an outpost settlement was attacked by a band of two dozen savages; and though the latter were eventually beaten off, it was not till they had secured the heads of three of Mackay's trading friends.

According to the unwritten law of the mountain villages, no man is permitted to marry until he has proved his prowess by bringing at least one head to his chief, while eminence in the estimation of the tribe always depends upon the number of skulls which a brave can display under the eaves or along the inside walls of his hut. Mackay tells of one famous chief who was captured at last by the Chinese authorities, and who said, as he was led out to execution, that he was not ashamed to die, because in his house in the mountains he could show a row of skulls only six short of a hundred.

A headhunter's outfit consists, in the first place, of a

long, light thrusting spear with an arrow-shaped blade eight inches in length. In his belt he carries a cruel looking crooked knife with which to slash off his victim's head. Over the shoulder he wears a bag of strong, twisted twine, capable of carrying two or three heads at a time. From the attacks of these bloodthirsty savages none who live or move on the borderland between mountains and plain are ever secure by day or by night. In the daytime the hunters usually go out singly, concealing themselves in the tall grass of the level lands, or behind some stray boulder by a path through a glen along which sooner or later a traveler is likely to pass. When his quarry is within spear-thrust, the crouching hunter leaps upon him, striking for his heart; and soon a headless corpse is lying on the ground, while the savage, with his prize slung round his neck, is trotting swiftly, by forest paths known only to himself, towards his distant mountain home.

But more commonly the attack is made at night, and made by a party of braves. In this case everything is carefully planned for weeks before. Watchers on the hilltops, or scouts lurking in the bush along the edge of the forests, report as to when a village festivity is likely to make its defenders less watchful, or when the fishermen have gone off on a distant fishing expedition, leaving their homes to the care of none but womenfolk. Having selected a house for attack, the savages silently surround it in the darkness, creeping stealthily nearer and nearer until, at a signal from the leader, one of them goes on before the rest and sets fire to the thatch. When the unfortunate inmates, aroused from sleep by the crackle of the flames and half stifled by the

ARMED HEAD-HUNTERS IN FORMOSA

Their victims are men, Chinese or even their own people who have been conquered and live amongst the Chinese. Their outfit of a spear, and knife, and a bag capable of holding two or three heads. No sleuth-hound is truer to the scent, no tiger stealthier of foot in the pursuit of prey.

smoke, attempt to rush out of the door, they are instantly speared and their heads secured. In a few moments, before the nearest neighbors have had time to come to the rescue, or even been awakened from their slumber, the hunters have disappeared into the night. These headhunters are pagan to the core and greatly in need of a Savior.

The return to the village of a successful headhunting party is a scene of fiendish delight, in which men, women, and children alike all take a part. Hour after hour dancing and drinking is carried on, as the Chhi-hoan gloat over the death of their enemies and praise the prowess of their warriors. On rare occasions cannibalism is even practiced. Dr. Mackay had himself been present in a mountain village on the return of a headhunting party, and had seen this barbaric practice.

One who goes among such people must literally take his life in his hands, for he may at any moment fall a victim to treachery or to the passion for human blood. But perfect courage and unvarying truth and kindness will carry a traveler far, and Mackay had the further advantage of being possessed of medical and surgical skill. He owed something, moreover, to his not having a pigtail. "You must be a kinsman of ours," the Chhi-hoan said, as they examined the missionary's back hair. And so by degrees Mackay came to live in close touch with these savages, and found that, apart from their headhunting instincts, they had some good and amiable qualities of their own. From time to time he visited them as he got the opportunity, and was even able in some cases to bring a measure of light to darkened minds.

One year, Mackay spent a Christmas holiday high up among the mountains as the guest of one of the barbarian chiefs. The house was a single large room, full thirty feet long, in which at night a fire blazed at either end. Around one fire the women squatted spinning cord for nets, around the other the braves smoked and discussed a headhunting expedition, which they proposed to undertake before long. On the walls were the customary rows of skulls, their grinning teeth lighted up fitfully by the flickering gleams from the burning fire logs. In the midst of this promiscuous crowd, which included a mother and her newborn babe, Mackay with his students had to sleep that night. But before the time came to lie down and rest, he proposed that he and his Christian companions should give a song, a proposal which secured silence at once, for the aborigines are much more musical than the Chinese, and are very fond of singing. And so on Christmas night, in that wild spot where no white man had ever been before, and to that strange audience, Mackay and his little band of Chinese converts sang some Christian hymns. And after that he told the listening savages the story of the first Christmas night, and of the love of Him who was born in the stable at Bethlehem for the headhunters of Formosa, no less than for the white men whose home was over the sea.

NOTES AND AUTHORITIES: The material for this chapter is derived from Dr. Mackay's book, *From Far Formosa* (Edinburgh: Oliphant, Anderson, and Ferrier).

"THE SAVIOR OF LIAO-YANG"

C H A P T E R   F I V E

FROM THE EDITORS: During the 19th century, China was a land humiliated and controlled by numerous foreign powers, all interested in economic gain. Austria, France, Germany, Great Britain, Italy, Japan, and Russia fought for trading rights and influence in governance, while the United States waited for its opportunities. Meantime, the Chi'ing Dynasty empress, Tsu His, was looking to rid her country of the foreigners and preserve her sovereign rule. Towards the latter part of the 1800s, the nation faced severe drought and social unrest, led in part by a secret revolutionary society known as the "Boxers." The empress used these unruly forces to her own ends at first, in order to hamper Western interests. For several years, the Boxers continued their destructive path unchecked by the royal army. In the year 1900, great throngs of Boxers attacked and killed many of the foreign missionaries and Chinese converts. Foreign leaders either left the country or fled to the capital for protection. Over 20,000 Boxers surrounded the city, seeking to kill the empress and the foreigners gathered there. The royal army and foreign refugees resisted the siege for two months. Finally, as the city approached mass starvation, a force of international soldiers, including 2,500 American sailors and Marines, liberated the capital. The empress fled, the power of the Chi'ing Dynasty was broken, and an "Open Door" policy remained in effect for foreign interests in China until the end of World War II.

While some of the Western powers fought the battle in the south, Russian forces moved into the Manchurian province. Japan felt threatened by the Russian encroachment and also sought control of this rich mineral region. This rising Eastern power sent forces into China to fight the Russians over Manchuria, between 1904 and 1905. This struggle, known as the Russo-Japanese war, was an extremely bloody affair, with over 160,000 combined casualties in the campaign's final land battle alone.

Into this fray stepped Dr. Westwater, a missionary under the auspices of the United Presbyterian Church, now known as the United Free Church of Scotland. Very little is known about his life before arriving in China. However, his "Free Healing Hall," in the city of Liao-Yang became renowned throughout Manchuria. Forced to leave his field of service in Liao-Yang during the Boxer Rebellion, Westwater served as a volunteer military doctor in the Russian army while they advanced through Manchuria. As the forces approached Liao-yang, Dr. Westwater was able to intercede with the commanding general to keep his troops from sacking and destroying the city upon their approach. Permission was granted, and the city hailed him as her rescuer.

Dr. A. Macdonald Westwater (dates unknown)

In an earlier chapter on the work of Dr. Chamberlain among the Telugus of southeastern India, something was said about the romantic aspects of even the ordinary routine of medical missions. Whether in the wards of his hospital or itinerating among scattered villages, the missionary doctor has an opportunity and an influence beyond any possessed by one who is only a preacher or teacher.

Jesus Christ, it has been said, was the first medical missionary. As He went about Galilee doing good, He not only "preached the Gospel of the kingdom," but "healed all manner of sickness and all manner of disease among the people." In this combination of healing with preaching lay a large part of the secret of our Lord's attractive power. The modern missionary doctor cannot normally work miracles. But through the progress of medical science he has acquired a marvelous power to heal sickness and relieve suffering. And by the quiet exercise of his skill amongst a heathen and sometimes hostile population, he inspires a confidence and calls forth a gratitude by which the solid walls of prejudice are rapidly broken down and locked doors are thrown wide open for the entrance of the Christian Gospel. Such methodology was the way in which Dr. A. Macdonald Westwater began his famous work.

The Boxer madness had swept up to Manchuria from the south, and had raged across the country with the swift destructiveness of a prairie fire. Hordes of Chinese soldiers joined the anti-foreign movement, and everywhere there was "red ruin and the breaking up of laws." Christian missions and native Christians suffered most, for they had to bear the full brunt of the savage hatred stirred up against the "foreign devils." But the rioters did not stop short with massacring Christians and destroying mission property. Boxerism soon turned to indiscriminate brigandage. And by and by the great city of Mukden, the capital of the three provinces of Manchuria, was looted, while for a distance of 500 miles the marauders marched along the railway line, tearing up the rails, destroying stations, plundering and burning houses and villas on either hand.

But the avengers were soon on the trail. Russian troops poured into Manchuria, and a terrible work of reprisal began. Advancing simultaneously from south and north, the Russians simply wiped out every village in which they found any railway material, and left the country behind them black and smoking on both sides of what had once been the railway line.

The terror of their name traveled before them. As they drew near to Hai-cheng the people fled *en masse*, though the better off among them, in the hope of securing some consideration for their property, took the precaution of leaving caretakers behind in their houses and shops. But the troops of the Czar treated Hai-cheng as they had already treated many a meaner place. Of the numerous caretakers left in the city only six escaped from the pitiless massacre that followed the military occupation. Hai-cheng itself was looted and left absolutely bare. And then the Russians moved onwards, still destroying as they went, and making their way now towards the important city of Liao-yang.

In Liao-yang, previous to the Boxer outbreak, Dr. Westwater, an agent of the United Presbyterian, now the United Free Church of Scotland, had carried on a splendid work for years. His "Free Healing Hall," as the name of his mission hospital ran in Chinese, had become a place of note in the city. In this hall, as one of the citizens, not himself a Christian expressed it, "the blind saw, the lame walked, the deaf heard; and all were counseled to virtue."

Compelled by the Boxer fury to lay down his work in Liao-yang for some time, the doctor sought and obtained permission to accompany the Russian punitive field force as a member of the Russian Red Cross Society with General Alexandrovski at its head. He was present in every battle fought during the campaign, and immensely impressed the Russian officers by his surgical skill, which quite surpassed that of any doctor of their own. In this way he gained the good opinion and respect of the general in command, and was able to do something towards checking the frightful excesses of which, at first, the army was guilty.

When the advancing troops reached Liao-yang, a small engagement was fought in which the Chinese were defeated. Following up their victory, the Russians were just about to enter the suburbs, when they were fired upon from the city walls and so brought to a halt. Meanwhile from the Korean Gate the inhabitants were pouring out in crowds, endeavoring to make good their escape before the Russians should take the city. Numbers of people were trampled to death in the panic stricken rush and many were pushed into the river and drowned. To crown the horrors of the scene, the Russian gunners recognized this black mass of struggling fugitives, and began to throw shells into the thick of it.

It now seemed certain that Liao-yang would share the fate that had already befallen Hai-cheng—the fate of being deserted by a terrified population and given up to massacre and loot at the hands of native brigands and Russian troops. Only one man stood between the city and destruction, but that man had the soul of a hero, and proved himself equal to the occasion. Before the Russian general had ordered an assault upon the city, Dr. Westwater had obtained an interview with him. His words were brief but to the point. "I will undertake," he said, "to enter Liao-yang by myself, and to persuade the people to surrender peacefully, but upon one condition." "What is that?" asked the general. "That I have your solemn word of honor that no harm shall be done to the person of man or woman within the walls, and that there shall be absolutely no looting."

To a Russian commander this was a new way of dealing with an obstinate Chinese town. But Dr. Westwater's personality by this time had made a strong impression on him, and he at once gave his word of honor to observe the stipulated terms. The doctor then mounted his pony, and rode on all alone towards the walls of this lately Boxerised city.

Obtaining entrance by one of the gates, and riding on through the streets, he could see no sign of any living creature. It looked at first as if the whole population had already vanished, though most of them, he afterwards found, had simply shut themselves up within their houses. At last a Christian schoolboy approached who had recognized him and had come out to meet him. From this boy Dr. Westwater learned that at that very time the members of the Guild—the City Fathers of Liao-yang, as they might be called—were gathered together to take counsel regarding the city's fate.

Riding on, the doctor came to their hall of meeting, and introduced himself as one whom most of them knew as a Christian doctor, but who was now come as an ambassador of peace from the head of the Russian army. And when he went on to inform them that the general had passed his deliberate word of honor to himself to do no harm to the place if it was quietly surrendered, a thrill of astonishment and relief ran through the meeting. The word was quickly carried through the streets, and the confidence of the city was restored as if by magic. The people no longer thought of abandoning Liao-yang to its fate, but prepared with perfect calmness to receive their conquerors.

The Russian general, on the other hand, was absolutely loyal to his word. To ensure that his promises should be observed to the letter, he appointed not sergeants merely, but commissioned officers to go about the streets with the patrols. And this was the altogether unexampled result. During the whole of the Russian occupation of Liao-yang there was not a single instance of crime committed by the soldiery against the person or property of any inhabitant of the city.

This gallant deed of the Scotch missionary doctor has been described by Mr. Whigham, the well known Eastern traveler and war correspondent, as "a fine thing done by a white man all alone," and as the bravest deed of which he knows (See *The Bravest Deed I Have Ever Seen* by Hutchinson and Co., pg 37). And it was this that gained for

Dr. Westwater from the people of Manchuria his enviable name of "The Savior of Liao-yang."

Upon the citizens of Liao-yang itself Dr. Westwater's action made a very deep impression. They felt that to him they owed the salvation of their lives and homes. On his return to the city after the conclusion of his period of service with the Red Cross Society, the heads of the native guilds called on him to express their gratitude. They offered him the choice of a number of compounds for a temporary house and hospital, stating their readiness to pay all the expenses of alterations, rent, and even of medicines. Finally, about a year after, when the doctor went home to Scotland on furlough, the city honored him with a triumphal procession. Banners waved, musical instruments brayed and banged. With native dignity and grandeur the gentry of the place accompanied the man whom they delighted to honor through the streets, out of the gate, and right up to the railway station, where they bade him their best farewell.

As the result of what he had done, the doctor's name and fame spread far and wide through the provinces of Manchuria. Some time afterwards the Rev. Mr. MacNaughtan, going on a prolonged and distant missionary tour, found that right away to the banks of the Yalu River, some 200 miles from Liao-yang, Dr. Westwater's was a name to charm with. Immediately on hearing it mentioned the people would say, "Oh, that was the man who saved Liao-yang."

Hardly less deep was the effect produced by the doctor's character and action upon the Russians in Manchuria. His opinions had weight with the authorities, while he himself became a great personal favorite with all who knew him. Being a Scotchman, Muscovite demonstrativeness often caused him some embarrassment, for a Russian admirer thought nothing of throwing his arms round him and bestowing a hearty kiss. Mr. Whigham tells how he met a Russian engineer, M. Restzoff, who, learning that Mr. Whigham was a Scotchman, said he was glad to make the acquaintance of one who came from Scotland, for the two greatest men he knew of were both Scotchmen— Dr. Westwater and Sir Walter Scott!

Much water has flowed under the bridges of Manchuria—water often mingled with blood—since the days of the Boxer rising. But the events over the following years only added to Dr. Westwater's reputation, and proved once more how much can be done in the interests of humanity and Christianity, amid all "the tumult and the shouting," and the unbridled savagery of war, by a brave, strong man who has devoted his life to the service of his fellow creatures as a medical missionary.

When the tremendous struggle began between Japan and Russia, Dr. Westwater and his colleague, Mr. MacNaughtan, together with their wives, were allowed to remain in Liao-yang. This decision in itself was a tribute to the Doctor's influence, for it is practically certain that but for him the Russians would have expelled the missionaries from the province with the opening of the war. It was the entire confidence felt in him—sufficiently proved by his being in constant demand at headquarters to prescribe for the officers of the army—that enabled the mission to retain its hold upon the city right through the long period of stress and conflict.

As General Kuropatkin had fixed his headquarters at Liao-yang, every fresh disaster to the Russian forces sent an electric thrill through the whole region of which the city formed the center. And as the opposing armies drew nearer and nearer, the Russians constantly retreating and the Japanese pressing on, the surrounding population began to flock into Liao-yang by tens of thousands. At this stage the doctor obtained General Kuropatkin's permission to open a refuge for these poor homeless creatures, and soon he had four thousand of them, all heathen, under his immediate care.

Meanwhile the tide of battle rolled nearer and nearer. From Mr. NacNaughtan's lips we have received a vivid account of the scenes which were witnessed by Dr. Westwater and himself from the city walls during that long drawn week of desperate and Titanic encounter which is known as the battle of Liao-yang. Everything lay before them as in a vast panorama—the great Manchurian plain rolling out its length towards the boundary of the distant low hills, the constant stream of ammunition and commissariat wagons flowing on steadily from the station to the battlefield, and the sad stream of wounded men flowing as steadily back, the deadly shells bursting nearer and nearer until at length it became no longer possible to stand in safety on the city walls.

Then, after the days of waiting and watching, followed the days of strenuous action. Men, women, and little children, horribly smashed up, began to be carried into the mission hospital, till not only the wards but also all the surrounding sheds were crammed with patients.

Meanwhile the doctor had his crowded refuge to think of and provide for and be anxious about, for the shells were falling thick, and five times it was hit, though by a merciful providence on every occasion not a single soul within the walls was so much as scratched.

In his *Empire of the East* Mr. Bennet Burleigh, the veteran *doyen* of military correspondents, describes Dr. Westwater as he found him in the thick of his work at this decisive moment of the war. "Brave as a lion," he writes, "Dr. Westwater went about alone, regardless of shellfire and bullets, succoring the wounded and doing good." And then he goes on to tell in more detail what kind of good the doctor was doing in those awful days; how he sheltered the homeless, fed the starving, performed under all the strain of multiplied duties scores of critical operations, and yet found time to show pity and kindness to the crowds of terrified women and helpless children whom war had cast upon his hands.

"I saw the doctor," he says, "just after he had completed seven amputations, and a score more of cases remained to be dealt with." It adds to the impressiveness of Mr. Bennet Burleigh's picture of a hero at the post of duty in a trying hour when he remarks; "He had no assistant—his only helpers a few Chinese who served as nurses." We should supplement Mr. Burleigh's statement, however, by mentioning that while Dr. Westwater was ministering to the heathen refugees, Mr. MacNaughtan, by previous arrangement with his colleague, was devoting himself to the service of the native Christians of Liao-yang in their hour of need.

When the Japanese at length entered the city, they paid

their tribute, like the Russians before them, to the value of Dr. Westwater's work. It was their fire, of course, that had wrought the havoc among the noncombatants, but this was an inevitable result of the fact that the Russians had made their last stand at the railway station, and no one more regretted the suffering caused to the people of Liao-yang than the victorious general. One of his first acts was to contribute 1,000 yen to Dr. Westwater's hospital (a large sum for that time).

We have shown something of Dr. Westwater's renown among Chinese citizens and English war correspondents, among the warriors of Russia and Japan alike. It is half amusing to learn that he holds a reputation hardly less distinguished among the robbers and bandits of the Manchurian wilds.

These outlaws, the pests of the country in troubled times, had a happy facility of becoming armed marauders or peaceful villagers at will. The advantages of the doctor's "Free Healing Hall" to a man with a broken limb or an unextracted bullet were not unknown to them, and now and then a robber wounded in some skirmish would find his way into the hospital at Liao-yang, representing himself as a poor peasant who had been attacked and wounded by cruel bandits.

A Christian colporteur from the city was traveling through the country districts with his pack of Bibles, Testaments, and tracts. He was passing along a road bordered by a field of ripe millet, when in a moment three or four robbers armed with revolvers sprang out from their hiding place behind the tall stalks. First of all they relieved him of the money made by his sales, then they

opened his pack and looked curiously at his books. "Who
are you?" one of them asked. "I belong to the Bible Society,"
he said. "What is that?" "It is a society of Christians," the
man replied. "Ah! Christians!" they shouted, "the society
of the foreign devils;" and with that one of them pointed
his revolver at the colporteur's head, fingering the trigger
meanwhile in a way that was decidedly nasty.

Just then another of the band suddenly stepped forward
and asked, "Do you know Dr. Westwater?" "I know him
well," the man answered; "he is a member of the Church
to which I belong." On hearing this, the robber turned to
his companions and said, "Do not touch this fellow. Dr.
Westwater is a good man. Two years ago he took a bullet
out of my ribs." Whereupon this robber band handed back
to the colporteur not only his pack, but every copper of his
money, and bade him go in peace on his way to Liao-yang.

Another experience of a somewhat similar kind befell
the doctor's colleague, the Rev. Mr. MacNaughtan himself.
About a fortnight before the outbreak of the Russo-
Japanese War, Mr. MacNaughtan, who had been itinerating
in the province, was riding back to Liao-yang. He was
drawing near to a strange village, and there was nothing
on the road in front of him but a Chinese cart rumbling
slowly along. All at once there shot out from the village in
a fan shaped skirmishing formation a band of about twenty
horsemen, all armed with rifles. Some of them galloped
furiously to right and left, so as to cut off any possibility of
escape, but five came straight down the road towards the
carter and the missionary.

They met the carter first. One of them, who was

mounted on a tall Russian horse, taken no doubt from a murdered Russian soldier, drew up his steed across the road, compelling the cart to stop, and then drawing a heavy whip, began to lash the unfortunate peasant from head to heel.

Mr. MacNaughtan's heart beat fast, for he knew that at that very time Russian outposts were being nipped off every now and then by bands of desperate bandits. He did not know what might be about to befall him. But he thought it best, trusting in God, to put a brave face on the matter and ride straight on.

When he reached the cart the five robbers were drawn up beside it on the road. One of them held his rifle across his saddle ready for use, and all of them looked at him keenly. That he was a European they saw at once, but the Chinese sheepskin robe he wore showed that he was not a Russian, but a missionary. "Where are you going?" they demanded. "To Liao-yang," he replied. "Then pass on," they said. And without the slightest attempt on the part of any one of them to deprive him of his money or to molest him in any way, he was allowed to continue on his journey.

Talking to the present writer of this incident, Mr. MacNaughtan said that he had no doubt whatever that, though not himself a doctor, he owed his escape to the influence of the Liao-yang medical mission. Even to the savage bandits of Manchuria Dr. Westwater is "a good man." Some of them, as has been said, have passed through his hands, and are grateful to him accordingly. Others have heard of his skill and generosity, and if on no higher grounds, entertain a kindly feeling towards him at least from the lower but still effective motive of that form of gratitude which has been defined as "a lively sense of favors to come."

And thus as we have seen, it is the gracious work of healing, steadily carried on from year to year that lays the foundations of a medical missionary's power. But sometimes in the history of a mission there come hours of crisis which bring with them the chance of doing something heroic, and in which a strong man's grandest qualities become revealed by the power of God. It was just for such an hour as this that we see the hand of God in preparing Dr. A. Macdonald Westwater, a simple Scotch Presbyterian missionary, to honor his Heavenly King and in doing so gained the name of "The Savior of Liao-yang."

NOTES AND AUTHORITIES: The materials for the above chapter have been derived partly from the pages of the *Missionary Record of the United Free Church of Scotland*, but chiefly from the personal narrative of the Rev. W. MacNaughtan, M.A., of the Presbyterian Mission in Liao-yang.

PART II

AFRICA

AFRICA

"THE HERO OF UGANDA"

C H A P T E R   S I X

FROM THE EDITORS: Africa, known as "the Dark Continent" — fully deserves her title. While a grand and mysterious land, rich in wildlife, geography, and ancient civilizations, it is also a continent abounding in the deepest pagan practices — witchcraft, superstition, and the worst cruelties imaginable. Those who dared explore Africa or who came with a heart for missions, more often than not were either martyred or perished from sickness. The famous Dr. Livingstone blazed the first trail through Africa, serving a dual purpose as a messenger of the Gospel of Christ and a pioneer explorer. Livingstone opened the door to Africa, but Satan was not about to let go his grip on the continent without an immense struggle. The following chapters are dedicated to the courageous sacrifice paid by a great many missionaries in order that the message of the Gospel might catch fire and produce followers of Jesus Christ.

While Dr. Livingstone might be the most famous of African missionaries, Alexander Mackay is often referred to as the "Second Livingstone" or the "Modern Livingstone."

Indeed, Livingstone was one of Mackay's heroes, a fellow countryman. His ministry in Africa was instrumental in Mackay's decision to be a missionary.

Mackay was born in Aberdeenshire, Scotland on October 13, 1849, the son of a minister. While a young man he developed his great talent for engineering and pursued those studies at Edinburgh University. In 1873 Mackay traveled to Germany to study the German language and to work with an engineering firm. His technical abilities were soon recognized, and he was promoted. However, in 1875 he read Henry Morton Stanley's challenge about the need for Christian missionaries in Uganda, and his heart was quickened to answer the call. Accordingly, on April 27, 1876 he set sail with four companions for Africa. Arriving in Zanzibar on May 30th, he set his sights on the Dark Continent, never to return to England again.

Right away Mackay applied his engineering abilities to assist the Africans and elevate their primitive living conditions. He reasoned that in building roads, bridges, boats, and by introducing various tools and engines, he could win a place in the eyes of the Ugandan leaders and thereby secure a position to preach Christ. In this goal he succeeded. Mackay never forgot that any influence gained must be used for the sake of his ultimate purpose — winning lost souls. But Mackay's work was not one of ease or quick success. He labored for several years under the rule of the cruel and pagan Ugandan king Mtesa, and then under his even more depraved son, Mwanga. With Mwanga's ascension to power came severe persecution against the Christians. Mackay and his fellow missionaries were daily confronted with death threats, and many of their early converts were tortured and often burned to death. After some time however, the testimony of the faithful martyrs began to bear fruit. New converts would inquire, and then they would offer their lives in service to Christ; and slowly, the Ugandan Church took form.

Eventually, Mackay's last remaining English companion obtained leave to return to England, and he was forced to remove himself far from the base of persecution. Mackay would not live to see the ultimate flowering of the Ugandan Church. He contracted a severe strain of malarial fever and died on February 8, 1890. He had served Africa without ceasing from the day he stepped foot on her shores fourteen years before. It is for his selfless work and sincere heart for this people that he is called "The Hero of Uganda."

Alexander Mackay (1849—1890)

In the days when the British flag flew proudly over the Commissioner's residence in what was known as the Uganda Protectorate in the equatorial regions of East Central Africa, and railway trains passed regularly to and fro through the wild regions that lie between the town of Mombassa on the coast and Kavirondo Bay on the eastern shores of the Victoria Nyanza, the grandest of all African lakes, most of the mystery which once hung about the kingdom of Uganda may be said to have disappeared. However, not so very long ago, shortly before the turn of

95

the 20th century, the case was very different. In the mid 1800's, one or two bold travelers, pushing on towards the sources of the Nile, had heard from Arab traders, not less bold, of the existence of an ancient, powerful, and half-civilized kingdom lying directly under the equator, and stretching along the coast of a great inland sea. These at the best were only hearsay tales.

But in 1862 Captain Speke reached Uganda, the first of all white men to enter the country; and in 1875 there came an explorer greater still—Henry M. Stanley. Stanley was much impressed by what he saw of Mtesa and his kingdom, and was especially struck with the great possibilities for the future of Christian missions in Africa that seemed to be opened up by the existence in the very heart of the continent of such a country as Uganda, ruled by a monarch so enlightened. On his return to England he wrote a historic letter to a great London newspaper, describing his visit to Uganda, and challenging the Christian churches of Britain to send missionaries to that land. It was this letter that led the Church Missionary Society, shortly afterwards, to undertake that work in Uganda with which the name of Alexander Mackay will always be associated.

Mackay was a young Scotchman, the son of a Presbyterian minister in Aberdeenshire, who at an early age had made up his mind to devote himself to the service of Christ in the foreign field, and had conceived the original idea of becoming what he called an "engineer missionary." From the first he saw, as most missionary societies have now come to see, that Christianity and modern civilization should go hand in hand, and that mechanical work is as legitimate an aid to missions as medical science. He had a natural bent towards engineering, and after studying it theoretically for three years at Edinburgh University, went to Germany and spent some time there as a draughtsman and constructor. So marked were his constructive talents that one of his employers offered him a partnership in a large engineering concern; but what would have seemed a tempting opportunity to most young men was not temptation to him. Already his heart was in the mission field. When he was twenty-four years of age, and hard at work in Berlin, he wrote in his diary on the first anniversary of Dr. Livingstone's death: "This day last year Livingstone died—a Scotchman and a Christian, loving God and his neighbor in the heart of Africa. 'Go thou and do likewise.'" It was in the year following that Stanley returned from Uganda and wrote the celebrated letter already referred to; and among the first to respond personally to the explorer's challenge was the young Scotch engineer who had drunk so deeply of Livingston's spirit, and whom Stanley himself described fourteen years later, when he had seen with his own eyes the kind of work that Mackay had done in the heart of Africa, as "the modern Livingstone."

According to Stanley it was the practical Christian teacher who was wanted in the Dark Continent—the man who, sailor-like, could turn his hand to anything. "Such a one," he wrote, "if he can be found, would become the savior of Africa." Mackay's practical teaching began long before he set foot in Uganda, for as soon as he reached the East African coast he set to work to cut a good road to Mpwapwa, 230 miles inland. It was a huge task for one white man to undertake in the teeth of countless natural difficulties, and in spite of frequent sickness and dangers from wild beasts and savage men. But in the words of the old Scotch proverb, the young engineer "set a stout heart to a stey brae"—fording swamps and climbing hills, bridging rivers and cleaving his way through forests. It was not till two years after he had landed in Africa that he arrived at Kagei on the south of the Victoria Nyanza, and caught his first glimpse of the great lake in the neighborhood of which the remainder of his life was to be spent. Two of the missionaries for Uganda, Lieutenant Smith and Mr. O'Neill, had been murdered shortly before by a neighboring king, others had succumbed to the climate one by one; and meantime he was left alone to hold aloft in this vast region the flag of Christianity and civilization.

His first business was to get across the lake, for Kagei is at the south end, while Uganda lies along the northwestern shores. In size the Victoria Nyanza is about equal to Ireland, and the only way of crossing this inland sea was by means of a sailing boat called the *Daisy*, which had been brought up from the coast in sections by Lieutenant Smith but in which not a single sound plank now remained, thanks to the burning rays of the sun, the teeth of hippopotami, and the ravages of armies of white ants. Mackay had to begin without delay those mechanical labors by which he was to produce so deep an impression on the native mind, and which by and by made his name famous all round the shores of the Victoria Nyanza. Day by day he toiled single handed on the beach with crowds of natives all around, willing to help so far as they could, but sometimes doing more to hinder, watching and wondering until, as they saw his turning-lathe at work, or beautiful candles growing under his fingers out of the fat of an ox, or a complete steam engine out of a heterogeneous collection of bars and rods and bolts and screws, they began to whisper to one another that the white man came from heaven.

But before his boat building was completed, Mackay impressed the natives in another way by paying a visit to King Lkonge, of the island of Ukerewe, by whose warriors the two missionaries had been murdered a short time before. The friendly people of Kagei entreated him not to go to Ukerewe, assuring him that by doing so he would only be putting his head into the lion's jaws. But he went, alone and unarmed, and got Lkonge to promise that he would allow the missionaries to come and teach his subjects; and then after a nine days' absence returned to Kagei, where he was received almost as one who had come back from the dead.

At length the *Daisy* was ready, and Mackay had now to undertake the duty of navigating her across the unknown waters. Even to an experienced sailor like the murdered Lieutenant Smith the task would not have been an easy one, for like the Sea of Galilee, the Victoria Nyanza is a lake of storms, while countless rocks and islets stud the broad expanse on every hand. And Mackay was not only no sailor, he had not the slightest acquaintance with the art of handling a sailing boat. Still there was nothing for it but to launch out into the deep with a native crew that knew even less about boats than he did himself. It was a terrible voyage. Soon after leaving Kagei a great storm came down and raged upon the lake for two days, during which the *Daisy* was driven helplessly before the fury of wind and waves, until she was hurled at last a mere wreck upon the western coast. The boat-builder's task had to be resumed once more; and the *Daisy* was repaired, as Mackay himself puts it, "much as one would make a pair of shoes out of a pair of long boots. Cutting eight feet out of the middle of her, we brought stem and stern together, patching up all broken parts in these with the wood of the middle portion; and after eight weeks' hard labor, we launched her once more on the Victoria Nyanza."

It was not till November, 1878, two and a half years after leaving England, that Ntebe, the port of Uganda, was sighted at last; and five days afterwards Mackay entered Rubaga, the capital of the land which had so long been the goal of all his hopes and efforts. On the earliest day on which there was a *baraza* or levee at Mtesa's court, he received a summons to attend. It was a striking succession of scenes that met his quietly observant eye as he passed along the magnificently wide road that led to the royal palace of this Central African city. In his *Two Kings of Uganda* Mr. Ashe, Mackay's colleague at a later period, gives a graphic account of one of Mtesa's levees, when, amidst the rolling tattoos of deep-toned drums and the blare of trumpets, lords and chieftains from far and near, villainous but smiling Arabs, runaway Egyptian soldiers from the Sudan, adventurers from the East Coast and Madagascar, mountebanks, minstrels, dancers, and dwarfs all gathered into the courtyard of the Kabaka, which was the native title of the king.

Mackay's presentation passed off very well, and it was not long till his great skill in all kinds of arts and crafts, and especially in ironwork, made him an object of wonder to the whole country and a special favorite with the king. But he never allowed himself to forget that, important as practical work was, there was something which was infinitely higher, and that all the influence that he gained by his mechanical ingenuity must be turned to the service of the Gospel of Christ Jesus he had come to Uganda to proclaim. So while during the rest of the week he practiced the arts of civilization and imparted them to others, when Sunday came he regularly presented himself at the court, and read and expounded the New Testament to a listening crowd in the presence of the king. At first Mtesa appeared to be in sympathy with his teaching, and to the ardent young missionary it almost seemed as if the whole nation of Uganda might be born in a day. It was not long, however, till adverse influences began to work. The Arab traders bitterly disliked Mackay, for they were well aware that all his influence went to undermine their very lucrative slave trade. There were some Roman Catholic priests, too, who had followed him to Uganda after he had opened up the way, and these men set themselves to prejudice both king and people against him as far as they could. But worst of all, Mtesa turned out to be a hearer of the type of that Felix to whom Paul preached. Up to a certain point he listened to Mackay willingly enough, but he did not like the missionary to get into close grips with his conscience. There was much that was good and amiable about Mtesa, and to the end he protected Mackay from all his enemies. But his previous life had been a training in cruelty, brutality, and lust; and though his mind was convinced of the truth of the

Christian Gospel, its moral demands were too much for his taste, and he remained a heathen in heart.

And so there came a time when Mackay discovered to his horror that while for more than two years the king had been listening to him with apparent interest, he had been permitting almost unimaginable cruelties to be practiced just as before. In particular, every now and then he gave orders for a *kiwendo*, i.e. a great massacre of human victims, in one of which as many as 2,000 persons were put to death in a single day. In anticipation of these great sacrifices, gangs of executioners prowled about the land by night, pouncing upon innocent and helpless people and marching them off to the capital; and by and by Mackay came to know that the deep roll of drums which sometimes awakened him in the dead of night was nothing else than the signal that a fresh batch of victims had been brought in. When the day of the *kiwendo* arrived, these wretched creatures were put to death by burning. But before being cast alive into the flames many had their eyes put out and their bodies mutilated in grotesque fashion.

Against these horrible deeds Mackay protested with all his strength, but only offended the king, who now declined to see him at the court, and no longer as at first supplied him with food, so that he and the two other missionaries by whom he had been joined were sometimes reduced to actual starvation. From time to time, however, the royal favor was regained in some measure by a fresh demonstration of the white man's mechanical power. Once in a time of great drought, when water was not to be had in the capital, Mackay sank a deep well—a thing which

had never before been seen in Uganda, and fitted it with a
pump—a thing more wonderful still. And when the people
saw the copious stream of water ascending twenty feet high,
and flowing on as long as any one worked the pump handle,
their astonishment knew no bounds, and they cried, *Makay
lubare* ("Mackay is the great spirit") again and again. But
their benefactor did not trade on their ignorance. He told
them that the pump was only a kind of elephant's trunk
made of copper, or that it was like the tubes they used for
sucking beer out of their beer jars, only much bigger and
with a tongue of iron to suck up the water. "I am no great
spirit," he assured them. "There is only one Great Spirit,
that is God; and I am only a man like yourselves."

Another of Mackay's tasks at this time was imposed
on him by the death of Mtesa's mother, and consisted
in the manufacture of what the king considered a fitting
receptacle for the corpse of so august a personage. It was a
triple series of coffins—an inner one of wood, a middle one
of copper, and an outer one of wood covered with cloth.
Everything had to be made as large as possible, and to fulfill
the office of undertaker on this Brobdingnagian scale the
handy missionary had to toil incessantly for thirty days,
and often all through the night as well. The outer coffin was
made of 100 boards nailed together, with strong ribs like
the sides of a schooner, and was so enormous that it looked
like a house rather than a coffin, and required the assistance
of a whole army of men that it might be lowered safely into
the grave, which, again, was a huge pit twenty feet long,
fifteen feet broad, and about thirty feet deep.

At last Mtesa died, worn out prematurely by his vices,

and was succeeded by his son Mwanga, a youth of about seventeen, who inherited his father's worst qualities, but none of his good ones. Then began a time of fiery trial for the mission. Mackay and his companions were daily threatened with death, and death was made the penalty of listening to their teaching or even of reading the Bible in secret. Many of Mackay's pupils and converts were tortured and burnt to death; but in Uganda as elsewhere the old saying came true that "the blood of the martyrs is the seed of the Church." Inquirers became far more numerous than ever; men stole into the houses of the missionaries by night and begged to be baptized; and there were cases where bolder ones went openly to the court and proclaimed that they were Christians, though they knew that their confession would immediately be followed by a cruel death. Sir H.M. Stanley said of this martyr Church of Uganda that he took it to be "a more substantial evidence of the work of Mackay than any number of imposing structures clustered together and called a mission station would be." Certain it is that it was by the tearful sowing of Mackay and his companions in those gloomy days that there was brought about that time of plentiful and joyful reaping which came in Uganda by and by.

And now we come to the culminating tragedy in this story of tyranny and bloodshed, and the moment when the faith and courage of the missionaries were most severely tested. They knew that Mr. Hannington had been consecrated Bishop of East Equatorial Africa (in the Anglican Church) and was on his way to Uganda from the coast. And they had heard with much concern that, instead of following the customary route to the south end of the lake, he was marching through the Masai country on the east towards the district of Usoga at the northern extremity of the Victoria Nyanza, with the intention of entering Uganda from that quarter. The ground of their concern lay in the fact that the people of Uganda looked upon Usoga as their private "back door," through which no strangers, and especially no white men, should be permitted to approach. There was an old prophecy among them that their country was to be conquered by a people coming from the east, and when word was brought that white men with a large caravan of followers had made their appearance in Usoga, Mwanga and his councilors grew excited and alarmed. Mackay guessed at once who the advancing travelers would be, and did everything he could to reassure the king as to Hannington's purpose in coming to his country. But in spite of all his efforts, a band of soldiers was secretly dispatched to intercept and massacre the Bishop and his followers; and soon the news spread throughout all Uganda that Mwanga's instructions had been literally fulfilled. The murder of the Bishop seemed to whet the tyrant's appetite for Christian blood, and a general persecution followed in which the very flower of the native converts were slain, while the lives of the missionaries themselves constantly hung by a single thread—the king being kept from ordering their instant execution only by the powerful influences of his Katikoro or Prime Minister, who urged him to remember all that Mackay had done for his father in the past.

At length Mr. Ashe, Mackay's only remaining companion, got permission to return to England, while

Mackay himself was allowed to withdraw to the south end of the lake. Much as he needed a rest, he could not be persuaded to turn his back on Africa at this critical juncture. Nor did he cross the lake from personal danger and fears, but only because he was convinced that it might be best for the native Christians that his presence should be removed for a time. He went accordingly to the district of Usambiro, south of the lake, and immediately started mission work there, devoting himself at the same time to the task of translating and printing portions of Scripture for the Uganda people, so that even in his absence the Divine Word might continue to win its way in many hearts.

It was while he was at Usambiro that Stanley and he first met. The distinguished explorer was then on his way back to the coast after his relief of Emin Pasha, and to him and his companions it was a welcome relief, as several of them have testified—an oasis in the desert of African travel—to come in the midst of their long and weary march upon Mackay's mission station at Usambiro. In his book, *In Darkest Africa* (vol. II, pp. 388—389), Stanley himself gives a graphic description of the meeting, and thus records his impressions of the young Scotch missionary and the work in which they found him quietly and steadily engaged:

"Talking thus, we entered the circle of tall poles within which the mission station was built. There were signs of labor and constant, unwearying patience, sweating under a hot sun, a steadfast determination to do something to keep the mind employed, and never let idleness find them with folded hands brooding over the unloveliness, lest despair might seize them and cause them to avail themselves of the speediest means of ending their misery. There was a big, solid workshop in the yard, filled with machinery and tools, a launch's boiler was being prepared by the blacksmiths, a big canoe was outside repairing; there were sawpits and large logs of hard timber, there were great stacks of palisade poles, in a corner of an outer yard was a cattle-fold and a goat pen, fowls by the score pecked at microscopic grains, and out of the Europeans quarter there trooped a number of little boys and big boys looking uncommonly sleek and happy, and quiet laborers came up to bid us, with hats off, 'Good morning!'"

And later he continues by saying:

"A clever writer lately wrote a book about a man who spent much time in Africa, which from beginning to end is a long-drawn wail. It would have cured both writer and hero of all moping to have seen the manner of Mackay's life. He had no time to fret and groan and weep; and God knows, if ever man had reason to think of 'graves and worms and oblivion,' and to be doleful and lonely and sad, Mackay had, when, after murdering his Bishop, and burning his pupils, and strangling his converts, and clubbing to death his dark friends, Mwanga turned his eye of death on him. And yet the little man met it with calm blue eyes that never winked. To see one man of this kind working day after day for twelve years bravely, and without a syllable of complaint or a moan amid the 'wildernesses,' and to hear him lead his little flock to show forth God's loving kindness in the morning and His faithfulness every night, is worth going a long journey for the moral courage and contentment that one derives from it."

Stanley spent twenty days at Usambiro, enjoying to

the full the society and hospitality of his missionary friend. On the day that the expedition left Mackay walked with the travelers for some distance, but bade them good-bye at last, and stood on the path waving his hat till they passed out of sight. One of Stanley's officers wrote afterwards, "That lonely figure standing on the brow of the hill, waving farewell to us, will ever remain vividly in my mind."

The end of this heroic life came not long after. Mackay was struck down in the midst of his labors by a sharp attack of malarial fever, which he had not the strength to resist, and after some days of delirium he passed quietly away. He has been called "The Hero of Uganda," and the record of his life shows that he would be worthy of the name, even though no great apparent fruitage had come from all his toils and trials. But the events that have followed since his death help us to a clearer estimate of the richness of the seeds he sowed, often in manifold pain and sorrow, in those first days of Christianity on the shores of the Victoria Nyanza. The Rev. J.S. Moffat, son of the celebrated Dr. Moffat and brother-in-law of Dr. Livingstone, writing in August, 1904, in the *Aurora*, the journal of the Livingstonia Presbyterian Mission on the west of Lake Nyasa, gives a vivid description of a recent visit to Uganda, and thus pictures the scene he witnessed on Easter Sunday in the Cathedral Church at Namirembe:

"From where I sat I could see at least three thousand faces. I was told that there was still a crowd outside—of those who could not find room: and there was a separate and simultaneous service being conducted in an adjacent building, at which at least five hundred younger people were assembled. In the cathedral we joined in the stately service of the Anglican Church, never so stately and impressive as when it is rendered in noble simplicity, free from the adventitious accompaniment and the vicarious performance of a highly artistic choir.

"There was something more real and solemn than this in the vast murmur, almost a thunder-roll, of thousands of responding voices, the voices of men and women who had been born in the most degraded and darkest heathenism, the people that sat in darkness but had seen a great light; the Easter sun shining upon the stone that had been rolled away, and upon the open grave."

NOTES AND AUTHORITIES: The chief authorities for Mackay's life are *Mackay of Uganda* and *The Story of Mackay of Uganda*, both written by his sister, and published by Hodder and Stoughton; *Two Kings of Uganda*, by Rev. R.P. Ashe, M.A. (Sampson, Low, Marston, and Co.).

THE LION-HEARTED BISHOP

CHAPTER SEVEN

...we seem to see him as he strides ahead with that springy step of his. Arms swinging, eyes ever on the alert to notice anything new or remarkable, now a snatch of song, again a shout of encouragement, a leap upon some rare flower or insect—the very life and soul of his company, while ever and anon his emphatic voice would be raised in the notes of some old familiar tune, and the wilderness would ring to the sound of a Christian hymn:

> Peace, perfect peace, the future all unknown;
> Jesus we know, and He is on the throne.

—Rev. Dawson

FROM THE EDITORS: It has often been said, "the blood of the martyrs is the seed of the Church." From an earthly perspective the death of a Christian witness seems a tragic event. Yet from a heavenly perspective it is but the continuation of that seamless plan, conceived before time began, by a just and loving God to accomplish his ultimate redemption of man. To the amazement of the persecutors, new converts to the cross of Christ are raised to fill the shoes of the martyr. The story of James Hannington and the martyrs for Uganda illustrates this fact. His life, in tandem with the work of his fellow laborer, Alexander Mackay, gave birth to the Ugandan Church in Africa.

Born at Hurstpierpoint, in Sussex, England, James Hannington was an adventurer. More at home studying natural history on his own and traipsing across the fields and glens than sitting in school, he was an outdoorsman to the core. However, upon his mother's death in 1872, he began to study theology and was ordained in 1873 into the Anglican Church. While serving as a curate, he was impacted by the story of the murder of two missionaries on the shores of the Victoria Nyanza. He felt called to take their place. Accordingly, in 1882 Hannington left his parish and family in England to take up the work with the Church Missionary Society in Africa and so began his brief missionary life. This is the story of the martyrdom of Bishop James Hannington, a seed sown for the Christian church in Uganda.

James Hannington (1847—1885)

There is no chapter in the story of modern missions which has more of the romantic and inspirational element about it than that which tells how the Kingdom of Uganda, within less than a generation, was turned from a land of heathen darkness and cruelty to one in which such scenes of devout Christian worship on the Lord's Day, as described by Rev. Moffat occurred. We have spoken of Alexander Mackay as the hero of Uganda; and undoubtedly it was he more than any other who sowed in that land the seed which has been reaped so plentifully since. However, the Church of Uganda must ever cherish the name of that lion-hearted man, Bishop Hannington, who literally laid down his life for her sake. It is true that Hannington never saw Uganda. And yet during his brief missionary career it was for Uganda most of all that he prayed and toiled and suffered, and it was for Uganda, too, that he died at last a martyr's death. When the soldiers of the cruel Mwanga were about to thrust their spears into his body as he stood on the very threshold of the land he had sought so long, he bade them tell their king "that he was about to die for Uganda, and that he had purchased the road to Uganda with his life."

James Hannington was the very ideal of a pioneer missionary. Full of physical vitality and strong spirits, and absolutely devoid of fear, he spent his boyhood in all kinds of adventures by land and water, which sometimes developed into schoolboy scrapes. When only twelve, he had the thumb of his left hand blown off by some damp gunpowder squibs or "blue devils," which he had manufactured with a view to taking a wasp's nest. And in after years, when a young curate, he often alarmed the parishioners by his reckless feats as a climber and egg hunter on the Devonshire cliffs.

But in the heart of "Mad Jim," as he had been called at school, there grew up a great love for Christ, and a desire to serve Him in the ministry of the Church. And when he took Holy Orders, after studying at Oxford, it proved that his adventurous spirit, his athletic habits, and his frank outspoken manliness gave him a power over many minds which the ordinary clergyman mostly fails to reach. By and by the stirrings of the heart began to urge him forth to a larger and more difficult field than he could find at home. In particular, when word came to England of the murder of Lieutenant Smith and Mr. O'Neill on the Victoria Nyanza, he felt the impulse of the brave soldier to step into the gap where a comrade has fallen. And when the Church Missionary Society decided to send a fresh party to Uganda to reinforce Mackay, who was holding the ground with a single companion in the face of infinite difficulties and discouragements, Hannington was one of the first to volunteer. He was most happily settled by this time as incumbent of St. George's Chapel, Hurstpierpoint, the home of his boyhood and youth, and had besides a wife and young children to whom he was passionately attached. But the call he heard was one to which he could give no denial. For Christ and Africa he felt that he must be willing to suffer the loss of all things.

Hannington was appointed leader of the new party, which consisted of six men; and his instructions were to endeavor to reach Uganda from Zanzibar by what was then the ordinary route, which was to the south end of the Victoria Nyanza, and thereafter by boat across the Lake to Rubaga, King Mtesa's capital. His first landing in Africa was thoroughly like himself. The thirty miles of channel between Zanzibar and the mainland was crossed in a filthy

Arab scow, but the water was so shallow that the vessel could not get within half a mile of the shore. A dugout canoe put off to their assistance, in which the rest of the passengers were conveyed to land two or three at a time. But as the sea was rough the waves broke constantly over the canoe, nearly filling it with water. Hannington said "that he preferred a regular bath to a foot-bath with his boots on. So he stripped off his clothes, put them into a bag which he carried on his head, and disregarding the sharks, he waded and stumbled and swam over the half-mile of rough coral and through the breakers which lay between the vessel and the beach. So he landed on the coast of Africa in a manner quite characteristic."

When Hannington went up for his examination before being ordained, he did not make a very brilliant appearance, and the Bishop, after looking him all over, said, "You've got fine legs, I see: mind that you run about your parish." His parish now was East Central Africa and it was well that he had good legs. Practically the whole of his life as a missionary was spent in journeying up and down this vast region. But to a man of his temperament, though the motive of carrying the Gospel to the heart of the African continent was the central one, exploration and adventure were very welcome in themselves, and he entered into his new experiences with much of the zest of his boyish days. Here is a description written to his nephews and nieces, and accompanied by one of those droll sketches with which he often embellished his letters to familiar friends:

"Fancy a set of savages regarding your uncle as a strange, outlandish creature, frightful to behold! 'Are those

your feet, white man?' 'No, gentlemen, they are not. They
are my sandals.' 'But, do they grow to your feet?' 'No,
gentlemen, they do not; I will show you.' So I would unlace
a boot. A roar of astonishment followed when they saw my
blue sock, as they thought my feet must be blue and toeless.
I pulled off the sock, and they were dumbfounded at the
sight of my white, five-toed foot. They used to think that
only my face and hands were white, and the rest of me black
like themselves. My watch, too, was an unfailing attraction.
'There is a man in it.' 'It is *Lubari*; it is witchcraft,' they would
cry. 'He talks; he says, Teek, teek, teek.' My nose they would
compare with a spear, it struck them as so sharp and thin as
compared with their own. Often one would give my hair a
smart pull to try whether it was a wig and would come off."

There were times when the experiences of the travelers
were more dangerous than amusing, for there were
murderous robbers in some of the forest, who were ever
on the watch to pounce upon unwary strangers, and there
were deep pits, cunningly covered over with twigs and
grass, and with upright spears at the bottom, which were
used by the natives as traps for the larger kinds of game. To
stumble into one of these means almost certainly a horrible
death. Hannington himself fell into one, but fortunately
in this case the spears were wanting; and he was not
dangerously hurt, though much shaken and bruised.

It was fitting that this lion-hearted missionary should
have more than one exciting encounter with lions. The
most thrilling of all took place one day when he had gone
out to shoot, accompanied by a single boy. Seeing a small
animal moving through the long grass in front, he fired,

and the creature rolled over quite dead. On coming up to
it he discovered that it was nothing less than a lion's whelp.
Immediately the boy shouted, "Run, master, run!" and
took to his heels as hard as he could. His terror was not
premature, for the next moment, with terrific roars, a large
lion and lioness came bounding towards Hannington out
of the jungle. His gun was empty, he had no time to reload;
but though his natural instinct was to run, he felt at once
that this would be fatal. So he stood his ground, and when
the lions came near growling and lashing their tails and
glaring at this intruder, he only glared back at them with
steady eyes. This unflinching courage completely subdued
them, and as they stood staring fiercely at him, he gradually
retreated backwards for a hundred yards or so, facing them
all the while, and then turned and quietly walked away.
Most men, however brave, would have been content with
this victory. But Hannington was not content, for he now
determined to go back and secure the young lion's skin if
possible. As he drew near again he saw that the lion and its
mate were walking round and round the dead body of their
whelp, licking it, and turning it over, and trying to restore
it to life. Throwing his arms into the air and yelling as loud
as he could, he rushed forward and the fierce beasts, which
evidently had never met such a person as this before, fairly
turned tail and leaped away into the brush. Whereupon
Hannington seized his prize, and by and by marched into
camp carrying it triumphantly on his shoulders.

The Victoria Nyanza was reached about Christmas,
1882, after a weary journey of several months, marked not
only by dangers from lions, leopards, rhinos, and buffaloes,

but by constant worries and anxieties due to the fact that the expedition was very badly provided with supplies. At first it seemed to Hannington that his journey was almost at an end, for only the great sheet of water now separated him from Uganda. But, like Mackay before him, he soon found that his worst troubles were yet to come. In the meantime

A VISIT FROM A HIPPOPOTAMUS

From a sketch by Bishop Hannington.

they had no means of crossing, and while Hannington toiled to make arrangements he took a violent attack of malarial fever, and was quickly reduced to such terrible weakness that his companions agreed that the only chance of saving his life lay in returning to England immediately. And so when almost within site of his goal he had to turn back, and allow himself to be carried in a hammock all the

dreary way back to Zanzibar. Catching a mail steamer, he
got safely home to England, and was received again into his
beloved circle at Hurstpierpoint "almost," as his biographer
Mr. Dawson puts it, "as one alive from the dead."

At first it seemed certain that he would never see
Africa again; but gradually his strength returned, and with
it a keen desire to resume the task he had undertaken.
Meantime the directors of the Church Missionary Society,
who had long been anxious to secure a Bishop to take
the oversight of all the churches they had planted in East
Central Africa, singled him out as pre-eminently qualified
for the position, and the Archbishop of Canterbury
cordially agreed to consecrate him. In the summer of 1884,
accordingly, he became Bishop of East Equatorial Africa, a
diocese which embraced not Uganda only, but the immense
region that lies between the Victoria Nyanza and the coast.
Uganda, however, was still his chief concern, and his failure
to reach it on the first attempt made him all the more
determined to visit it now without delay, and to endeavor to
bring some comfort to its persecuted Christians and some
help to brave Mackay, who still held the fort for Christ and
the Church in that unhappy land in which the debased and
cruel Mwanga was now king.

Having set things in order at the stations near the coast,
and paid a flying visit to Mount Kilimanjaro for the purpose
of planting the banner of the cross upon its very slopes,
the Bishop therefore began at once to make preparations
for his second and last journey towards Uganda. And
now he came to what proved to be a fateful decision.
Hitherto the missionaries had started from Zanzibar and

made for the south end of the lake, thereafter crossing the Victoria Nyanza in boats. But Hannington knew by painful experience the difficulties of that route—its undue length, its exasperating delays, the deadly influences of its fever-haunted swamps. He conceived the idea of a new line of march which, starting not from Zanzibar but from Mombassa, about 150 miles nearer the Equator, should aim not at the south of the lake but at the north. For one thing, this route would be considerably shorter. Moreover, as his brief visit to Kilimanjaro had shown, instead of passing through a low lying country, it would lead to a large extent over healthy uplands where traveling would be safe for Europeans. The one great difficulty he thought of, a difficulty which until lately had seemed insurmountable, was the fact that he would be obliged to traverse the country of the Masai, whose very name was a word of terror for hundreds of miles around. But not long before, that intrepid young Scotchman, Mr. Joseph Thomson, had explored the Masai country without coming to any harm; and a close study of his fascinating book, *Through Masai Land*, had set the Bishop thinking. If an explorer could make his way among the Masai, why not a Christian missionary? Anyhow, he meant to try, for he was convinced that if this route was at all practicable, the choice of it in the future would mean to the Society an immense saving of time and money, as well as of precious lives.

Unfortunately there was one element in the case which escaped all Hannington's calculations, and brought about the tragedy of which we have to tell. He did not know that the kings of Uganda regarded the country of Usoga, to the

ENCOUNTER WITH AN ELEPHANT AND A RHINOCEROS

north of the lake, through which he would have to pass, as their "back door," by which no white man must be allowed to enter. Nor was he aware that that very journey of Joseph Thomson's, from which he was drawing encouragement, had caused a great flutter at the court of Mtesa, and that it was well for that bold traveler that he had turned back after merely touching the lake at its north-eastern extremity, without attempting to advance farther. No blame, however, can be ascribed to the Bishop for his ignorance, nor can he be accused of acting rashly. His plans were made with the approval of both the Sultan of Zanzibar and Sir John Kirk, the British Consul, with the latter of whom he had frequent consultations before starting on his ill-fated journey.

In the meantime something like his old strength and vigor had returned, as may be judged from the fact that, on a preliminary tramp up country in connection with some of his Episcopal duties, he marched back to the coast, a distance of 120 miles, in exactly three days and half an hour—forty miles a day on average—a feat which is perhaps unexampled in the annals of African travel.

It was in July 1885 that he finally set off from Mombassa at the head of a caravan 200 strong. He knew that he must be prepared to face many dangers. "Starvation," he wrote, "desertion, treachery, and a few other nightmares and furies hover over our heads in ghastly forms." But nothing disturbed the flow of his spirits. His biographer gave us this glimpse of the Bishop on the march: "All the way during that march to Taita his letters reveal him to us, till we seem to see him as he strides ahead with that springy step of his. Arms swinging, eyes ever on the

alert to notice anything new or remarkable, now a snatch
of song, again a shout of encouragement, a leap upon some
rare flower or insect—the very life and soul of his company,
while ever and anon his emphatic voice would be raised
in the notes of some old familiar tune, and the wilderness
would ring to the sound of a Christian hymn—

"Peace, perfect peace, the future all unknown;
Jesus we know, and He is on the throne."

By and by his correspondence ceases, as he vanishes
into a region which knows not the post office even in its
most primitive forms. Fortunately, however, his little pocket
diary was recovered from one of the band that murdered
him, and Mr. Jones, a newly ordained native clergyman
whom he had taken with him as his companion, has shed
much additional light upon that last journey.

The new route proved to be less easy than Hannington
had hoped, and the caravan, besides having to fight its
way through obstinate jungles, had a good deal of trouble
with unfriendly natives, even before reaching the land
of the much dreaded Masai—the scourges at that time
of East Central Africa. The Masai are not Negroes, or
members of the great Bantu family by which the greater
part of the African continent is inhabited, but belong to
what ethnologists call the Hamitic race. Up to the age of
thirty, Mr. Joseph Thomson tells us, every young Masai is a
warrior, and these warriors, or El Moran as they are called,
live in huge kraals or military barracks large enough to
accommodate 2000 of them at a time, from which they issue
periodically on murdering and marauding expeditions. The

arrogance and insolence of the warrior class is unbounded, while any attempt at resenting it is met at once by the uplifting of a forest of their great broad-bladed spears.

With these Masai Bishop Hannington had a trying time. It was quite impossible to keep the young warriors out of his tent, and they came crowding in at their pleasure demanding *hongo*, which is the name for an enforced present, and making themselves free with everything. His chair, his bed, his washtub, his biscuit-boxes were all covered with dirty, sprawling figures, and he himself was subjected to impertinences of every kind. They stroked his hair, pulled his beard, felt his cheeks, and tried on his clothes; and not only fingered all his personal belongings, but spat upon them, that being the Masai token of appreciation. Again and again destruction seemed to be hanging over the camp by a single thread, for the El Moran like nothing better than an excuse for slaughter, and if any one had lost his temper for a moment, it might have been the signal for a wholesale massacre. But at this time the Bishop and his men were mercifully preserved. He notes in his diary, "I strove in prayer; and each time trouble seemed to be averted." And it would appear that even those fierce people felt the power of Hannington's brotherliness. They were by no means agreeable company, with their spitting habits, and the grease and red earth with which they daubed their bodies and so smeared everything they touched. But once when three of them had come with an ox for sale, Hannington invited them to stay with him all night, as it was getting late and their kraal was far off; and, rather to his surprise, they consented quite gratefully. So the

HANNINGTON A PRISONER SHORTLY
BEFORE HIS MARTYRDOM

He was kept in a fair-sized hut with about twenty men around him.
The place was very dirty, and quite dark but for the firelight.

Bishop and the three warriors lay down side by side on the floor of the little tent, and though the Masai slept with their spears beside them, he neither showed nor felt the slightest fear. He writes, "They packed themselves away like sardines in a box, and I covered them over first with a leopard's skin, then with a grass mat, and finally a waterproof sheet. They fell almost instantly into a most gentle sleep. I followed their example and, with one exception, I did not wake up until time to start. Wherever we meet we are to be brothers."

Soon after passing through the Masai country the travelers came to Kavirondo, a region which no white man but Mr. Joseph Thomson had ever visited, while even he had not attempted to go farther. Between them and Uganda nothing now lay but the forbidden land of Usoga. At this stage, owing to the uncertainty of the route, Hannington decided to leave Mr. Jones with the bulk of the caravan encamped in Kavirondo, and to push on himself towards Uganda with fifty of his men.

News travels swiftly even in Africa, and the cruel Mwanga was by this time perfectly aware of the white man's advance, and, as we learn from Mackay, was greatly concerned about it. Mackay did all he could to reassure the king and his adviser, but without effect. Mwanga decided that this daring stranger must die, and sent orders to Lubwa, an Usoga chief, who was his puppet in the matter, to have him and his followers arrested. For fully a week they were kept in close confinement, until a band of Mwanga's soldiers arrived with secret orders to put them all to death.

The Bishop was led through the forest to a place some miles distant from the scene of his imprisonment, and there he found his men before him, stripped naked and bound with thongs. His own clothing was then roughly torn off; and he saw that the end was near. Although weak with fever and greatly reduced by his trying imprisonment, his courage never failed him in that awful hour. He gave his murderers the message to their king to which we referred at the beginning of this chapter; and then kneeling down, he committed his soul to God. A moment after the fierce soldiers rushed upon their victims with their stabbing spears. Two of them, who had been told off for the purpose and were stationed one on either side of Hannington, plunged their weapons into his heart, while all around him the ground was covered with his dead and dying men.

The diary which he kept during his imprisonment is exceedingly touching, especially the entries of the last two days. It was on a Thursday that he died, and on Wednesday we find him writing: "A terrible night, first with noisy drunken guard, and secondly with vermin, which have found out my tent and swarm. I don't think I got one sound hour's sleep, and woke with fever fast developing. O Lord, do have mercy upon me and release me. I am quite broken down and brought low. Comforted by reading Psalm XXVII." The last entry of all is very brief. It must have been written just before soldiers came to lead him out to die.

"Oct. 29th, Thursday (Eighth day's prison).—I can hear no news, but was held up by Psalm XXX, which came with great power. A hyena howled near me last night, smelling a sick man, but I hope it is not to have me yet."

Our knowledge of the final scenes comes partly from the testimony of three or four of Hannington's men, whose lives were spared on condition that they would show the murderers how to open his boxes, partly from the evidence of some of the soldiers themselves, who subsequently became members of the Uganda Church, but especially from one of his porters, a young coast Christian, who was with the Bishop to the very last, and was speared by his side and left on the ground for dead. During the night he revived and crawled for miles through the forest, with his bowels protruding from a dreadful wound, till he reached the tent of a native who was a friend of Mackay's and by whom he was kindly received and tended until his recovery.

So died the lion-hearted Bishop at the comparatively early age of thirty-eight. But "we live in deeds, not years;" and the brave simplicity of his character, together with this martyr death, will keep his name alive as one of the truest of the many missionary heroes of "Darkest Africa."

NOTES AND AUTHORITIES: *James Hannington* and *Lion-Hearted*, both by Rev. E.C. Dawson, M.A. (London: Seeley and Co.); *Through Masai Land*, by Joseph Thomson, London: Sampson Low, Marston, Searle, and Rivington.

VORTREKKERS IN BAROTSELAND
C H A P T E R   E I G H T

FROM THE EDITORS: In the great mission thrusts into Africa during the late 1800's and early 1900's, the various British mission societies were not alone in the work of sending out missionaries. The following story traces the efforts of the Rev. Francois Coillard sent out into the mission field by the Paris Evangelical Mission Society in France. Born to French Huguenot parents, he was educated at the University of Strasbourg and ordained for service in the Dark Continent, in the Basutoland region of South Africa.

In 1877, Francois Coillard took his wife over the Limpopo River in search of service among new tribes. As providence would have it, their travels brought them to what is now Zambia. The King of Barotseland formally requested that they establish a mission work in his country. It became quickly evident that the King cared little for religion, but only wanted some economic benefit for his people through trade and Western technology. However, Coillard steadfastly preached the Gospel and fought hard against the horrors of the slave trade and pagan life. Through many years of hardship and by steadfast perseverance, a successful mission was developed.

Francois Coillard served in the Barotseland region until 1895 when he suffered a severe illness that required him to return to Europe for recovery. He returned to his beloved Africa in 1899 where he continued the work until he went to be with the Lord in 1904.

Francois Coillard (1834—1904)

On an autumn day in the year 1875 three horsemen rode out of King William's Town in the Cape Colony, and turned their faces to the north for the long journey to Basutoland, a distance of 300 miles, which lay before them. As they rode side by side, they talked earnestly about a movement, in which they were all deeply interested, for extending the influence of the French Protestant Mission in Basutoland into the vast region to the north between the Limpopo and Zambezi rivers—virgin soil in those days so far as Christian teaching was concerned. Of the three one was a soldier, Major Malan by name. He was Swiss by birth and had become an officer in the British Army, but had resigned his commission in order to devote himself to Christian work among the natives of Africa. The other two, M. Coillard and M. Mabille, were Frenchmen, agents of the celebrated Basutoland Mission carried on by Protestants from France. These two had already done their part in building up a strong native Church among the valleys of that "Switzerland of South Africa," and now they were lifting up their eyes to wider horizons and thinking of the needs of the tribes to the far north.

When the trio reached the Great Kei River they plunged in and made the crossing. As they mounted the northern bank a common impulse seized them, and springing from their horses they knelt down under the shadow of a bush and devoted themselves before God to the new enterprise on which they had set their hearts. Then when they had remounted, Major Malan, as if he had been leading a cavalry charge, waved his hat, spurred his horse, and galloped up the hill with his two friends fast at his heels, shouting in his enthusiasm, "Three soldiers ready to conquer Africa." These stalwart men meant what they said. That incident marked the origin of the Barotse Mission, and it is of one of the three, M. Coillard, and how he fulfilled the vow he took beneath the bush by the Kei River, that this chapter is to tell.

When the honor of leading an expedition to the north of the Limpopo was entrusted to M. Coillard by the Church of Basutoland, he was no stranger to the work of the pioneer. In fact he had been pioneering already for twenty years. For most of that time he and his wife, a brave Scotch woman, had been content to live in a wagon, after the fashion of the South African "vortrekker," or at best in a poor hut. He had lately built himself a comfortable house and planted a garden round it; but of the fruit of that garden Madame Coillard and he were never to eat. The rest of their lives were spent in seeking to do for the tribes of the Zambezi what they had already done for the Basuto people.

Starting from Basutoland with four native catechists as well as with his wife and niece, a girl of eighteen, M.

Coillard trekked with his ox caravan right through the territories of the Transvaal Republic, crossed the Limpopo, and plunged into a trackless wilderness where, like sailors on the ocean, they had nothing to guide them but their compass and the stars. Their first rude experience was at the hands of Masonda, a cowardly and treacherous Mashona chief. He received them with great protestations of friendship, but the very next day tried to decoy them to the edge of a frightful precipice, with the view of hurling them down. Being frustrated in his murderous plan, he sought some compensation in robbing them of seventeen of their oxen before he would allow them to leave his country.

They had not long escaped from the clutches of this rascal when they fell into the hands of a savage still more dangerous because he was much more powerful—the redoubtable Lobengula, king of the Matabele. A band of Lobengula's men seized them and dragged them off to Bulawayo, at that time the capital of the Matabele, on the charge of having entered the king's territory without his permission. For three weeks they were hurried by forced marches across a very rough country, while every comfort was denied them. Even to wash in a wayside stream was a crime, respect for this black monarch requiring them to appear in his presence with all the dirt and sweat of the three weeks upon them as a proof that they had obeyed his summons with the utmost alacrity. When they came in sight of Bulawayo they were met by a witch doctor who performed a ceremony of exorcism. Dipping a gnu's tail in a slimy green mixture, applying this spiritual disinfectant liberally to every member of the company, back and front. For M. Coillard, as a rival sorcerer, he reserved a double dose of his medicine, dashing the liquid into his face and all over his clothes.

For nearly four months Lobengula kept the Coillards prisoners, but finally he contented himself with expelling them from his country, and forbidding them ever to return to Matabeleland. There seemed no alternative now but to retreat, and so with heavy hearts the little caravan made their way for hundreds of miles to the southwest till they reached Khama's country, where that well known Christian chief, then quite the young man, received them with the utmost kindness. He warmly approved of their purpose to push northwards, and did all in his power to further their plans. And as a good deal of communication went on between his own country and that of Lewanika, king of the Barotse on the Upper Zambezi, he sent a body of envoys along with M. Coillard all the way to Barotseland, to urge upon Lewanika the advisability of welcoming the white teachers. It was largely through Khama's influence that the way was thus finally opened up for an advance to the very threshold of Central Africa.

Having returned to the south and also having made a voyage to Europe for the furtherance of his new plans, M. Coillard was at length in a position to trek to the north again. This time he was accompanied not only by Basuto helpers, but also by a young Swiss clergyman, M. Jeanmairet, and by two white artisans, one English and the other Scotch, whose service proved absolutely invaluable to the enterprise. In the interval, Barotseland had been visited by Mr. F.S. Arnot, of whom something will be said in another chapter. He had spent a considerable time in

Lewanika's capital, facing endless privations and trials, but had at length been compelled by illness to leave the unhealthy Zambezi basin and start on that long march to Benguela which led him eventually to the Garenganze country. It was to take up and carry on the work that Arnot had tried to begin that M. Coillard now turned his face towards the Upper Zambezi.

Having once more reached Khama's country, the caravan next crossed the Makari-kari Desert, with its swamps and sands, its almost impenetrable jungles of thorn, its dreary death-like solitudes. Here dwell the Bushmen, the Masaroa, as they are called by the tribes of the Zambezi basin. These people would have proved troublesome but for the fact that Khama, whose strong arm was respected over all that region, had once more sent a party of his men to accompany the travelers all the way to their destination. After the desert came vast virgin forests. Through these forests the cumbrous wagons with their long teams of oxen, so suitable for movement on the open veldt, could only be forced with heartbreaking toil and to the destruction of nearly everything that was breakable. Constant zigzags were indispensable, but in spite of all care in trying to get around the trees, an unexpected branch would every now and then make a clean sweep of a wagon, so that portmanteaus, trunks, tool boxes, books, and haberdashery lay in wide confusion on the ground.

At length to their intense delight they came in site of the great river just where the Upper Zambezi joins its waters with those of the Chobe. But their difficulties were far from over. The cruelties of Lewanika had brought about a revolution in Barotseland; the king had been driven into exile, and the whole country was in a state of anarchy. It was impossible in the meantime to proceed up the river to the capital, and for months the expedition could do little but wait on the turn of events. At length there came a counter-revolution. Lewanika was restored to the throne, and signalized his triumph by a massacre of the rebel chiefs, their children also being put to death without exception, while their wives were divided among the conquerors. After all this had taken place, Lewanika gave permission to M. Coillard to advance into the heart of Barotseland and to begin work not far from Lealuyi, as the capital was called.

Seldom has pioneer work been carried on in the face of more crushing difficulties and bitter disappointments than those that were encountered for several years by this heroic Frenchman and his colleagues. It soon turned out that Lewanika cared nothing for the introduction of Christianity among his people; all that he wanted was to reap material advantages from the presence of the white men in his country. Whatever was theirs he considered to be his, and when he found them less pliable than his own cringing subjects, he treated them to threats and studied insults, or tried to starve them out by a system of boycott in which all the markets were closed against them. Meanwhile they had to witness day by day the worst horrors of African barbarism—the inhumanities of the slave trade, the fruits of a universal believe in witchcraft, the open practice of murder. Slave children were offered to the Coillards whom they could not buy, and yet they knew that to refuse might be to sign the death warrant of a child. It was impossible to walk a few steps from their door without striking their feet against a skull or a collection of half-charred human bones, marking the spot where men and women had been burned alive. Whoever gave the slightest offense to Lewanika was at once ordered off to execution. But most painful of all were the witchcraft ordeals which constantly went on. If misfortune came to anyone he had only to accuse a neighbor of having used sorcery against him, and the accused must submit to trial by ordeal. The method in Barotseland was by boiling water. A pot of water was set on a large fire. As soon as the water boiled, the poor wretch had to plunge his hands into it, and if the skin pealed off, as of course it almost invariably did, he was at once dragged away to a cruel death. From this fate no one was safe, man or woman, young or old, chief or slave.

But the power of the truth, backed by such patience and heroism as were shown by the Coillards, gradually began to tell. Lewanika grew ashamed of his cruelties, and came to have a larger sense of his responsibilities as the mast of a vast territory stretching from Kalahari Desert on the south to the watershed between the Congo and the Zambezi systems on the north. He was naturally a most intelligent man, possessed of a mechanical skill exceedingly rare in an African prince. He had a workshop of his own in which he spent his leisure hours, and could turn out almost anything he wanted, from a canoe to a harmonica or a delicately carved ivory bracelet. Canoe building was a specialty of the Barotse, for like all the Zambesians they are essentially a river people. But the state-barge of the king's own designing, sixty feet long and manned by fifty rowers,

was a structure of which the whole nation was proud.
Though his heart was difficult to reach, his intelligence
and ambition could be appealed to, and by and by he grew
eager to see education, industry, and civilization develop
among his people. Lewanika came to trust M. Coillard and
his colleagues as the representatives of all these good things
and to favor the progress of Christianity among his subjects.

When he had at length secured a firm footing in the
capital, Coillard began to think of the various tribes on the
higher reaches of the Zambezi, which were more or less
under Lewanika's sway, and one of the most interesting
chapters of his striking book, *On the Threshold of Central
Africa*, is that which tells of a voyage of exploration far
up towards the sources of the river. He was accompanied
by forty men in a flotilla of ten canoes, and, in order that
canoeing might be easy, the expedition was made at a time
shortly after the height of the annual floods, when the
Zambezi Valley was all under water. The plain at this season
"is a floating prairie, enameled with flowers; rosetted water-
lilies, with their delicate tints of blue, pink, and white; and a
kind of convolvulus which proudly erects her great magenta
trumpets, only dipping them reluctantly as our canoes go
by. But it is also diversified by tall grass and reeds, through
which we have to force our way."

Far up the river they met a venerable man, nearly
blind, who had seen Livingstone, and who pointed out a
spot where the great traveler had camped and which was
still known by his name. When Coillard spoke of Jesus he
listened attentively and said, "It is just what Nyaka (i.e. 'The
Doctor') used to say."

In one place where the Mission party held a meeting with the people and sang a hymn, they were astonished to find that all present could join in it heartily. "Who taught it to you?' they asked; and the people shouted, "Bangueta." Then M. Coillard saw how the seed he had been sowing had silently spread like "bread cast upon waters," for Bangueta had been a pupil in his own school at Lealuyi.

At length they reached a district so far up the river that Lewanika's name was no longer the protection it had hitherto been. They were now in the country of the Balubale, whose chief was called Kakenge. A mob of young men armed with guns met them, who demanded to know what the white man meant by coming into Kakenge's country with a band of Barotse, and without having obtained his permission. They also sought to exact the homage or tax that Kakenge imposed upon all traders coming to that land. Coillard told them that he was not a merchant or even a traveler, but a *Moruti*, i.e a teacher, and that he had come among them to teach the things of God. They took him into the presence of the king, who was throned on a stool, clothed in a colored blanket, and shaded by an enormous blue cotton umbrella held by a slave. All Coillard's explanations were treated by Kakenge as lies, and after breaking into a passionate speech, he suddenly turned his back on the missionary and disappeared into his harem.

Things were looking bad, especially as the expedition had been refused all food since coming to Kakenge's country, and by this time they were nearly starving. But the situation grew still more serious when two of M. Coillard's men, who had contracted blood-brotherhood with some of the Balubale, obtained secret information that out of pure hatred for the Barotse people, Kakenge had sworn to destroy the whole party, and had already given orders for their massacre.

That night not one of the company slept. All of them, heathen and Christian alike, were praying to God. And the next day a wonderful change had come over Kakenge's mind, for he sent them a plentiful supply of millet and fowls and sweet potatoes, and when they went in a body to the court to thank him for his kindness, he told them that he had come to believe in their good intentions, and asked them to forget his ill-temper of the past days.

Balubale was the farthest point reached by M. Coillard in his advance from the south towards the heart of Africa; and at this point our account of the labors and wanderings of this brave and devoted Frenchman must stop. Those who wish to know more about him and his work will find the story fully told in his own book *On the Threshold of Central Africa*.

Over the years, there have been wonderful changes on the Upper Zambezi. By the time of this publishing (1907), The Barotse Kingdom now forms a part of that vast stretch of British African territory which is known as Rhodesia. King Lewanika himself has paid a visit to England and been presented at King Edward's Court. A mighty bridge now spans the Victoria Falls. Through the regions where Coillard once toiled slowly with his laboring teams the Cape to Cairo railway now carries its passengers in swift and luxurious ease. But nothing can dim the honor of the heroic Christian "Vortrekker" who left his home in the fair Basuto valleys, and turned the poles of his ox-wagon towards the land beyond the Limpopo.

NOTES AND AUTHORITIES: The material for the above chapter is drawn from M. Coillard's *On the Threshold of Central Africa* (Hodder and Stoughton).

A PIONEER IN GARENGANZE

CHAPTER NINE

"He was a remarkable man.... He was the simplest and most earnest of men.... I have seen many missionaries under varied circumstances, but such an absolutely forlorn man, existing on from day to day, almost homeless, without any of the appliances that make life bearable, I have never seen. He was imbued with one desire and that was to do God's service.... And I have honored recollections of him ever since as being as near his Master as anyone I ever saw."

—Sir Ralph Williams, Governor of Newfoundland

FROM THE EDITORS: Frederick Stanley Arnot was born a Scotchman, on September 12, 1858. He and his family were neighbors of the family of David Livingstone, who quickly became Arnot's boyhood hero. Livingstone's travels and pioneering exploits fired Arnot's imagination and gave him a desire to one day follow in his footsteps. He spent much time as a boy studying Livingstone's maps and artifacts, and his heart soon settled on the course he was to pursue. After his schooling and preparation for missionary work, he left for Africa just two months before his 23rd birthday. Landing in 1881, Arnot disappeared into the interior, not to be heard of for seven years. During that time he rivaled Dr. Livingstone's exploits as an explorer, covering the broad strip of central Africa made up of Angola, the southern Congo, and Zambia. He traveled through the hostile kingdom of Botswana, journeyed across the Kalahari Desert, crossed the watersheds of both the Zambezi and Congo Rivers, to finally reach the Angolan coast. He finally settled for two years in the kingdom of the great chief, Msidi of the Congo. He built a small clinic, a church, a school, and a small orphanage, all without regular funding and simply living a life of faith trusting in God for his provision.

Returning to England in 1888, Arnot found himself a famous personage. For his pioneering travels and exploits, the Royal Geographical Society had him present a paper and named him a Fellow of the Society. Capitalizing on the popularity, he was able to recruit thirteen young men to join him in the work. He returned to Africa in 1889, in the company of his newly wedded wife, Harriet Jane Fisher. Ill health kept Arnot from settling in Msidi's kingdom at Garenganze, but they set out right away to work at a mission in Angola. By 1891 the Belgian's King Leopold II had annexed Garenganze into the Belgian controlled Congo-Free State following the planned assassination of King Msidi. A reign of terror soon followed as the indigenous tribes were subdued. Throughout these years, Arnot was disturbed by the political turmoil and European greed. His commitment to the principles of the Open Brethren kept him from interfering in these affairs however.

Arnot again returned home to England with his family in 1892. He could not stay away from Africa, however, and he returned to South Africa and after more years of service. Arnot died on May 14, 1914 at the age of 56.

Upon his death the words recorded from Sir Ralph Williams were offered as a tribute. Later to become Governor of Newfoundland, Sir Williams had met Arnot at Victoria Falls in 1884 and was genuinely impressed by his life of service for his Savior. While Arnot may not have seen large numbers of natives won for Christ, his services in opening up Africa for successive groups of missionaries, was a key factor for the eventual civilization and evangelization that would come to Central Africa. He was truly "the pioneer of Garenganze."

Frederick Stanley Arnot (1858—1914)

In 1884 a young Scotchman, Fred S. Arnot by name, who was traveling from the Upper Zambezi towards Benguela on the West African coast, met a company of men from the far interior with a letter in their charge. The letter was sent by Msidi, king of Garenganze, and contained an earnest appeal that white men would come to his country. Arnot did not doubt that by white men Msidi meant traders, by whom he and his people might be enriched. He was no trader, but a pioneer missionary who had already crossed Africa from east to west seeking to do good to the native tribes, and who at that very time was wondering where it would be best for him to settle down more permanently as a Christian teacher. Yet Msidi's appeal came to him with all the force of a personal call, and he decided that, as soon as he reached Benguela, he would make preparations for a march to the Garenganze country.

Garenganze lies to the west of Lake Moero and Bangweolo, near the latter of which Dr. Livingstone died. It is thus in the very heart of Central Africa, some 1,500 miles each way from the Indian Ocean and the Atlantic. It was since absorbed by the Congo Free State and is now known as the Belgian Congo, but at that time it was a powerful independent kingdom. The people, judged by an African standard, had attained to some measure of civilization; and King Msidi, in the same comparative sense, was an able and enlightened monarch. The country was one of the most densely populated in that part of the continent, famed far and near for the abundance of its corn, rice, sugarcane, and other agricultural products; and not less for its copper mines, which were worked by the inhabitants, who cleansed and smelted the copper out of the ore with remarkable skill. Up to 1886, the year of Arnot's arrival, only two Europeans had visited Msidi's dominions—a German traveler from the east and a Portuguese from the south; and in both cases the visits were very brief. Livingstone had never reached Garenganze, though he was drawing near it when he died at Ilala, not far from the shores of Lake Bangweolo.

But though Livingstone himself never entered Garenganze, it was a pioneer of Livingstone's own type who first brought the Christian Gospel to Msidi's people. Fred S. Arnot may be described as one of the most remarkable of the many heroes of African travel, not so much for what he actually accomplished as for the manner and spirit in which he accomplished it. It is here that he especially reminds us of Dr. Livingstone. His methods of progress were not those of the well-equipped and hustling explorer, but of the lonely wanderer who makes his way, quietly, patiently, and in the spirit of love, from village to village and from tribe to tribe. He had already served his apprenticeship to African travel. Landing in Natal in 1881, he had slowly trekked through the Orange Free State and the Transvaal to Khama's country, had next crossed the awful Kalahari Desert, and so made his way to Zambezi. A whole year was occupied in this journey, which brought with it many experiences of danger and suffering. Repeatedly he had been on the point of perishing from hunger or thirst. Once, after marching in the desert for three days and nights without a drop of water, he met some Bushmen, who supplied him with a drink after their own fashion. They dug a pit in the sand, and sank long tubes made of reeds into the ground at the bottom. By and by water began to gather, as they knew it would, at the sunken end of the tube. They invited Arnot to drink. He tried, but was quite unable to suck the water up the long tube. The Bushmen, whom frequent practice had made adept in the art, accordingly sucked it up for him, and then spat it out into a tortoise shell and handed it to the stranger. "It was frothy stuff," he writes, "as you may imagine; but I enjoyed it more than any draught I ever took of Loch Katrine water."

His ways of getting food had sometimes been peculiar also. On the Zambezi he often depended for his supper on the crocodiles, which are very plentiful in that great river. Not that he ate those loathsome reptiles, but he was thankful at least to share their meals. When one of the larger game comes down to the river to drink, the crocodile creeps up stealthily, seizes the animal by the nose, drags it under water, and then hides the body under the river bottom until it becomes almost putrid. When it is "high" enough to suit his taste, Master Croc brings it to the surface and enjoys a feast. The hungry traveler used to lie on the bank and watch one of those animals as it rose, with perhaps a quarter of an antelope in its jaws. Then he fired at its head and compelled it to drop its supper, and in this way provided himself with his own. He admits that it was anything but a dainty repast.

Coming at last to the malarious Barotse Valley on the Upper Zambezi, he settled down there for two years, doing what he could to teach the people and to wean them from their habitual cruelties. But at last his health completely broke down, and he decided to march for the west coast in the company of Señor Porto, a Portuguese traveler who was going in that direction. It shows the stuff of which Arnot was made that, in spite of his reduced condition, he decided to ride on an ox, instead of being carried like his fellow traveler in a *machila* or hammock. The reason he gave was that "that would be too comfortable a way of traveling, and might make me discontented and extravagant at other times." It was on this journey from the Barotse Valley to Benguela that he fell in with the messengers of King Msidi, as mentioned above, and resolved to make Garenganze the goal of another expedition in the interior.

It was in the beginning of June 1885, that he set out on this journey, which was to occupy between eight and nine months. In its earlier stages the march lay along a well-trodden route in Portuguese territory, from Benguela to Bihé. First came the low-lying desert region between Benguela and Cantumbela, which are just at the foot of the hills that mark the beginning of the lower section of the characteristic African plateau. These hills climbed, he found himself for a time in a fertile tropical country; but by and by another and higher table-land rose before him, on climbing which he passed so suddenly out of the climate of the tropics that he could almost mark the line of demarcation between trees like the baobab and the more familiar vegetation of the temperate zone.

At Bibé Arnot had no end of difficulty in getting porter to accompany him on his tramp into the unknown regions, which now stretched before him like an unexplored ocean. But at length he succeeded in gathering a motley company, some of the members of which he has sketched for us in typical African characters:

"Chipooka stammers as he speaks, but is lively under all circumstances; has a bad festering toe, which, however, does not prevent him carrying his sixty-pound load. Though limping badly, his only response to expressions of sympathy is a broad grin. Saombo is another representative man, perfectly hideous in his looks, but vanity has made his ugliness appear comical. All who came to the camp, he seems to think, have come to see him. So, as soon as a few strangers gather, he is not prepared for more hut building or wood-cutting, but must go and sit down in front of them, laughing and clapping his thighs with delight, and trying to crack jokes. Then we have the sulky grumbler amongst us, who has always something to complain of. Now his load is not right, next his rations, then his pay; or a thorn pricks his foot, and he can carry no longer that day. The work has to be done, but certainly not by him."

Besides his men and his horned steed, for once more he took an ox as his bearer, Arnot numbered on his camp roll a faithful dog and a parrot. Señor Porto, his recent companion, was accustomed to carry a cock with him on his travels by way of an animated chronometer, whose morning crows announced to all that it was time to commence the day's march. Arnot found a cock unnecessary, the cooing of the wood pigeons being a sufficient signal to his men that day had come and that it was time to be stirring. But he recommends a parrot as a valuable addition to the resources of an African caravan. His Poll was of great service in keeping up the spirit of his men. It was a true Mark Tapley of a bird, seeming as if it watched for opportunities when there would be some credit in being jolly. When everyone was dull and depressed it would suddenly make some ridiculous remark or break out in imitation of an old man's laugh. So it relieved the monotony of the march, and put the weary carriers into good humor again.

Mr. Arnot gives us a clear picture of the daily routine of an African journey. By break of day the camp is astir, for the porters are always anxious to get well along the road in the cool of the morning. Breakfast they do not trouble about, being content to have one good meal at the end of

IN THE FOOTSTEPS OF THE SLAVE TRADERS

the day. They buckle on their belts, shoulder their loads of 60 lbs. each, and trot off through the forest. Probably some one begins a solo in a high key, and all join lustily in the chorus. One or two halts are made, and there may be considerable delay when rivers have to be crossed. But for the most part all press on steadily for the next camping place, which is generally reached by noon. When a site for the camp has been fixed upon, some of the party are sent out to the nearest villages to buy food—the staple diet being maize meal made into a thick porridge, of which an African will consume an astonishing quantity. Meanwhile the others busy themselves with erecting shelters for the night. Poles are cut down in the forest, and stacked after the manner in which soldiers pile their rifles. Against these, branches are rested, and if it is the rainy season a thatching of the long African grass is added. Then fires are kindled to cook the supper, and these are kept up through the night to scare away wild beasts. "An African camp at night," says Mr. Arnot, "would make a fine picture on canvas—the blazing fires; the black faces clustered round them; the men singing, talking, laughing; and all about a pitchy darkness, made doubly deep by the dense shadows of bush and forest." Every night it was the leader's habit to sit with his men around the campfires, trying in every possible way to convey to them intelligent thoughts as to his mission. He felt that it was of the first importance that they should understand something about his message and his motive in bringing it, and so should be able to give an answer to the thousands of natives who would be sure to bombard them with questions as to who this white man was and why he had come.

One of the districts traversed by the caravan was the Chibowke country, a land of beeswax hunters, who spend weeks on end in the depths of the forest gathering beeswax to sell to the Bihé traders, and living meanwhile on little else than wild honey. A high region was crossed where one day, in the space of two or three hours, they saw the fountainheads of streams that flow respectively into the Congo and the Zambesi, and so ultimately into the Atlantic on the one side of the continent and the Indian Ocean on the other. Then came a wide tract where population was scanty and food scarce, and Arnot had a good deal of trouble with his men. They demanded more rations, and especially more meat. One day they flung down their loads crying, "Monare" (their name for Arnot), "give us meat. Why don't you hunt? You are staving us." Anxious though he was to press on, he saw that there was nothing for it but to devote the day to hunting. He seized his gun, forgetting that it was loaded, and as he was pulling off the cover, the charge suddenly went off, shattering the point of his left forefinger. There was no one with him who could dress a wound, and he thought it best to get one of the men to cut off the top joint according to his directions. The accident had a subduing effect on the men, who felt as if they were to blame for it; and in spite of hunger they tramped on bravely. Starvation, however, had begun to stare them in the face when Arnot succeeded one day in shooting two warthogs, one of which weighted over 200 lbs., and had tusks over a foot long. A time of feasting followed. And as the men marched along once more, their leader heard them saying: "Don't you remember what things we said of the white man and his God? What names we called them! But the white man's God has been with us, and has filled our bodies with pig-meat."

The trials of the long journey were now nearly over. A few days more brought them to the Garenganze country, where, after so many days in a desert region, it was a delight to see fields of grain and abundance of food, and still more to be hospitably received on every hand. On reaching the capital Arnot expected to have an early interview with the king. But it was not Msidi's habit to welcome strangers all at once. For some time the white man was placed in a sort of quarantine, while various tests were employed by witch doctors and diviners to see whether his intentions were good or bad, and "whether his heart was as white as his skin." A little piece of bark, for instance, was placed at night in a certain decoction. If next morning the bark appeared quite sound, that showed that the heart of the newcomer was equally so. If, on the other hand, it was in the least decomposed, the inference was that his heart was rotten, and that he must not be trusted. Fortunately, after several days had been spent in experiments of this kind, everything turned out in Arnot's favor, and the king accorded him a public reception.

The reception was both friendly and imposing. Msidi, an elderly man with a white beard, folded his arms around the traveler in the most fatherly manner, and then introduced him to his wives, of whom he had 500, as well as to his numerous brothers, cousins, and other relatives. Arnot found that Livingstone's name was one to charm with. Msidi had hear of the Doctor's approach from the east in 1873 and of his death at Ilala, and was pleased to

ARNOT DEFENDING HIS FOOD FROM WILD BEASTS

Food was scarce, so he went out shooting accompanied by a native. He succeeded in bringing down three antelopes, and then he sent the native to get help to carry the game to camp. Meanwhile he had to mount guard. With no fire and no cartridges left, he had to keep cheetahs and hyenas at bay by shouting and stamping his feet right through the night. Fortunately no lions happened to come by.

learn that his visitor was a man of peace and goodwill like Livingstone, and that he hailed from the same country. He begged Arnot to remain in Garenganze and to build himself a house on any site he pleased; and this was the beginning of the Garenganze Mission.

For two years Arnot toiled on all alone in that remote land, making tours of exploration from the capital into the surrounding districts. In most places the people had never seen a white man before, and his appearance created a great sensation. The very print of his boots on the path was a portent. "His feet," they said, "are not a man's feet; they are the feet of a zebra." He had many strange adventures and not a few narrow escapes. But perhaps his most trying experience was when he spent a whole night in the open, alone and in pitch darkness, surrounded by a ring of hungry wild beasts.

He had gone out in the company of a native to shoot antelopes at a time when food was scarce, and after a long tramp had succeeded in getting near to a herd and bringing down three. By this time, however, the sun was setting, and the dismal howl of the hyena began to be heard. The nearest village was far off, but Arnot sent his companion to bring assistance, resolving to keep guard himself over the game throughout the night. He had no means of kindling a fire, and to make matters worse, his ammunition was all expended, so that he had no weapons but an empty rifle and a hunting knife. One of the antelopes, which lay at a distance of about a hundred yards from the rest, he soon had to surrender, but he marched up and down beside the other two, shouting and stamping and making as much noise as possible. The cold grew so intense by and by that he drew his hunting knife and skinned one of the antelopes as best he could in the dark, rolled himself in the warm hide, and lay down on the ground. But no sooner had he done this than he heard stealthy footsteps approaching so that he had to spring up again. Only by rushing up and down for several hours, shouting all the time, was he able to keep his savage assailants at bay. When daylight came he saw from the footprints that he had been surrounded through the night by a band of hyenas and cheetahs. It was fortunate for him that no lions had been attracted to the spot.

For two years, as we have said, Arnot held this missionary outpost single handed before any reinforcements arrived, and during all that time he never had a chance of receiving even a letter from the outer world. The oppression of this loneliness was increased by the heathen vices and cruelties that went on in Garenganze just as in other parts of Darkest Africa. All around him in particular the horrors of the slave traffic prevailed and infants were constantly stoned to death because their owners had no use for them. The slave traders regarded them as positive nuisances, not only encumbering their mothers on the march, but also preventing them from carrying loads of ivory or some other commodity. And as no one wanted to buy the helpless little creatures, the slaves quite constantly flung them into a river or dashed them fiercely against the trunk of a tree. As we read of the sights that were to be seen in Garenganze day by day, we do not wonder that the saying passed from mouth to mouth among the slave population: "Cheer up, slave! The Emperor (death) is coming along to save you."

One day the body of a fine little boy, with a fatal spear gash through and through, was picked up on the road. It was a child whose owner shortly before had pressed Arnot to take it. Another infant whom he had felt unable to accept was thrown into the bush and devoured by the beasts. And so he was led to resolve that he must at all costs save these poor slave children—a decision which soon brought him a strange and demanding family of youngsters to whom he had to take the place of both father and mother.

Not less painful than the accompaniments of slavery was the prevalence of human sacrifice. Msidi never entered upon any enterprise without seeking to ensure himself of success by putting someone to death. No one knew beforehand who the victim might be. The king simply said that So-and-So was to be taken, and straightaway the appointed man or woman was led to the slaughter.

There is heroism of patient endurance and continuance as well as of heroism of bold achievement. It sometimes needs more courage to hold the trenches than to lead the forlorn charge. Arnot showed himself a hero in both kinds. His marches through Africa, first from Natal to the West Coast, and then again from Benguela to Garenganze, reveal some of the best qualities of the intrepid explorer. But his quiet persistence in his chosen work as a messenger of Christ, through loneliness and sickness, through danger and disappointment, tells of other qualities which are nobler and finer. It is men like this hero of Garenganze who are the true saviors of Africa.

NOTES AND AUTHORITIES: Mr. Arnot's book, from which the

above sketch is drawn, is entitled *Garenganze, or Seven Years' Pioneer Mission Work in Central Africa* (London: James E. Hawkins).

AFRICA

A TRAMP THROUGH THE GREAT PYGMY FOREST

CHAPTER TEN

FROM THE EDITORS: Buried deep in the forests of Central Africa dwell a fascinating race of humans, so unique and intriguing as to set them apart from any other tribal group known to man. These tribes are dispersed through a zone directly across equatorial Africa from Uganda, and the Belgian Congo, to Angola, and Gabon, and are found especially in the "Great Forest of the Congo," a region six times the area of England, now known as the Ituri Rainforest. These people are the Pygmies, a group of humans of extraordinarily small size.

The following story takes a look A.B. Lloyd's interesting march across Africa, directly through the Great Forest of the Congo and his encounter with Pygmy people. Though rumors of Pygmies had circulated in the civilized world from time to time among Arab traders, most Europeans doubted their existence until shortly before the turn of the twentieth century. The explorer Henry Morton Stanley came upon Pygmies in the Aruwimi River region shortly before this story takes place. Rev. A.B. Lloyd was a missionary with the Church Missionary Society of London, but his services in Africa were of a varied sort. He worked with the British army as a war correspondent, an interpreter, and a makeshift surgeon.

In 1897, A.B. Lloyd set out on a remarkable missionary journey from Uganda deep into the forests of the Congo. It was during these travels that he came into contact with the Pygmy tribe. In his journals he poured out his heart for these peoples in the heart of Africa, "The time has come when we in this civilized land of ours should stretch out our hands to these poor ignorant cannibals, and seek to lift them out of their darkness and gross superstition into the light of the Gospel of Christ. Their blood will surely be upon us. . . if we knowing their state, seek not to break their age-bound chains of heathenism and proclaim liberty to the captives, and the opening of the prison to them that are bound."

To this day, the Pygmy tribes are every bit as much in need of the light of the Gospel as they were during A.B. Lloyd's time. Relatively few missionaries have worked for extended periods of time in the pygmy villages. Would that God may stir the hearts of those readers who hear of this that they might carry the blessed good news of Christ to those little people discovered by A.B. Lloyd.

Albert B. Lloyd (1875?—1947)

Of Stanley's different expeditions to Africa the greatest, though in some respects the least successful, was the last, when he marched by way of the Congo for the relief of Emin Pasha. And of all the thrilling chapters of *In Darkest Africa*, where he tells the story of that long struggle against frightful difficulties, none are more fascinating than those in which he describes his march through the vast primeval forest of the Upper Congo and its tributary, the Aruwimi, and his encounters with the strange dwarfish people who dwell in that region of interminable gloom. Rumors of the Pygmies had come to the civilized world from time to time, especially through the reports of Arab traders, but few persons believed those rumors to have much more reality behind them that the tales of Baron Münchausen. Stanley proved, however, that the existence of the Pygmies was a fact and not a fable. And it was natural that a later traveler, who, in addition to Stanley's courage and love of adventure, possessed a large share of the missionary spirit, should visit the Great Forest with the view of learning something about the religion of the Pygmy folk, and particularly of seeing what prospect there might be of carrying the light of Christian civilization with success into that shadowy world in which this unknown people lived and died.

Mr. A. B. Lloyd, the hero of this enterprise, was a young missionary of the C.M.S. who had been working for some time in the district of Toro on the western side of the Uganda Protectorate, under the very shadow of the giant snow-capped peaks of Ruwenzori, anciently known as the Mountains of the Moon. His experiences already had been of an exciting kind, for he had been in the thick of the fighting in Uganda during the year 1897, when the Sudanese troops mutinied, and Mwanga, the dethroned king, himself raised the standard of rebellion against British rule. Primarily Mr. Lloyd's duties in the campaign had been to act as interpreter to the British forces and to give the wounded the benefit of such surgical skill as he possessed. But he was a good shot with a Martini rifle, and a "handyman" generally, who could work a Maxim gun in case of need. He did not hesitate, accordingly, as a loyal British subject, to play his part like a soldier in the suppression of the rebellion, along with the handful of white men who at the time represented Queen Victoria and the British flag in the heart of Africa. His companion and friend, the Rev. G. Pilkington, fell in the course of the fighting, and Mr. Lloyd himself had several narrow escapes in the eleven engagements in which he took part. At last, after a long period of great strain, a reaction came, and he was laid down with malarial fever. On recovering from the attack he was ordered to give up his work for a time and leave for England in order to recruit.

In these circumstances ninety-nine men out of a hundred would have made for home from Uganda by the ordinary East Coast route, via Zanzibar. But Mr. Lloyd was the hundredth man, and he decided to strike westwards right across the continent, by way of the Pygmy Forest of the Upper Aruwimi. His preparations were soon made, for unlike Stanley he had no intention of advancing at the head of a small army. He secured as a guide a man who had once before passed through the forest; furnished himself with provisions for three months; gathered a few porters; and with a bicycle, a camera, a donkey, and a faithful little dog named Sally, set out upon his tramp into the unknown.

For the first stages of the journey the way was plain. The mighty mass of Ruwenzori, which barred direct progress to the west, had to be circumvented, and thereafter the route lay through a charming plain abounding in game, where to the delight of his followers Mr. Lloyd was able to supply them plentifully with elephant steak and antelope joints. After five or six days' pleasant marching, a river was crossed which forms the boundary between the Uganda Protectorate and the Congo Free State, and four days' progress through King Leopold's territory brought the party to a Belgian fort called Mbeni, where they rested for two days. Here they saw running along the western horizon a long dark belt which, they were told, was the commencement of the Great Forest. Leaving Mbeni they made for the center of this black line, and soon plunged into a mysterious region of darkness and solitude from which they were not to escape for many days.

The Great Forest of the Congo has an area of no less than 300,000 square miles—about six times the area of England not including Wales. Mr. Lloyd describes the scenery that meets the traveler's eye as possessed of a beauty of its own—a beauty that is thoroughly weird and uncanny. Majestic trees tower up toward the sky to a height often of 200 feet, interlacing their foliage so closely that not even the rays of the tropical sun are able to pierce through the dense barrier. The day at best is a dull twilight, while at night blackness falls which might almost be described as solid. In spite of the want of sunshine, however, the vegetable life is wondrously profuse. Strange ferns and flowers spring on every hand, and gigantic creepers, with cables that are sometimes a foot in diameter, climb up the trunks and along the branches from tree to tree until the whole forest becomes a confused tangle of luxuriant growths.

The animal life is not less exuberant. Insects swarm and chirp and buzz on every hand. Birds of the most variegated plumage flit from bough to bough, some of them uttering deep musical sounds like the tolling of a bell, others of the parrot tribe whose only music is the harshest of screams. And there are other denizens of this vast woodland. "Elephants and buffalo are met with constantly, sometimes in herds, sometimes singly; wild pigs and forest antelope, many species of gazelles, chimpanzee, gorilla, and vast quantities of monkeys of every kind are seen; leopards, panthers, wildcats, civets, hyenas, and reptiles. Deadly snakes will be found hanging from the branches of the trees, or curled up amongst the decaying vegetation beneath. Huge black adders, pythons, bright green snakes with wicked red eyes, and whipcord snakes which look for all the world like green twigs. The forest is threaded with a network of rivers and stream, and all seemed full of fish. There are also crocodiles and hippos, water-snakes and lizards, leaches and slow-worms."

With the great majority of these animals the traveler was quite familiar, for, by the necessity of his calling, a pioneer missionary in Central Africa is something of a sportsman, since the very life of his followers and himself when on the march may depend on his skill in shooting game. Elephants, buffalos, and antelopes he had often dealt with. The roar of the lion and the yelp of the leopard in search of its prey were familiar sounds to his ears. But he had not long entered the forest when evidence came of the near presence of the gorilla, an animal which is only to be found in Central Africa, and there only in the depths of "the forest primeval."

They had reached a particularly dark bit of the forest where no light at all seemed to come from the sky, so that, though it was only one p.m., a gloom as of night was all about them. Suddenly they heard a strange noise not far off, as of deep voices angrily quarreling. For a moment everyone was scared, but the guide assured them that it was nothing else than *nkima nkubwa* ("big monkeys"). The Belgians at Fort Mbeni had told Mr. Lloyd that he would probably meet with gorillas, and gorillas these doubtless were. But for the present he was quite content with hearing their voices, having no desire at the head of his unarmed porters to make their closer acquaintance.

For six days the little expedition fought its way through wood and jungle without meeting with any adventures of an especially thrilling kind. Every day, however, the difficulties of steady progress grew greater. The undergrowth seemed to get thicker and thicker as they advanced, and Mr. Lloyd had to walk in front of the line with an old sword-bayonet, chopping a way for himself and the porters who followed with the loads. The guide, too, it soon turned out, was helplessly at sea as to direction. And so, Mr. Lloyd had further to pilot his company as best as he could with the help of a compass, trying to keep a north-westerly course with the view of striking the Ituri River, a principle affluent of the Aruwimi, and then of proceeding along its banks until they should emerge from the forest. Besides overcoming the obstacles presented by the tangles of bush and creepers, the caravan had every now and then to cross one or other of the numerous marshy streams which find their way through the forest, most of them being deep enough to take a man up to his armpits, and some of them so polluted with rotting vegetation as to be highly offensive to the smell.

A day's march under such conditions was very exhausting; but the work of the day was far from over when the day's tramp was done. A piece of ground had to be cleared where a tent could be pitched, and a strong zareba or fence built round it as a protection against wild animals—leopards, panthers, and elephants—which gave the travelers many an uneasy moment. Through the night they often heard elephants squealing loudly, and trampling through the bush in the immediate neighborhood of their little camp. And one morning when Mr. Lloyd had risen early and gone out of the tent before any of his men were awake, he found a huge old tusker with his head over the zareba, "evidently in deep thought, and wondering what on earth this could mean."

Six days had passed since entering the forest, and not a trace of the Pygmies had anywhere been seen. Mr. Lloyd began to wonder if the Pygmy stories were really true. But on the seventh day, as he was walking in advance of the caravan, rifle in hand, accompanied by his black boy and

looking out for a shot at some wild pigs which had been
sighted shortly before, the boy stopped of a sudden, cried,
"Monkey!" and pointed towards the top of a high cotton-
tree beneath which they were passing. Mr. Lloyd looked
up, and there sure enough was a creature, which from its
size he took to be a gorilla. Now his men had been glad to
eat monkey meat before this when nothing better was to
be had. So he raised his rifle to his shoulder, took careful
aim, and was in the act of pulling the trigger when his boy
hastily pulled his arm and exclaimed, "Don't shoot—it's
a man!" At once he saw that the boy was right. It was a
strongly built little man, who, seeing that he was observed,
ran along the branch on which he stood, and jumping from
tree to tree with the agility of a monkey, soon disappeared
in the depths of the forest.

They had pitched their tent that same afternoon, and
Mr. Lloyd had sat down at the tent door with a book in his
hand intending to read for a little, when looking up, he saw
a number of little faces peering at him through the thickets
in front, and one in particular which was nearer than the
rest, peeping round the trunk of a huge tree that grew
opposite. The boys, who were cooking food for the evening
meal, noticed the little people at the same time and sprang
up in alarm, for they knew the Pygmies only by report, and
thought of them as a kind of devil. For some time the white
man and the dwarfs remained motionless, gazing silently
at one another in a mutual fascination, though Mr. Lloyd
felt all the while that at any moment he might be transfixed
with a shower of poisoned arrows from the bows with
which the Pygmies were armed. Stanley had characterized

them as "malicious dwarfs," and his warlike company had been greatly harassed by them again and again. But at length it occurred to the missionary, still sitting peacefully in his camp chair, to call out the ordinary salutation of the people of Toro; and when he did so, to his great surprise, one little man immediately returned the greeting in the same language. He then said, "Come here and let us talk together;" and, very shyly, the nearest of the dwarfs crept forward, followed by a few of the others, half covering his face with his hand and staring through his fingers at the white man in a sort of amazement.

As the Pygmies approached, Mr. Lloyd was struck first of all by their extreme shortness of stature, four feet being the average height of a full-grown man, but next by their exceedingly well-knit figures and powerful limbs. The one who replied to his salutation turned out to be the chief of the party. This man had once come in contact with some people from Toro, and hence knew a little of the Toro language. With him, Mr. Lloyd was able to carry on an imperfect conversation, in which he learned something of the Pygmies and their ways. One of the first things that the chief told him was, that for six days he and his people had been following the caravan and keeping it under constant observation. "But we never saw you," the traveler objected. Whereupon the little man laughed with great glee, accepting this as a high complement to the forest-craft of himself and his followers. During the whole of that time the Pygmies had the caravan entirely in their power; but the very smallness of the company and the evident peacefulness of its intentions had disarmed their suspicions. Mr. Lloyd's experience in the forest, so different from Stanley's, showed that the dwarfs are by no means so "malicious" as that great explorer imagined. As his testimony, like that of Dr. Livingstone or Mr. Joseph Thomson, points to the conclusion that where no warlike demonstrations are made, the African savage of whatsoever tribe is in ordinary circumstances a good natured fellow, who was ready to give the right hand of fellowship to those who show themselves peaceful and friendly.

With the Pygmies Mr. Lloyd struck up a friendship on the spot. The chief testified to his goodwill by presenting him with an antelope he had just killed, and also with a pot of wild honey, of which great quantities are gathered by these people from the hollows of the trees. That night the two parties encamped in the forest side by side, and they parted next morning on the best of terms, after Mr. Lloyd had made several ineffectual efforts to obtain photographs of the strangers. He found that snapshots were impossible in the forest twilight, while the Pygmies were too restless to submit to time exposures. And so, after spoiling about a dozen plates, he had to give up the idea in despair.

After this, different parties of Pygmies were met with at various times in the further course of march through the forest, some of whom even brought their women to see the white traveler. The women were comely little creatures, averaging 3 feet 10 inches in height, with light tan colored skin. Like Stanley, Mr. Lloyd was much struck by the beautiful eyes of the Pygmy women. These are singularly large and lustrous, but so quick and restless that they never seem to fix their gaze upon any object for one second at a time.

A VISIT FROM THE PYGMIES

I called out, "Come and let us talk together." First one man came creeping towards me, then some of his companions who dodged

The Pygmies are essentially a wandering people. They never think of clearing the ground and cultivating the soil, and are content to wander from place to place, gathering the honey which the bees have stored and the fruit and beans and nuts which grow plentifully on the trees, but above all living on the spoils of the chase. They are fearless and expert hunters, who do not hesitate with their little bows and arrows to attack the largest elephants. Sometimes they have to follow one of these forest monsters for days, and shoot hundreds of arrows into it before it falls down and dies from exhaustion and loss of blood. Then they camp around it and feast upon its flesh day after day. When nothing but the hide and skeleton are left they seize their weapons once more and go in search of another quarry.

Particularly interesting to this traveler were the evidences he discovered of the Pygmy worship. It has sometimes been alleged that these Congo dwarfs have no religion; but Mr. Lloyd had abundant evidence that this was not the case. Sometimes at the foot of a huge tree there might be seen a bundle of food neatly tied up and a piece of bark cloth, or a pot of honey, or a humble offering of forest beans. The Pygmies venerate the Spirit of their forest home, and look upon a giant tree as enshrining that Spirit's presence. And besides their tree shrines Mr. Lloyd came upon temples of their own building-little huts, roughly fenced in from the forest, and hardly better than the tiny shelters of boughs and leaves in which they lie down at night, but holy places in their eyes, because there they deposit the gifts they wish to offer to the invisible Spirit of the woods.

Having successfully struck the river Ituri, the

expedition made its way along the banks, and at length issued from the forest at a place called Avakubi, where there was a Belgian station with an officer in command. Here the white traveler was kindly received, and stayed for two days, thoroughly enjoying the comforts of civilized life after all the privations of camp arrangements in the Pygmy forest. And now it was a comfort to think that though he still had some 1,500 miles of African travel to face, no more tramping would be necessary. Fifteen days' paddling down the Aruwimi would bring him to the Congo. Reaching that great river, he would connect with a service of steamers running between Stanley Falls and Leopoldville. At the latter place a passage would be secured by another steamer to Boma, at the Congo mouth, and from that place the Belgian mail boat would carry him homewards.

This was a comparatively tame program for one who had just fought his way for weeks through all the dangers and terrors of the Great Forest; and yet the journey, especially in its earlier stages, was full of interest, and not without adventure. More than once the canoe came to grief in shooting the rapids, for the African boatmen are not such experts at this kind of work as the North American Indians; and once at least Mr. Lloyd was all but drowned. Moreover, the Aruwimi for a long distance runs through a country in which cannibalism is practiced almost as a fine art by a bold and warlike race known as the Bangwa. More than once on landing at a Bangwa village Mr. Lloyd had to face a trying experience. A crowd of tall savages, each with a cruel looking knife shaped like a sickle, walked round him, looking him up and down, as if taking stock of his condition and considering whether he was worth killing.

Apart from disagreeable sensations on his own private account, Mr. Lloyd often had to witness scenes which were horrible and sickening. The visitor found, however, that the cannibalism of the Bangwa was not simply a depraved appetite, but in large part the result of superstition. They firmly believed that the spirit of the dead warrior passes into the body of the men who eats him, so that by partaking of the flesh of his slain foe a man will increase his own strength and courage. It is in keeping with this that a woman is seldom, if ever eaten by the Bangwa.

The donkey with which Mr. Lloyd started from Toro not only proved to be of no use as a steed, but was a source of infinite trouble through her habit of floundering into swamps and sticking fast in the bush on every possible occasion, and he was glad to sell her on the first opportunity. His little dog Sally, after many exciting adventures and hairbreadth escapes, came to an untimely end in the jaws of a crocodile, but his bicycle, which had been carried safely through the forest in sections, he was now able to put together again, and one day in a large Bangwa community inhabited by some thousands of people he appeared suddenly in the village street pedaling along at the top of his speed. The sensation he produced was enormous. The cannibals rushed about in consternation, knocking each other down in their eagerness to get out of the way, and crying, "The white man is riding on a snake." By and by he dismounted, and calling to the chief, he tried to persuade him to come and examine this strange flying creature. But his assurances that it was perfectly harmless were of no avail. The cannibal declined to come any nearer, saying, as he pointed to the long trail left by the wheels on the village street, that he always knew a snake's track when he saw it.

The intrepid traveler reached Boma safely at last, and caught the mail steamer for Europe. He had suffered many hardships, but he had also had not a few experiences that were pleasant—especially in the retrospect. And not the least pleasing of his impressions was the conviction which had grown upon him day by day, whether in the forest of the Pygmies or among the cannibals of the Aruwimi river, that great as was the darkness in which those people lived, they had many fine characteristics of their own, and offered a fresh and splendid field for the messengers of the Christian Gospel.

The rapidity of his march, combined with this complete ignorance of the languages of the Congo region, so different from those of Uganda, made it impossible for Mr. Lloyd to engage during his journey in any kind of Christian work among the natives. But it was a missionary purpose which carried him through the Dark Forest, and that missionary purpose had not been fruitless.

The C.M.S., it is true, has not hitherto felt justified in taking up work among the Pygmies. But Mr. Lloyd may be said to have claimed that strange people for Christ. Stanley had shown that, so far from being on the plane almost of the brute creation, they were a people of a quick intelligence. Mr. Lloyd proved that they were also possessed of religious ideas which offer a foundation for a higher faith and worship than their own. An American missionary traveler, the Rev. Mr. Geil, has followed in Mr. Lloyd's steps by traversing the forest, and has added something further to our knowledge of its very interesting inhabitants. There is every reason to hope that Pygmyland, like many another part of the Dark Continent, will one day be brought into the Kingdom of Christ.

NOTES AND AUTHORITIES: The book which contains Mr. Lloyd's narrative of his remarkable journey is entitled *In Dwarf Land and Cannibal Country*, and is published by Mr. T. Fisher Unwin. The present author has to thank Mr. Unwin for his kind permission to make use of Mr. Lloyd's narrative.

PART III
AMERICA

AMONG THE INDIANS AND ESKIMOS OF HUDSON BAY

CHAPTER ELEVEN

FROM THE EDITORS: Imagine living and working in a land of ice, a frozen world both spectacular and potentially deadly. The summertime heat in this place, sometimes exceeding 100 degrees Fahrenheit, would melt the snow and ice. In the depths of winter temperatures would sink to 50 degrees below zero. Such a land does exist in Canada; it is the Hudson Bay region, in which our next story takes place.

On August 25, 1851 Mr. John Horden and his wife, missionaries sent out by the Church Missionary Society, arrived in their new home, the Hudson Bay Company's settlement called Moose Factory. At 23 years years of age, John Horden would serve the native Indians and Eskimos (an indigenous people group in Canada who today prefer to be called Inuit) for the next forty-two years. It was an exciting, but dangerous life that he lived. Upon arriving in Canada, he found that the region in which he was to serve would be comprised of 2,250,000 square miles. Undaunted, he threw himself into his labors, traversing as much of the country as he could on foot, by dogsled, canoe, and any other mode of travel by which he could reach the unsaved. Each trip was an extraordinary adventure. Often, he would barely escape death in the most remarkable ways.

Horden was also blessed with unusual linguistic abilities, and within just a few months of arriving he had mastered the Cree Indian language and developed a special rapport with the natives. Over time, he acquired a "working knowledge" of the Chipewyan, Ojibwe, Inuktitut, and Norwegian languages, each of which proved useful for sharing the Gospel. In 1872 John Horden returned for a brief visit to England, at which time he was consecrated as bishop of the Moosonee region by the Anglican Church. Soon thereafter, he journeyed back again to his adopted home and the needy Indian peoples whom he loved. His new title meant little to him; it was simply a greater responsibility to establish missions, train native pastors and teachers, and demonstrate a life of faithful service.

Throwing himself back into his work, he continued to travel throughout the Hudson and James Bay regions, in spite of the worst of conditions. An excerpt from one of his journal entries indicates the nature of much of the travel: "Feb. 5th. — Cold still more severe; wind as yesterday, right in our teeth; could not travel after eleven o'clock, when we encamped at the edge of Stoney River Plain. With the exception of myself, all were frozen; the guide and James Isaac, my special attendant, very severely. Temperature, 36 degrees below zero."

John Horden's greatest legacy may very well have come by his literary work. During his life, he accomplished two literary feats. The first was *A Grammar of the Cree*

Language, as Spoken by the Cree Indians of North America
published in 1881. The second was even more important
— the translation of the New Testament into the Cree
Indian language. Persevering even when requiring an
assistant to do the writing, he completed his translation on
his deathbed, just prior to his departure into the heavenly
realm to meet his Master. John Horden died on January 12,
1893, at the age of 65, in Moose Factory, Canada, the place
where his missionary labors first began.

John Horden (1828—1893)

To those who as boys have read Mr. R.M. Ballantyne's
Ungava and *Young Fur Traders*, the name of Hudson
Bay will always suggest a world of glorious adventure and
excitement. They have visions of Indians shooting swift
rapids in their bark canoes, or of Eskimos on an ice floe
fighting a fierce polar bear or lying in wait for an unwary
seal. They see the trapper on a winter morning, with his
gun on his shoulder, skimming lightly on broad snowshoes
over the powdery snow, as he goes his rounds from one trap
to another through a forest which has been transformed by
icicle and snowflake into a wonderland of glittering beauty.
Or they remember the traders in a lonely fort, doing their
best to keep their hearts jolly and their noses free from
frostbite, at a time when the thermometer is fifty degrees
below zero, and the pen cannot be dipped into the ink
bottle because the ink has turned into a solid lump of ice.

The present writer has a vivid recollection of a sunny midsummer season spent in the Orkneys. In Stromness Harbor he saw some strongly built but old-fashioned vessels preparing to set sail, and felt an almost boyish thrill of delight as he learned that these were the Hudson Bay ships about to start on their annual voyage for the coasts of Labrador, from what is their last port of call in the British Isles. He thought of that solitary route, where sometimes never a sail is sighted from one side of the Atlantic to the other. And he remembered that, though the bright summer sun might be shining on our islands, these ships would have to struggle with many a bristling iceberg before they could discharge at Moose Fort or York Factory the precious cargo on which depended the comfort and even lives of those who held the outposts of the British Empire along the frontiers of the Frozen North.

Let us go back to the year 1851, and imagine ourselves on board of a stout old wooden ship of the whaler type, which has fought its way from Stromness across the North Atlantic and through the floes and bergs of Hudson Straits, and is now entering the wide expanse of Hudson Bay itself. She is squarely built, and armed at her bows with thick blocks of timber called ice-chocks, to enable her to do daily battle with the floating ice. On board of her as passengers are a young Englishman named John Horden and his wife. Horden is a teacher who is being sent out from England by the Church Missionary Society to try to bring some Christian light into the minds and hearts of the Indians and Eskimo scattered round the shores of this great inland sea. The vessel is nearing her destination, but the danger is not yet over; indeed the worst dangers are yet to come. Horden himself describes their experiences:

"Ahead, stretching as far as the eye could reach, is ice—ice; now we are in it. More and more difficult becomes the navigation. We are at a standstill. We go to the masthead—ice; rugged ice in every direction! One day passes by—two, three, and four. The cold is intense. Our hopes sink lower and lower; a week passes. The sailors are allowed to get out and have a game at football; the days pass on; for nearly three weeks we are imprisoned. Then there is a movement in the ice. It is opening. The ship is clear! Every man is on deck. Up with the sails in all speed! Crack, crack, go the blows from the ice through which we are passing; but we shall now soon be free, and in the open sea. Ah! No prisoner ever left his prison with greater joy than we left ours."

A few days after, the voyagers reached Moose Fort, at the extreme southwest corner of Hudson Bay, and the young teacher found himself on the spot that was to be his home for the rest of his life.

And now let us look at the task which lay before him. When John Wesley said that he took the whole world for his parish, he was speaking figuratively; but this inexperienced young man found himself literally responsible for the education and religious welfare of a district 1,500 miles long by 1,500 broad. Indeed, lengthwise his parish stretched out indefinitely into space, for though bounded on the south by the settled parts of Canada, it might be said to extend in the opposite direction right up to the North Pole. Within this huge area, and planted along the coasts of Hudson Bay, a few trading posts of the Hudson Bay Company were scattered several hundred miles apart. And here and there small bands of Indians and Eskimo were settled, who gained a precarious livelihood by hunting and fishing. Apart from those who lived in the neighborhood of Moose Fort, or visited it from time to time to barter skins and furs for English goods, Horden could reach the people of this vast territory only by toilsome and dangerous journeys, performed in summer in a bark canoe, and in winter on snowshoes or in a sledge drawn by a team of Eskimo dogs.

First of all, however, he had to learn something of the language, or rather of the languages, for there were several of them. Around Moose Fort the Indians were Crees, but in other parts of the country there were Ojjibeways and Chippeways, each of whom spoke an entirely different dialect. Farther north, on both sides of the Bay, were the Eskimo, whose speech bore no resemblance to any of the Indian tongues. The language difficulties did not trouble Horden very seriously. Most Europeans are greatly puzzled by the peculiarities of the agglutinative family of languages used by the native tribes of North America. But though Horden confessed that Cree was a jaw-breaking speech, and that Greek and Latin in comparison were tame affairs, he had so much determination, combined with such a knack for picking up new words and forms of expression, that in a very few months he was able to preach to the people without the help of an interpreter. He made mistakes, of course. Once he was speaking of the creation of Adam and Eve. All went well till he came to describe Eve's manner of coming into the world, when he observed that his hearers were "smiling audibly." He found that instead of saying that

the woman was made "out of one of Adam's ribs," he had
said "out of one of Adam's pipes." *Ospikakun* is "his rib," and
ospwakun "his pipe." But by and by he was able to speak
with correctness as well as fluency, not in one language,
but in several. And having taught the people to read, and
himself learned how to work a printing press, he scattered
abroad thousands of Gospels and other books which he had
translated into the various tongues.

Mr. Horden showed such aptness for his work that
before long he was ordained as a clergyman by the nearest
bishop—the Bishop of Rupert's Land, who had to make
for this purpose a journey of six weeks, mostly by canoe.
And now Horden himself began to make those constant
and arduous expeditions to all parts of the territory which
form the most striking feature of the story of his life.
"Arduous," his biographer says, "is but a mild expression for
the troubles, trials, privations, and tremendous difficulties
attendant on travel through the immense trackless wastes
lying between many of the posts—wastes intersected by
rivers and rapids, varied only by tracts of pathless forest
swept by fierce storms."

Sometimes he went on from day to day for four or
five hundred miles, without ever seeing tent or house
or even the trace of a human being by the way. Often he
encountered men who delighted in bloodshed, and thought
little of killing and eating their fellow-creatures when other
means of subsistence failed. Once he met an Indian who
during the preceding winter had murdered and devoured,
one after another, his whole family of six children, in order
to satisfy the cravings of hunger. As for his own food on

these journeys, he was obliged to take whatever he could get. "I have eaten," he says, "white bear, black bear, wild cat; while for a week or ten days I have had nothing but beaver, and glad indeed I have been to get it."

Far up the eastern side of Hudson Bay lies the region of Ungava, with the Little Whale and Great Whale rivers flowing through it to the sea. For the Eskimo of this district Horden always had a special affection and regard. He loved his Indian flock too; but he found these Eskimo more responsive, more eager to learn, and more teachable in every way. Bleak and desolate as the country was around Moose, it was colder and wilder still towards Ungava, where from year's end to year's end the snow never entirely disappeared, and the white bear of the floes took the place of the black bear of the forest. In summer the Eskimo lived in tents made of sealskins; but in winter, like their Greenland cousins, in houses built of slabs of frozen snow. Bears and seals were hunted in winter, but in summer there came the fiercer excitements of a great whale drive. The whales would come over the river bars in vast numbers, and then every kayak was afloat, and with harpoon and line the eager sportsmen followed their prey to the death. On one occasion Mr. Horden himself took part in a whale fishery in which no fewer than a thousand prizes were secured—a world of wealth and feasting to the poor Eskimo.

But no matter what the Eskimo were about, if they heard that the white teacher had come they dropped spear and harpoon, and trotted off to listen, to sing, and to pray, in a fashion which showed how deeply interested they were. By and by Horden was able to obtain for them a missionary of their own, who settled on the spot, and under whose teaching the whole colony around the Whale River region became not only thoroughly civilized, but earnestly Christian.

Still farther north than Ungava, but on the opposite side of Hudson Bay, is a station called Fort Churchill. Horden dubbed it "the last house in the world," for there was no other between it and the North Pole. There the cold in winter is as intense almost as in any spot on the surface of the globe. The diary of an expedition to this lonely outpost, undertaken in the depth of winter, is especially interesting. Horden traveled in a cariole, or dog sledge, accompanied by Indian guides. The temperature was never less than thirty, and sometimes nearly fifty degrees below zero. The greatest precautions had to be taken against frostbite. Every evening, when they encamped in the forest, about an hour and a half was spent in erecting a thick, high barricade of pine branches as a protection against the piercing wind. An enormous fire was also necessary, for one of ordinary size would have made little impression on the frozen air. When a hearty supper had been cooked and eaten, and the Indians had lighted their pipes, the little company would sit around the blazing pine-logs and tell of hunting adventures, or of hairbreadth escapes from the perils of the forest and the flood. As bedtime drew near, all joined earnestly in a short service of praise and prayer, and then lay down to sleep under the open sky, which glittered with frosty stars, or glowed and throbbed with the streaming rays of the brilliant Northern Lights.

Though the last house in the world, Fort Churchill had a heterogeneous population of English traders, Indians, and Eskimo. The Eskimo of the west were a fiercer people than those on the eastern side of the great bay, and were much feared even by the Chippeway Indians—themselves dangerous customers to deal with. Often an Eskimo would come to the station with his face marked with red ochre, a sign that he had recently committed a murder. This red mark was their peculiar glory, for while they prided themselves on their prowess in killing a walrus or a polar bear, they thought it a much higher honor to have slain a human being. Churchill was thus a very needful field of operations in the eyes of Horden, and he did not rest until a church had been planted there, with a minister of its own to attend to the wants of the variegated flock.

In spite of its rigors and occasional tragedies, life at Churchill was not without its own small humors, too. Horden was fond of telling his friends farther south about the Churchill cows. There were three of them. The first was a dwarf. The second was so lean and supple that she could milk herself with her own mouth, and was therefore condemned to go in harness, carrying a bag round her udder which effectually prevented her from enjoying a drink of fresh milk whenever she pleased. The third member of the dairy had been despoiled of her tail one winter night by some hungry wolves. The result was that when summer came and the flies began to swarm—and in the brief, hot summer they *do* swarm around Hudson Bay—they threatened to eat up all of her that the wolves had left; for without a tail she was perfectly helpless against their assaults. But an ingenious trader bethought himself of a dead cow's tail which was lying in the store:

"Why not use that? The suggestion was at once acted upon; the tail was attached to the stump by means of some twine, and over it was tied some canvas, well saturated with Stockholm tar. It was a great success, and the creature was again able to do battle with her diminutive but persevering foes."

In the course of his constant journeys in such a land, John Horden, as will readily be imagined, had many a narrow escape. Shooting the rapids in a bark canoe is one of the most exhilarating of experiences, but sometimes one of the most dangerous. Horden, who traveled thousands of miles by water almost every year, had full taste of the dangers. Once a large canoe in which he was ascending a swollen river was caught in a strong current and dragged down towards some difficult rapids, while the Indians, with faces upstream, dug their paddles into the water and strained their muscles nearly to the bursting point. Their efforts, however, were quite fruitless. The canoe went back and back, and at length was swept at lightning speed in to the boiling flood. Fortunately, the crew were equal to the emergency. In a moment they all turned swiftly round in their places, thus converting what had been the stern into the bow, and by careful steering through the rocks the canoe shot safely out at last into the smooth water beneath the rapids.

On another occasion, a smaller canoe struck with a heavy crash upon a rock right in mid-stream. A great hole was made, and the water came pouring in. But by great exertions the canoe was brought to shore before it had time to sink; and in an hour or two was sufficiently patched up again. For if an Indian canoe is easily damaged, it is easily repaired.

"One goes to a birch tree and cuts off a large piece of bark, another digs up some roots and splits them, a third prepares some pitch, and in the course of an hour or two the bark is sewn into the bottom of the canoe, the seams are covered with pitch, and we are once more loading our little vessel."

But the narrowest escape that Horden ever made was connected with the sudden breakup of the sea-ice. They were crossing a frozen inlet on the south of Hudson Bay, when the cold season was rather far advanced for a short cut of this kind to be altogether prudent. Just in the middle, when they were about ten miles from the nearest point of land, the guide gave a sudden exclamation and pointed seawards. As they looked, they saw mass after mass of ice rise up and fall back into the sea; and they knew that, with the approach of the warmer weather, the solid surface was going to pieces before an incoming tide. The guide next struck his stick sharply on the spot on which they stood, and the stick went clean through. Everyone knew what that meant—the ice was quite rotten. "Get into the cariole at once!" the guide cried to Mr. Horden. The Bishop jumped in, but his weight forced the hinder part of the sledge downwards into the sea. Both sledge and occupant might have disappeared in a moment if it had not been for the prompt action of the sagacious dogs. They seemed to realize at once Horden's danger and their own. Straining on their harness, they quickly drew the cariole out of its terrible position, and made for the nearest shore at full gallop, while the Indians ran behind not less swiftly. Eskimo dogs and Indians are both good long-distance runners, and we are not surprised to be told that neither men nor dogs ever thought of halting until they felt the solid ground once more beneath their feet.

There were many trials and anxieties, as well as dangers, in John Horden's life. Once the annual ship from England, so eagerly expected, was wrecked on a reef, and a large part of the provisions and other goods on which both traders and missionaries depended to carry them through another twelve months was utterly lost. Sometimes there came a bad season—no game in the forest, no wild geese for the goose-hunters along the shore—and the poor Indians died by the dozens. Above all, there was the great trial of parting from his wife and children, for Mrs. Horden, his faithful companion and helpmate from the very first, had to take the boys and girls to England to receive their education. But the good man never lost his cheerfulness or relaxed his activity. He was true always to the motto of his life: "*The happiest man is he who is most diligently employed about his Master's business.*"

Even on his deathbed his diligence did not cease. His last letter, dictated when he was no longer able to write himself, shows him, like the Venerable Bede in the well-known narrative of his pupil Cuthbert, busy to the last with the task of New Testament translation. He suffered dreadful torture from rheumatism, the natural result of forty-two years of "roughing it" in a climate where the temperature varies from 100 in the shade at the height of the brief summer to 50 degrees below zero in the depth of the winter. But in the intervals between the sharp attacks of almost intolerable pain, he pushed eagerly on with a revised version of the New Testament in the Cree language: "Picture me in my work," he writes to his friends in England. "I am lying on my back in my bed, Mr. Richards is sitting at a table by my side. I have my English Bible, the Revised Version, in my hand; Mr. Richards has my translation before him, which he is reading to me slowly and distinctly. Every sentence is very carefully weighted, and all errors are corrected. This is a glorious occupation, and I cannot feel too thankful that I am able to follow it in these days of my weakness."

The end came suddenly, but it did not come too soon. Horden had accomplished his task, and left behind him a splendid record of heroic work heroically done.

John Horden's monument is to be seen in the presence of a pervasive Christian civilization all around the shores of Hudson Bay. When he went there first, he found the people living for the most part under the cruel spell of their conjurers. It was a common thing to strangle the sick with a bowstring in order to save further trouble. Aged parents were got rid of in the same way to avoid the expense of supporting them. Murder for gain was rife on every hand. When Bishop Horden died, a complete change had passed over the great part of the Hudson Bay region. More than one Indian had been educated and ordained for the work of the ministry. Twenty-six native lay teachers, Indian and Eskimo, were busily engaged in various parts of the diocese. Thousands of persons had been baptized into the membership of the Church, and showed by peaceable and upright lives that they were

Christians in fact as well as in name.

NOTES AND AUTHORITIES: *Hudson Bay*, By R.M. Ballantyne; *Forty-two Years amongst the Indians and Eskimo*, by Beatrice Batty (the Religious Tract Society); *John Horden: Missionary Bishop*, by the Rev. A.R. Buckland, M.A. (London: The Sunday School Union).

THE "PRAYING MASTER" OF THE REDSKINS

CHAPTER TWELVE

"The letters, during the period of service over which we have been looking, include many testimonies to the character and worth of the Christian Indians, both men and women. The "noble Red man" does not always appear in fiction or in fact with much true nobility of character; yet under the Gospel of Christ, men and women such as had once killed their own kindred, to save themselves from starving, proved themselves genuine heroes."

—Rev. A. R. Buckland, M.A

FROM THE EDITORS: By the Indians he was known as "The Praying Master." His English and Canadian admirers often called him "The Apostle of the North," but in his own mind he was simply a servant and soldier of the Cross of Christ. Born the son of a ship's captain on January 18, 1801 in Kingston-upon-Hull, England, James Evans was trained for the grocery business as a youth. At 21 years of age, he set off to Canada to find better employment. There, he quickly discovered his preference for teaching. In 1828, after a conversion at a Methodist camp meeting, Evans accepted a position to teach at a mission school for Indian children. Armed with a natural aptitude for picking up the Ojibwe and Cree Indian languages, he began ministering to the Indians, teaching and sharing the Gospel on various circuits.

In 1840, the Hudson Bay Company, having obtained the rights to all the Canadian frontier fur trade, saw the need for missionaries to minister with the Indians with which they did their business. This they hoped would provide a stabilizing factor for future trade opportunities in the area. Identified as the best man in the region for the job, Evans was appointed by the Wesleyan Methodist Missionary Society to the post at Norway House, Manitoba. This work perfectly accommodated his desire to travel, and reach as many of the Indians as he could with the Good News of Jesus Christ. By the time of his death on November 23, 1846, he had spent twenty-four years of service among the Indians in Canada. During his service, he had completed a speller for the Ojibwe Indian language, *A Bibliography of the Algonquian Language, A Bibliography of the Languages of North American Indians*, a hymn book of Christian songs for the Indians, as well as providing an alphabet in the Cree language, and publishing portions of the Bible in the Indian tongues. In spite of the high and low points experienced during his missionary career, the contributions of James Evans in spreading the Gospel most certainly warrants the honorary title of "The Apostle of the North."

James Evans (1801—1846)

We have seen how, through the influence of John Horden, Christianity was spread among the Indians and Eskimo around the inhospitable shores of Hudson Bay. But we have now to follow the story of a man whose journeys and adventures amidst the "snowflakes and sunbeams" of the Far North throw even those of Horden into the shade. James Evans, "The Apostle of the North" as he has been called, was not confined to a certain diocese or area of service, and so was free to minister throughout the length and breadth of half a continent. From Lower Canada to the Rocky Mountains, and from Lake Superior to the Arctic Circle, he pushed ever forward as a pioneer of Christianity to the Indian races of British North America. It is over 150 years since he began those incessant labors which made him the successor of Brainerd and Eliot. The wheat fields of Manitoba now wave where in those days vast herds of buffalos roamed over the plains. The fur trader's lonely fort in the wilderness has been supplanted here and there by the flourishing, up to date Western cities. And yet, after all, civilization has done little more than fringe the borders of those vast territories of the Canadian Northwest through which James Evans journeyed unwearied, whether in the long winter or the short summer, as he bore his message of peace and goodwill to the tribes of the Assiniboine and the Saskatchewan, to the fierce Blackfeet and Mountain Stonies of the Rockies, and even to those of the redskin peoples whose hunting grounds lay under the North Star by the shores of Lake Athabasca or along the banks of the great Mackenzie River, which pours its mighty flood of waters into the Arctic Sea.

James Evans was an Englishman who, like many another, had gone to Canada in search of a career. Finding it difficult to get employment in business, he became a backwoods schoolmaster. It was a fine training for the life that lay before him, bringing not only experience as a teacher, but familiarity with those arts of the hardy backwoodsman which were by and by to stand him in good stead. He was a Wesleyan, and as the leaders of the Wesleyan Church in Canada came to know his talents and enterprise, as well as his Christian zeal, they offered him a post as a teacher in one of their Indian schools in the Lake Ontario district. It was pioneer work of the purest kind, but Evans thoroughly enjoyed it and lived happily in a tent with his young wife until he had felled cedar trees and sawn them into logs and built both school and schoolhouse with his own hands. His success as a missionary teacher led before long to his being ordained as a minister, and appointed to labor among the Indian tribes on the northern shores of Lake Superior. This involved a dangerous journey of many days in an open boat, but Evans was now an expert canoeist, who could handle a paddle as if to the manner born. He reached Lake Superior in safety and began his lifelong fight against the superstitions and cruelties of Red Indian paganism at a place that bore the appropriate name of Devil's Hole.

To any ordinary man the far stretching coasts of the greatest of all the American lakes would have been a field sufficient for a life's labors. But Evans was not an ordinary man. Like Livingstone in Africa, he was never satisfied unless he was continually pressing on into new regions, and carrying the name of Jesus Christ where it had not been heard before. And in the most unexpected way there came an opening and a call to a new and larger sphere such as he longed for.

The fur traders of the great Hudson Bay Company, whose forts where scattered right across the continent from the Atlantic to the Pacific, and from the Great Lakes to the Arctic Ocean, had noticed for some time that many of the Indians of the north where drifting steadily southwards. This gave them much concern, for it was from the northern part of their territories that they got a large proportion of their most valuable furs, and this southerly movement of the native hunters threatened the Company with serious loss. At first the migration was set down simply to a desire to escape to a more congenial climate, but fuller investigation revealed that the true reason was very different. The Indians of the north had heard some word of a new and wonderful religion, which had come to their brothers in the south—a religion given by the Great Spirit to the red man as well as to the white. Around many a campfire the tidings had been discussed. And at last religious curiosity became so strong that, in the words of Mr. Egerton Young, the biographer of Mr. Evans, "family after family embarked in their birch canoes and started for the land of the South Wind, in order to find the teacher and the Book."

And so it occurred to the directors of the Company that it would be to their advantage to bring the missionary to the Indians, instead of leaving the Indians to go in search of the missionary. They applied accordingly to the Wesleyans in England to send without delay several suitable men to work among the tribes of the Northwest. This the Wesleyan Society at once proceeded to do, and as the most competent man to be the leader of the movement their choice fell upon Mr. Evans. He lost no time in transferring himself from Lake Superior to Norway House, which is situated at the northern end of Lake Winnipeg, "The Lake of the Sea," and in those days was one of the Hudson Bay Company's most important forts.

As illustrating the conditions of life at that time in those remote regions of the British Empire, it is interesting to know how Norway House received its name. So great were the hardships and loneliness that had to be faced in the service of the Hudson Bay Company that few Englishmen cared for such employment. Hence, as a matter of fact, it was largely Scottish Highlanders and Islanders, or men from the fiords and fields of Norway, who manned the outlying forts. Norway House was originally occupied by a contingent of Norwegians, and it was in compliment to them that the title was given to the fort.

We cannot dwell on the long canoe journey of 1500 miles to the northern lake, though it included perils in the rapids, and adventure with a black bear, and dangers on Lake Winnipeg itself, which got its name from the Indians because of its great size, and the sudden storms which burst upon it and raise its waves to the height of ocean billows.

On reaching his destination, Mr. Evans was received with great kindness by the officials of the Company, and was soon plunged into the kind of work he delighted in. For here were Indians from far and near. Those of the district around the fort were called Swampy Crees, and were a

splendid class of men both in physique and intelligence.
But in addition to these there came to Norway House
large bands of hunters from the warlike tribes of the Rocky
Mountains, men who had come down the Saskatchewan in
their canoes for more than 1,200 miles. And here too were
Indians of a more peaceful blood from the Mackenzie and
Peace Rivers in the distant north. All came on the same
errand. They brought for sale the skins and furs of bears
and beavers, otters and ermines, black and silver foxes, and
many other animals. And in exchange they carried back
English goods which had come across the Atlantic and
through the ice packs of Hudson Straits and Hudson Bay,
and, after being landed at York Factory, had been brought
up country for many hundreds of miles with infinite toil by
canoe and dog-train.

Evans turned his attention in the first place to the
Indians of Lake Winnipeg itself. Their minds were full of
superstitions. They believed in a *Kissa-Manetoo* or Good
God, but also and still more strongly in a *Muche-Manetoo* or
Evil Spirit, whose power was thought to be the greater of the
two. They listened eagerly to the good news which the white
preacher brought to their wigwams of a divine love which
conquers all evil, and a Father in heaven to whom every one
of His children, whether whiteskin or redskin, is equally dear.

It was more difficult, however, for the *Ayumeaookemow*,
or "praying-master," as Evans was called, to get them not
only to believe in the divine love, but to give up their own
hatreds and cruelties and other wicked ways. There was one
chief named Maskepetoon, a man of magnificent stature
and strength, who liked Mr. Evans greatly, but said that this

new religion was only fit for old women. "I will never be a Christian," he cried, "so long as there is a scalp to take or a horse to steal from the Blackfeet." He was a man of such an ungovernable temper that he scalped one of his own wives in a fit of displeasure. And yet this same man by and by met the murderer of his son on the prairie, and riding up to him, tomahawk in hand said: "By all the laws of the Indian tribes you deserve to die; but I have learned that if we expect the Great Spirit to forgive us, we must forgive our enemies, and therefore I forgive you."

But Evans not only taught the Indians religious truth, he taught them to work—a very necessary lesson. No doubt there were times when work seemed quite superfluous, for deer abounded in the forest and multitudes of buffaloes browsed on the prairie. There were seasons, however, when game was scarce, and times when the Indians perished by the score for lack of some other means of subsistence. Hitherto they had thought it degradation for a hunter to engage in any kind of manual toil. But Evans introduced new ideas. He won their respect by his own skill as a shot, and then by his example induced them to till the fruitful soil and build themselves comfortable houses. By the shores of the Lake, and not far from Norway House, there sprang up the neat Indian village of Rossville, with its houses and gardens and school and church, one of the finest Indian missions in North America. Those who have read Mr. R.M. Ballantyne's *Hudson Bay* will remember his humorous and yet sympathetic account of an Indian school festival at Rossville, of which Mr. Evans was the presiding genius, and at which the famous writer of boys' story-books was

himself present, when he was a young clerk in the service of
the Hudson Bay Company.

And now Mr. Evans began to turn his attention to those
far-off tribes which had their settlements along the foothills
of the Rocky Mountains or the banks of the Mackenzie River.
Now began those great expeditions by waterway or dog-
trail which surpassed in extent even the historic journeys
of the Apostle Paul, for Evans would undertake a circuit of
five thousand or six thousand miles in a single season. It is
these immense journeys through the unknown wilderness
that provide the most romantic elements in the story of
his life. It was by them that he became known among the
Indians through all the regions of the Northwest not only,
like other Christian preachers, as the *Ayumeaookemow*, or
"praying-master," but as the *Keche Ayumeaookemow*, the
"great praying-master." At one time we find him in his canoe
toiling upstream, or darting down the swift rapids with a
thrill of dangerous delight to which the artificial joys of the
modern waterslides cannot be compared for a moment.
Again he is camping out on those rolling plains of the Far
West which are now some of the most fruitful cornfields
in the world, but were then the special preserves of the
buffalo. Sometimes, as he lay down at night, the roaring of
the bulls in the immediate neighborhood would be so loud
and incessant that it was impossible to fall asleep. And often,
as he closed his eyes, he knew that if the herd should be
seized with a sudden panic and stampede in the direction of
his little camp, nothing could save him and his companions
from being trampled to death.

But it is his winter journeys by dog-train over the

HUNTING BUFFALO IN WINTER TIME

frozen snow that strike us most with a sense of adventure. His favorite team of dogs was famous all over the land. They were hybrids—half dogs, half wolves, possessed of such strength that they could do their eighty or ninety miles a day, dragging a load of three hundred pounds or more. In harness they were easily controlled, and yet they were so fierce that they had always to be chained up at night; while through the summer, when sledging was over for the season, they were carefully shut up in a high stockade. Their savage disposition brought about their death. One morning an old chief who had come to look for Mr. Evans opened the gate of the stockade-yard, thinking he might be inside. In a moment the wolf dogs sprang upon him and mangled him to death before they could be beaten off. For this crime, of course, they were immediately shot.

Let us take one or two glimpses of a tour in the depths of winter. The sledge which glides so swiftly over the snow is shaped like a boy's toboggan, but is eight or ten feet long, about eighteen inches broad, and is drawn by a team of four powerful dogs. On a long journey two or three of these sledges are necessary, for a plentiful supply of provisions must be carried, as well as bedding and camping utensils.

As the train sweeps forward there is often not a landmark to be seen—nothing from horizon to horizon but a vast unbroken sheet of snow. But the Indian guide pushes on with confidence, led by an instinct that never fails him and is almost as mysterious as that by which the swallows flying south find their way across the trackless sea.

After a long day's drive through air which is trying enough at 40, 50, or even 60 degrees below zero, though infinitely worse when accompanied by a wind sufficiently strong to raise the fine, powdery snow into a blinding, choking blizzard, both men and dogs are thankful when camping time comes with its prospect of rest, warmth, and food. The camp is nothing more than a square hole in the deep snow, scooped out with snowshoes that have to serve as shovels. On three sides the snow is banked up, while on the fourth a huge fire is kindled with logs cut from the forest. The kettles are then filled with snow, and as soon as the snow is melted, a goodly chunk of frozen buffalo or bear or beaver is popped into the largest kettle to be boiled. Meanwhile, the dogs are being fed, mostly with frozen fish, which has first to be thawed before the fire; and if the night is unusually cold they are allowed to get on their dog-shoes, which are not unlike socks. For the privilege of getting on their shoes they often beg by howling piteously.

Supper is never luxurious, and is always taken under difficulties. When the cold is 50 degrees below zero, meat taken out of the kettle freezes so fast that it has sometimes to be thrust back into the water two or three times in the course of a meal. The tea is flavored with milk which is quite sweet, though it may be several months old, and is presented not in a milk-jug but in a bag, from which pieces of it are broken off with a hatchet as required. There is no lingering over the tea-cups, or rather the pans that do service in the wilderness for those symbols of civilization; and that for the very good reason that if the tea is not quickly drunk, it cannot be drunk at all, having already become solid.

After evening prayers and the evening song, there comes the process of going, or rather being put, to bed. An

Indian has a knack of rolling himself up securely in a warm rug of rabbit skins, but a white man is better for being tucked in. Mr. Evans's Indians always attended to this duty most carefully. They spread blankets and rugs over him, and tucked in his head as well as his shoulders and feet, leaving not the least chink for the entrance of the outer air at any point. Under such treatment Mr. Evans felt at first as if he were being suffocated, but he soon learned to adjust himself to the necessary conditions of safety. For there is a real danger to the sleeper in neglecting these precautions. Mr. Egerton Young tells of one restless traveler who could not lie still in his camp bed, and so shook his face free from the protecting blankets. Wakening by and by, he put his hand up and felt what he took to be the icy handle of an axe. It turned out to be his own frozen nose.

Sometimes in the night a snowstorm would come on, and the travelers would waken in the morning to find themselves completely buried; but to those properly wrapped up the dry snow did little harm. It was more discomposing when the wolves, as often happened, gathered in a grim circle round the campfire and kept up their blood-curdling howl through all the hours of darkness. Then it was necessary that a watch should be kept, and that the watcher should rise every now and then and pile on a fresh supply of logs, for there is no better protection against a pack of wolves than the glow of a blazing fire.

On a long march Mr. Evans frequently slept during the day and traveled through the night. The reason for this was that the intense white glare of the snow, with the sunshine reflected from it, was apt to bring on a distressing

SHOEING DOGS IN NORTHERN CANADA

Dog shoes are long mittens without the thumb. They are fastened to the leg by a piece of deerskin. They are put on when a dog

complaint of the eyes called snow blindness. At night there was no similar risk. Besides to a lover of nature there was a peculiar charm about the winter nights, especially in the sub-Arctic zone. Those northern nights were nearly always beautiful, whether the moon was flooding the world with a soft radiance, or the frosty stars sparkled like diamonds through an atmosphere of absolute purity, or the aurora flashed and blazed, sending its mysterious ribbons of colored light pulsing up to the very zenith and filling even those who had seen it times without number with a sense of awe in the presence of a glory so unearthly.

But from the romantic wanderings of the "Apostle of the North" we must pass to notice another feature of his varied activities and another great item in the debt owed him by the Indians of British North America (as it was then called). He was not only an intrepid and indefatigable traveler, but also a remarkable linguist and a man also of real inventive genius. A matter which troubled him greatly was the difficulty of teaching the Indians to read in the ordinary way. He brooded for years over the problem of inventing a simpler and easier path than that of the alphabet and the spelling book, and at last hit upon the plan that is known as the Cree Syllabic System. Taking the Cree language as his model, he found that it contained only thirty-six principal sounds, and by devising thirty-six simple characters to represent these sounds, he made it possible for any Cree Indian who learned to identify the characters to read at once without further difficulty. No spelling was necessary, only the pronunciation of the sound that corresponded to the character.

The result was that in a very few days old and young alike were able to read. But next came the difficulty of supplying them with books. Evans had no materials for printing and no experience in work of this kind. But he begged from the traders at Norway House the thin sheets of lead with which their tea chests were lined. Then, having carved out models of his syllabic characters and made casts of them in clay, he melted the lead and poured it into the molds; and so, after many failures, obtained a sufficient supply of type. Printing ink he manufactured out of soot mixed with sturgeon oil. Paper he could neither get nor make, but he found that sheets of birch bark would serve his purpose very well. Finally, in lieu of a printing press he begged the loan of a jackscrew used for packing bales of furs, and with no better equipment than this, turned out the first books which his Indian flock had ever seen.

The excitement produced by these printed sheets of bark was immense, for it seemed to the people nothing less than magic that birch bark could "talk," and something still more wonderful that it could bring them a message from the Great Spirit Himself. The result was that thousands, young and old, became readers of God's Word. And when the Society in England realized the value of Mr. Evans's invention, he was furnished with a properly equipped printing press, from which, year by year, there came a steady supply of Bibles and Testaments in the native tongue.

"The syllabic characters," says Mr. Egerton Young, "are still in use. The British and Foreign Bible Society now furnish all these Northern missions with Bibles and Testaments free of cost. Hundreds of Indians are reading out of them every day of the year. Missionaries to other tribes have utilized these syllables for other languages by adding additional signs for sounds not found among the Crees. Methodists, Episcopalians, Moravians, and others use these syllabics of James Evans, and find them of incalculable value."

As illustrating both the remarkable character of the hero of this chapter and the kind of influence he exerted even over Indians who remained heathen, a tragic incident in his history is worthy of notice.

One day he was out in a canoe shooting ducks, along with a young Indian named Hassel, who had become a Christian. By some accident, which he never understood, his gun went off. The full charge entered the head of poor Hassel, who fell back dead into the canoe.

Mr. Evans's grief was terrible. The Indian was a Chippewayan, and all his people were heathen. As such they retained their superstitious beliefs and cruel customs, and held in particular that blood must be given for blood and life for life. But his sorrow and sense of responsibility for his companion's death made him feel that he must surrender himself to Hassel's relatives, even though, as he well knew, it might result in his being put to death himself. Accordingly he wound up all his personal affairs, made arrangements for the management of the Mission, and after a trying scene of farewell with his wife and daughter, set out all alone for the distant part of the country in which the Chippeways lived.

Reaching the encampment of the tribe, he asked for the wigwam of Hassel's father. When it was pointed out to him he entered, and sitting down on the ground told his sad story, tears of sorrow meanwhile trickling down his face. At once the tent was full of excitement. Grasping their tomahawks and drawing their knives, the men of the family cried out for the blood of this paleface who had slain their kinsman. But there was one person in the tent who had already resolved that the paleface should live. This was no other than Hassel's old mother herself. She had been stricken with anguish when she heard of her son's death, but she had watched the stranger's countenance, and listened to the tones of his voice as he told his story, and she knew by the instincts of love and of grief that Evans was the true friend of her boy, and that his sorrow for what had happened was not less sincere than her own. And so when the avengers of blood were about to spring upon him as he sat unresisting on the ground, she ran forward and, putting both her hands on his head, said firmly:

"He shall not die. There was no evil in his heart. He loved my son. He shall live, and shall be my son in the place of the one who is not among the living."

And so the Christian missionary was actually adopted, after the Indian custom, into the tribe and family of these heathen Chippeways. For a time he remained in the wigwam with his new father and mother. And after he returned to his own family and work he still regarded himself as their son, given them in place of the son he had shot. He knew that Hassel, after becoming a Christian, had been very thoughtful of his parents, and had sent them a present from time to time. And though himself a poor man at the best, he made a point to the end of his life of sending regularly to his foster-parents what he regarded as their rightful share of his own yearly income.

And so, from living with the heathen Indians, to printing the Bible in their native tongue, to traveling the immense region in search of new converts, James Evans demonstrated by word and by deed how one might live his life as a missionary of Christ.

NOTES AND AUTHORITIES: *The Apostle of the North*: Rev. James Evans, by Egerton R. Young (London: Marshall Brothers); *Hudson Bay*, by R.M. Ballantyne (Thomas Nelson and Sons).

IN THE LAND OF THE DAKOTAS

FROM THE EDITORS: Consider the young missionary couple called by God to leave all behind and travel to a distant land in order that they may share the Gospel of Jesus Christ with the most savage Indian tribes. The man is tasked with clearing the land and building a small home on the prairie, under constant threats from surrounding Indians who look to rob him of his provisions. His wife travels separately to join her husband. But, within a days' journey of joining her husband on the field, is stopped by a war party prominently displaying a collection of fresh scalps. Another war party confronts her along the way, kills her horse, and forces her to complete the journey on foot. Only days later, her brother drowns in the nearby river. After all this, we learn of the missionary couple that, "the devoted pair never lost heart."

This story is no imaginative tale. It is the true story of Stephen and Mary Riggs upon their arrival at Traverse des Sioux in 1842, to serve as missionaries to the Sioux peoples of the Dakota Tribe. It is a remarkable adventure that unfolds in this chapter, showing how the power of the Holy Spirit, through the work of faithful men and women, can miraculously change heathen life and culture. This missionary couple did not lead an easy life; they had few converts in the first twenty years of service. It was the strenuous life that the Christian is called to live, forsaking all to serve wherever the Master leads. When hope languished and sorrows multiplied, God brought forth fruit in an unusual way.

Born in Ohio on March 23, 1812, Stephen Riggs attended college and seminary in Pennsylvania before he joined an American mission society in 1837. He ministered to the Indians at various Sioux villages and American military outposts. His wife Mary was born in 1813, and from the time they were married and traveled together to live among the Dakota tribes, they dedicated their lives completely to the cause. In the sovereign plan of God, Mary died in 1869 at the age of 56 before seeing the full fruits of their labors take hold. However, one of the greatest tributes to the work and faithfulness of Stephen and Mary as missionaries and godly parents, is seen in the lives of their six children who went on to do missionary work. Several continued Stephen's work among the Indians and one crossed oceans to share the Gospel among the native Chinese.

The Riggs's work among the Sioux was varied. They did everything from running a school for Indian children, to preaching on Sundays, to serving as a military chaplain, to visiting and encouraging other missionaries at the various mission stations, to finishing a translation of the

Bible in the Dakota language. A man who made use of every single minute of time to the fullest, at his death in 1883, Stephen Riggs had completed nearly fifty literary works including everything from his personal biography called *Mary and I: Forty Years with the Sioux*, to works on the customs of the Dakota Indians, grammars and dictionaries of the Dakota language, hymn translations, and of course, the translation of the Bible. This husband and wife team, while hardly known by most Christians a hundred years after their death, are still an inspiration to those couples who wish to unite in ministry for the cause of Christ, though they may experience extreme conditions, and be confined to a simple lifestyle.

Stephen Riggs (1812—1883) and Mary Riggs (1813—1869)

The title of the present chapter will remind those who have read Longfellow's *Hiawatha* of one of the most frequently recurring lines in that poem of melodious repetitions—repetitions which are intended to suggest the steady "rushing of great rivers," and the waterfall's monotonous music:

> In the land of the Dacotahs,
> Where the Falls of Minnehaha
> Flash and gleam among the oak-trees,
> Laugh and leap into the valley.

But Longfellow's picture of the Dakotas and their country, though beautiful as poetry, is very misleading as to the realities of life among the uncivilized Western Indians of the United States of America. He deliberately put their cruelty and squalor out of his mind, and set himself to weave their legends and traditions into a song of pure romance. The tale we have to tell in the following pages may justly claim to be a story of romance and adventure. It takes us to the land of Hiawatha and Minnehaha, the land of lakes and prairies and primeval forests, where "the curling smoke of wigwams" is seen rising through the trees. But it is in the first place a story of sheer reality. The merely imaginative side of the story quite disappears, in the presence of Indian life as it was actually lived in the land of the Dakota Indians. The true adventure is seen to lie in the heroism and self-sacrifice of the young American missionary and his wife, who went out to the Far West in connection with the American Board of Foreign Missions to spend their days in the midst of those fierce savages. Their life was one of constant toil, of frequent alarms, of hope long deferred. But they had the courage of faith, and also its quiet patience. And one of them at least was spared to see a transformation among the Dakotas that went beyond anything for which they had looked.

It was in the year 1837 that the Rev. Stephen Riggs and his wife Mary left their home in the eastern United States and started westwards to begin work among the Sioux, the leading branch of the great Dakota family of Indians. Their first destination was Fort Snelling, a lonely military outpost at the junction of the Minnesota Falls of Minnehaha, and on the very site of the future city of Minneapolis. The greater part of this journey of 3,000 miles they were able to make by water—first down the Ohio River and then up the Mississippi. But so slow was traveling at that time, especially on the Upper Mississippi, that it was not until three months after leaving Massachusetts that they reached Fort Snelling.

Not far from the Fort there was a mission station, soon afterwards to be broken up by a furious and bloody war between the Sioux on the one side and the Ojjibeways and Chippeways on the other. Here the Riggses stayed for a few months to learn a little of the Dakotas and their language, and then set out with a wagon across the prairies towards a lake known as Lac-qui-parle, "The Speaking Lake," which lay some 200 miles farther to the west and near the border line between the present states of Minnesota and the Dakotas. For thirteen days they pushed steadily towards the setting sun, and at length reached the lake with the mysterious name. There they joined another pioneer missionary, Dr. Williamson, and had a room assigned them in a log cabin which he had built in the midst of the *teepees* or wigwams of the Sioux nation.

Their first task was to seek the acquaintance of the inmates of those teepees that were scattered along the shores of Lac-qui-parle. Approaching a Dakota village of that time, one saw a number of conical tents made of buffalo skins, with smoke issuing from holes left at the top. Lifting the little door of skin, the only shelter of the inmates against a temperature which in winter often sank to twenty degrees below zero, the visitor found himself in a cold, smoky lodge about twelve feet in diameter, where, besides a dirty lounging warrior with his pipe, there might be "a mother and her child, a blanket or two, a skin, a kettle, and possibly a sack of corn."

The Indians did not give the white men any welcome. On the contrary, they regarded them as intruders into their country, from whom it was legitimate to steal everything they could lay their hands on. They resented, too, any attempts to interfere with their ancestral habits, and especially with their deadly feuds and murderous attacks upon the Indians of other tribes. There was a notable chief called "Eagle Help," a war prophet and war leader among the Dakotas, a man of unusual intelligence, and the very first of all the Sioux nation who learned from Mr. Riggs to read and write his own language. But, when the lust of battle came upon him, as it periodically did, he was the most bloodthirsty of savages. Once, when he was about to lead out a war party against the Ojjibeways for the purpose of slaying and scalping the men and carrying off the women as captives, Mr. Riggs argued with him in vain, and finally said that if the Sioux went on the war trail he would pray that they might not be successful. This so offended the chief that just before starting he and his men killed and ate two cows that belonged to the Mission. And when they returned from their expedition, after a long tramp during which they had not fallen in with a single Ojjibeway, he attributed this failure entirely to the white man's charms, and held himself justified accordingly in killing and eating another cow that still remained.

After spending five years at Lac-qui-parle in hard and

unpromising labor, Mr. Riggs decided to push out still farther into the wilderness, and so removed to a district called Traverse des Sioux, where no missionary had ever been before. But if his experiences at Lac-qui-parle had been trying, those which he had to encounter were ten-fold worse. Accompanied by his wife's brother, a fine young man of twenty-two, by whom they had been joined, he went on in advance and pitched his tent among the Traverse Indians. Many of them objected to his coming, and even tried to drive him away by threats. But his mind was made up to stay, and with the help of his companion he began to cut and haul logs to build a little cabin. The Indians did not interfere with this; but as soon as the two men had felled their logs and painfully dragged them to the spot where they proposed to build, they came down in force demanding payment for the wood taken from the forest, and Mr. Riggs was obliged to give up some of his scanty stock of provisions.

Before the cabin was finished Mrs. Riggs and the children arrived and their arrival was marked by an incident which left a deep and painful impression on the lady's mind. She was attended by three young Dakota Indians who had become Christians. Some distance from Traverse the road crossed the Chippewa River, and this point, as one of the three Indians, whose Christian name was Simon, was riding on ahead of the little company, a war party of Ojjibeways suddenly emerged from the forest, carrying two fresh and bleeding scalps. They came up to Simon and flourished their trophies in his face, but did him no harm, probably because they saw that he was in the company of white people, and vanished across the river as suddenly as they had appeared. Two miles farther on the road, Mrs. Riggs and her escort met a band of maddened Dakotas in wild pursuit of the Ojjibeways. They told Simon that one of the two scalps he had just seen was that of his own brother; and when they learned that the Ojjibeways were now beyond their reach, they turned their fury on Mrs. Riggs and her three Indian companions for not having tried to kill or stop the scalping party. Brandishing their muskets in the air, they clustered with savage faces and angry cries round the wagon in which the lonely white woman sat with a child in her arms. Finally, they shot one of the two horses that composed the team, so that she had to get out and walk the rest of the way in the heat of the broiling sun, carrying her little girl in her arms. This was Mrs. Riggs' introduction to Traverse des Sioux, and it was only one of various similar episodes which helped to turn her dark hair to prematurely gray.

A few days after, her brother was drowned while bathing in the swift river that flowed in front of the cabin. He was a youth of a joyful Christian spirit, and all that morning, while hard at work on the unfinished house, had been singing again and again a couplet from a simple but very appropriate hymn:

> Our cabin is small and coarse our fair,
> But love has spread our banquet here.

By and by he went down to the stream and plunged in for a swim before dinner, but took cramp, and was carried away by the current and drowned. And now in the midst of her weeping for the dead brother, Mrs. Riggs had to take his place in the task of finishing the log house, working with her husband at the other end of the crosscut saw, because there was no one else who could be got to do it.

It was a sad beginning to life in the new sphere, the forerunner too, of many another hard experience, but the devoted pair never lost heart. The Dakotas killed their cows and horses, stole their goods, and sometimes threatened their lives. But they worked patiently on, doing their best to live down enmity and opposition. Gradually they made friends with one and another through the power of kindness, but found it difficult to get even the most friendly to become Christians. A redskin might acknowledge that Christianity was true, but the Christian commandments were too much for him. He could not give up his killing and stealing and polygamy. Or if he promised to live a Christian life and actually made a start upon the straight path, a visit to some white trader's settlement where whisky was to be had was enough to turn him into an incarnate devil once again, ready for the worst of his old evil ways, and using vile and insulting language even to the white lady who had done so much for his own women and children. In each case, proof that while one can have a "faith" in Christ and knowledge of Him, unless the Spirit of God gives true saving faith to believe in his Son, true conversion and Christian life and walk can never take place. It is truly a miracle of God.

At length after several years had been spent at Traverse, the departure of Dr. Williamson to another station made it necessary in the general interests of the Mission to the Dakotas that the Riggses should return to Lac-qui-parle. Their trials and hardships, however, did not cease with the change. The Indians robbed them as before, though sometimes, it must be confessed, the thieves had the excuse that they and their children were almost starving. Fortunately, this excuse for stealing was taken away not long after their return. For several years the vast herds of bison, on which the Indians chiefly depended for their subsistence, had migrated farther and farther to the west, seeming to justify the complaint of the Dakotas that a curse fell upon their country with the coming of the white man's foot. But now the bison came back again, and all around Lac-qui-parle the hunters might be seen armed with bow and arrow and riding forth over the prairie to shoot down the noble game. For two years the Dakotas reveled in fresh buffalo meat, and were content to leave the white man's horse and cow alone. The children playing around the teepees grew sleek and fat. The very dogs got plump, and peace and contentment reigned on every hand.

But by and by the buffalos began to move westwards again—a circumstance which the Dakotas might very well have attributed to their own deadly arrows rather than to the white man's foot. The redskin thieves resumed their work in the dark nights; and of all the forms of theft that they practiced none was more trying than the spoliation of the gardens of the palefaces. It was hard to sow and plant, to weed and water, and after weeks of toil and months of watching to rise some morning and find that a clean sweep had been made of all the fruits and vegetables during the night. It almost seemed an allegory of what had been going on for years in the larger sphere of missionary labor. "We have sown our seed in toil and tears," Mr. Riggs and his wife said to each other, "but where is the fruit?" And yet it was just when the hope of much fruit was almost disappearing that fruit came most abundantly, though not in any anticipated way.

In the autumn of 1862 a body of 4,000 Dakota Indians had gathered at an agency called Yellow Medicine to receive certain annuities from the Government to which they were entitled. But through some mismanagement at headquarters (not greatly to be wondered at, seeing that the tremendous struggle with the Southern States was absorbing all the energies of President Lincoln's administration at that very time) the annuity money had not come, and the agent could not say when it would arrive. He wished the Indians in the meantime to disperse again to their homes. But as their homes in many cases lay at a distance of a week's journey or more, they refused to go back, and they also demanded that while they were kept waiting they should be fed. By and by they grew unmanageable, and began to attack the stores and help themselves to provisions. Resistance being offered, they became violent, and several white men were killed. As soon as word of this outbreak reached the nearest fort, an officer of the United States Army hurried off with fifty men, hoping to quell the rising. But the Indians met this little company with alacrity, and easily defeated it. Half of the soldiers were killed, and the rest had difficulty in making good their escape. Their victory over the regulars set the prairie on fire. All over the land of the Dakotas the red men rose against the whites.

Fortunately for the missionaries, the Indians who knew

HUNTING BUFFALO ON HORSEBACK

them best proved friendly towards them at this crises, and did what they could to shelter them from the storm of savagery which had burst over the country. The Riggses were smuggled stealthily to an island in the Minnesota River, where for a time they lay concealed. But their situation there was too precarious, and flight to the east was decided on. A terrible flight it was, especially for the women and children. The nearest place of safety was the town of Henderson, far down the Minnesota. They had to make their way cautiously, often in the dead of night through the long grass of the trackless prairie, grass that was heavy and sodden with water, for it rained incessantly for nearly a week. Starvation stared the fugitives in the face again and again, but they found food more than once in cabins which had been hurriedly deserted by white settlers, and once, coming upon a cow left in a stable, they did not hesitate to kill it and cook themselves a hearty meal. All the time, by day and by night, there lay heavy upon their hearts the horror of the Indian pursuer with his tomahawk and scalping knife. But they reached Henderson safely at last, where they were received by the inhabitants as persons alive from the dead. "Why, we thought you were all dead!" was the first greeting they had received. And they found that a telegram had come from Philadelphia saying, "Get the bodies at any cost."

The Sioux rebels were defeated at last in a pitched battle, and 400 of them were taken prisoner. When brought before a military commission, 300 of these were found guilty of having deliberately taken up arms against the U.S. Government, and were sentenced to death. President

Lincoln, however, who had the right of reviewing the findings of the commission, leaned towards clemency, and gave instructions that in the meantime only those should be executed who were proved to have taken party in individual murders or in outrages upon white women. These special crimes were brought home to thirty-eight of the prisoners, and an arrangement was made by which they were all hanged simultaneously in full view of the camp by the cutting of a single rope.

Through the crevices of the walls of their log prison house, the rest of the captives saw their comrades hanged. And the sight produced a profound impression upon them, an impression not only of fear, but also in many cases of guilt. Mr. Riggs and Dr. Williamson, who had been present in the camp as interpreters from the first at the request of the commanding officer, found their time fully occupied in dealing with the prisoners, who listened to their message of the love of God and salvation through Christ for the sinful as no Indians had ever listened to them before. Formerly, even in church on the Lord's Day, the Dakotas had heard the most earnest preaching with an air of stolid indifference. They would never rise to their feet at any part of the service, and they continued smoking all the time. Now their whole demeanor was changed. And as the days passed, a wonderful wave of conversion passed through the camp, in which there were now gathered, in addition to the prisoners, some 1,500 other Dakotas who were anxious about the fate of their friends. It was not long till 300 adult Indians in that camp made public profession of their faith in Christ, and were baptized into the communion of the Church.

Eventually the prisoners were pardoned by the President and allowed to return to their homes. But the work begun by the missionaries under such strange circumstances at the close of the war still went on, and resulted in the Christianization of the greater part of the Dakotas.

A few years after the Sioux war was over, brave Mary Riggs passed away, worn out by labors and trials. Her husband, however, was spared to see his name become an honored one in American and not only among the friends of Christian missions, but in academic circles as well. For this bold pioneer of the Cross had also the instincts of an original scholar. Through all his years of frontier toil and peril, often with no better study than a room which served at the same time for kitchen, bedroom, and nursery, and no better desk than the lid of the meal barrel, he had carried on laborious researches into the language of the Indians, which resulted at last in his *Dakota Grammar* and *Dakota Dictionary*, and brought him the well deserved degrees of D.D. and LL.D. But his highest honors were written not in the records of the Universities but in the changed lives of the Dakota people. In his old age, looking back over forty years of service, he could trace a wonderful contrast between *then* and *now*. In 1837, when he came to the Far West, he was surrounded by the whole Sioux nation in a state of ignorance and barbarism. In 1877 the majority of the Sioux had become both civilized and Christianized. Previously in the early days he and his young wife had seen the dusky form of Indian warriors flitting past on their way to deeds of blood. Now the same race was represented not only by sincere believers, but by native pastors in the churches and native teachers in the schools. And on the same prairie where the war-whoop of the savage had once been the most familiar sound, the voice of praise and prayer might be heard to rise with each returning Day of Rest from Indian cabins as well as Indian sanctuaries.

NOTES AND AUTHORITIES: The story told in this chapter is drawn from Mr. Riggs's book, *Mary and I: Forty Years with the Sioux* (Chicago: W. G. Holmes).

IN THE FORESTS OF GUIANA

CHAPTER FOURTEEN

FROM THE EDITORS: In the year 1498, Columbus passed by the coast of Central and South America, and on sighting one area of the northeast coast of South America, named it "Guiana." Soon after, Spain claimed all the region of the Caribbean Sea and the South American coast. In the 1620s the Dutch obtained a charter for settlement and began to colonize the region. Between 1666 and 1803, numerous European wars involving the English, the French, and the Dutch ended in these colonies finally falling under the purview of the British Empire.

By the 1820s, the British had begun to organize new towns and build plantations, and missionary works were established among the native tribes. With the discovery of gems and precious metals, colonization came into full swing. It was in the early 1840s that we meet the subject of this story, known by some as the "Apostle to the Indians of Guiana," the Rev. William Henry Brett. Born in 1818, he would serve for almost forty years in the jungles and swamps of South America, laboring among the Caribs,

Waraoons, and Arawaks tribes. Gifted in languages and equipped with a heart for seeing unreached people groups brought to know the Savior, he settled in Guiana.

Mr. Brett had the pioneering, adventurous spirit imminently necessary for this sort of work. Whether it required traveling up alligator-infested rivers in dugout canoes paddled by natives, or wading barefoot through muddy swamps, crossing over ravines bridged by tree trunks, or braving the terrible swarms of mosquitoes — he courageously pressed forward to explore, visit, and minister to the various tribal people.

After decades of service, Mr. Brett passed on his work to a younger fellow missionary, Mr. Heard. In 1878 he returned to Guiana for one last trip to visit the Indian missions that he had established. He returned to England and there died in 1886 at the age of sixty-six. William Brett recorded the following scene in his own words from that last visit to Guiana:

"It was a lovely and peaceful Sunday evening. My first visits to these rivers had taken place nearly forty years before. Each had its peculiar association. At Washiba Hill, near the head of one, the Caribs had, soon after that visit, made their first attempt at 'church' building; on the other I had met with a most unfriendly reception from the uncouth Waraus…A great change had taken place since those days. The people of those races, and of two others, had joined our congregation on that hill, no longer hostile to us, or to each other, but all worshipping together in peace. They were just then departing after even-song, and their clean white garments formed an agreeable spectacle as they streamed across the plain or entered the paths which led to their forest homes."

"To bid, without emotion, a last adieu to those old scenes, with their heart-cherished associations, was impossible. But the time had come. Increasing bodily infirmities had warned me that my forest journeys were all ended, and that I must now, with deep thankfulness to Him whose undeserved mercy had protected me so long, leave canoe and wood-skin voyages to younger and stronger men. May the Divine blessing be on all who seek to spread the knowledge of the Savior's name amongst the many races and languages of Guiana."

William Henry Brett (1818—1886)

Four hundred years ago, when the beautiful West Indian Islands were first discovered by the white men, they were inhabited by various native races of which the most powerful were the Caribs, a fierce and cannibal people. The original home of the Caribs, according to all their own traditions, was on the mainland of South America, in the dense forests which stretch along the lower reaches of the great river Orinoco. From the wide mouths of that river they had issued from time to time in their war-canoes and swept like a storm cloud on the nearer islands of the West Indian Archipelago, killing and devouring the gentle and peaceful Arawaks and Waraoons who were in possession before them. In *Robinson Crusoe* we have the most vivid description in English literature of those cruel Caribs of long ago. For though Alexander Selkirk served as the prototype of Defoe's immortal story, and Juan Fernandez in the South Pacific was the island in which that Scottish buccaneer was marooned for several years, it is really one of the West Indian islands, perhaps Tobago, that Defoe takes as the stage of Crusoe's exploits and experiences. The incident of the footprint on the sand, as well as the decidedly tropical vegetation of the island, is undoubtedly adopted from West Indian sources. And the cannibal scenes which are described with so much realism are probably derived from the writings of the early voyagers, who told of the inhuman habits of that savage Indian race which gave its name to the fair waters of the Caribbean Sea.

From the Caribbean Islands the old Indian races, both the conquering and the conquered, have now almost entirely disappeared. To find a pure-blooded representative of those primitive people whom Columbus and the other early discoverers found there at the close of the fifteenth century, we have to go to the forests of the South American mainland, to which the broken relics of the aboriginal West Indian peoples—Caribs, Arawaks, Waraoons, and the rest—were long since driven by the tyranny of the Spaniard. Within the recollection of the present writer (1907), Waraoons of the Orinoco used still to come paddling once a year across the blue Gulf of Paria on a visit to the old home of their fathers in Trinidad—the nearest of all the West Indies to the South American Continent. He can remember as a boy, going down with his father to the wharf at San Fernando to see these Waraoons arriving—statuesque, sad looking savages, absolutely naked, who brought with them

for barter articles of their own manufacture—hammocks
of great strength such as they swung to the trees in their
forest homes, baskets ornamented with stained porcupine
quills skillfully woven into the framework, mats similarly
embellished with wild seeds red, black or brown.

In the forests of Guiana the Society for the Propagation
of the Gospel has long carried on a most interesting work
among the Caribs, Arawaks, Waraoons, and other Indian
tribes which still represent those island aborigines around
whom gathers so much of the adventure and tragedy of early
West Indian history. None of the Society's agents have been
more diligent or successful than the Rev. Mr. Brett, whose
Mission Work in Guiana is a standard book on the subject
of the Indian races of Venezuela and British Guiana. We
shall follow Mr. Brett as he tells of something of his canoe
voyages on the rivers and itabbos of the Essequibo district,
of his tramps through the tropical forests and swamps, of
dangers from pumas and jaguars by land and alligators and
camudis by water, of the ways and thoughts of the Indian
folk, and the power of Gospel truth to deliver them from the
tyranny of the immemorial superstitions and make them
Christians as well as law abiding British subjects.

Today, it is more than 170 years since Mr. Brett began
his labors among the Indians of Guiana, and his task was
beset in those early days by many serious difficulties. One
was the wild character of the people, and their hostility,
the hostility especially of their sorcerers, to the teachers
of a new religion. Mr. Youd, a predecessor of Mr. Brett's,
had received a gift of poisoned food from one of those
sorcerers, with the result that he and his whole family

were poisoned. His wife and children all died, and though he himself lingered on for a few years, it was in shattered health; while he too eventually succumbed to the fatal influences in his blood.

Another difficulty was caused by language, for in penetrating into the country the traveler, as he leaves the coast and plunges into the forest, passes rapidly from one tribe to another, all speaking different tongues. Nearest to the sea are the Waraoons and Arawaks, farther inland are the Caribs, beyond these are the migratory Acawoios, who do not live in villages, but wander through the woods with their deadly blow-pipes, by means of which they bring down from the highest trees the birds, monkeys, and other animals that they use for food. Mr. Brett found it necessary to learn four Indian languages, none of which had ever before been reduced to a written form. And not only did he master them for himself, but prepared grammars and vocabularies which made the task of his successors infinitely easier, and also translated into all of them large parts of the New Testament.

Not the least of the difficulties was that of traveling in such a country. It involved laborious and often dangerous canoe voyages, and weary tramps through dense forests which at certain seasons were converted into dismal swamps. But Mr. Brett had the true enthusiasm and pluck of the pioneer missionary, and seems to have considered the hardships that fell to his lot as all "in the day's work."

Guiana is a land of many rivers, and this makes canoeing the chief method of traveling, especially as the forests themselves become inundated after the rains, and it is then possible to cross from river to river by means of passages called itabbos. In this way, for example, an Indian crew can paddle across the country from the Essequibo to the mouth of the Orinoco, a distance of two or three hundred miles.

It is not all plain sailing, however, in a voyage of this kind. Every few minutes the Indians have to use their cutlasses to lop away the network of interlacing branches and creepers which the prodigal growth of the tropics weaves so quickly from side to side of the narrow waterway. Sometimes again a great fallen tree blocks the passage, and then the missionary must lie down in the bottom of the canoe while his boatmen try to thrust it underneath the barrier. This has to be done as quietly and swiftly as possible, for fear of disturbing any venomous snake that may have taken up its abode in a hollow of the decaying trunk.

But canoeing was not always feasible, and then would begin the tramp through the forest—those mysterious and awesome "high woods of the tropics" of which Kingsley writes with such enthusiasm. To the inexperienced traveler in the wilderness of rank vegetation there sometimes comes the fear of being lost, for he feels his own helplessness as to direction, and knows that but for the instinct of his Indian guides he would soon go utterly astray. He is bewildered, too, by the multiplicity of strange sounds. Parrots are screeching, monkeys are chattering, cigales are piping on a high note which suggests a shrill steam whistle, insects innumerable are chirping and whirring; while at times perhaps, there comes a noise like a muffled crash of thunder, which tells that some ancient giant of the woods has fallen at last.

The forest of Guiana are full of swamps, and when Mr.

Brett came to these there was nothing for it but to take off his shoes and socks, sling them round his neck, and wade on through mud and slime. Repeated soakings often made his feet swell so badly that it was hardly possible to pinch them into shoes again, and he found it easier simply to go barefooted like an Indian. But this also had its disadvantages, for alternate wading through marshes and walking with bare feet over the burning sandy soil brought on painful blains, which, unless great care was taken, would pass into ulcers. Sometimes the swamps were so deep that they could not be waded, and the only means of crossing was by trees cut down and thrown across. These primitive forest bridges, which are also used for crossing the smaller streams and ravines, are often of considerable length. Mr. Brett tells of one that he measured, the trunk of a mora tree, which was 108 feet long from the place where the trunk was cut to the point at which the lowest branches began to spring. The Indians are quite expert at walking on these slippery pathways, but to a European with his boots on they present a formidable task. Mr. Brett's Indian companions were sometimes quite anxious about him, and on one occasion exhorted him to "hold on with his feet," forgetting that toes encased, as his were, in a good thick sole are of no use for prehensile purposes.

Apart from the malarial fevers to which in those low-lying tropical regions a European is constantly liable, the chief dangers encountered by Mr. Brett in his journeys into the interior came from the wild animals which swarm in Guiana, both on land and water. There are alligators of various sorts which, as amphibious creatures, are dangerous on both elements. Mr. Brett tells of one which made its nest in his own churchyard, and rushed savagely one evening at an assembly of mourners gathered round a grave, just after he had finished reading the burial service, scattering them in all directions. But not less dreaded than the alligator is the great anaconda, or camudi, as the Indians call it, a species of water-boa which swims like an eel, and grows to the length of thirty feet. In the water the camudi is more than a match for the alligator itself, and has been known even to attack persons who were inside a canoe. One Sunday morning an exciting fight took place in mid-stream between an anaconda and an alligator, exactly in front of a chapel on the bank of the river Pomeroon in which Mr. Brett was conducting divine service. At the news of the fight his congregation deserted him to a man, and even he could not resist the temptation to follow them as speedily as possible to the scene of action. The battle went on desperately for a long time, but at last the anaconda succeeded in getting that deadly grip with its tail which gives it full purchase for its gigantic strength, and then it drew its coils tighter until the life of the alligator seemed to be completely squeezed out. At this point one of the onlookers, who had a gun and was a good marksman, fired and killed the anaconda, which sank to the bottom. The alligator drifted ashore by and by, with its ribs crushed in, and in a dying condition, where it too was dispatched.

Besides the labaria, a very deadly snake that lurks among bushes or in the holes of old trees, the traveler through the forest has always to be on his guard against the puma and jaguar. The puma is a formidable beast, but the great spotted jaguar is the tiger of South America, and is not much inferior in size or ferocity to the tiger of the Indian jungle. It is very destructive of goats, sheep, and cattle; and Mr. Brett tells us that he has often seen its footmarks in the morning on the moist ground all round a house—showing how it had been prowling about through the night in search of prey. The jaguar does not hesitate on occasions to attack men, and within Mr. Brett's own knowledge several persons lost their lives in this way, being killed and devoured. Its habit of concealing itself in a tree and making its deadly spring from that place of vantage upon any animal that passes underneath renders great caution necessary in going along the forest ways. It has a wholesome dread of the rifle, however, and the march of civilization is driving it farther and farther into the recesses of the woods.

But there are smaller creatures of the tropics for which civilization and the rifle have no terrors. There are myriads of butterflies, of course, which flutter past on wings of crimson and gold; darting hummingbirds, with ruby or emerald breast gleaming in the sunlight; fireflies which come out at dusk, and flit to and fro with their soft twinkling lights in the warm night air that is heavy with the breath of flowers. If the tiny creatures of the tropic woods were all like these, the traveler might fancy himself in a kind of Earthly Paradise. But what of the marabunas—which Trinidad boys used to call "marrowbones," from some idea that the stings of these fierce wasps, which are fond of building their clay nest in the corners of the white man's veranda, would penetrate to that region of the juvenile anatomy? What of scorpions, centipedes, tarantulas, blood-sucking bats, bêtes rouges, chigoes or "jiggers," and biting ants, whether black, white, or red? Worst of all, what of the ubiquitous irrepressible, unconquerable mosquito, which sometimes almost drives its victims mad, and whose victories over man, its mortal foe, deserve to be sung in the notes of its own musical humming and written with the blood of its helpless victims in some epic of the jungle? Mr. Brett does not exaggerate in the least when he records insect and other small annoyances among the most serious trials of missionary life in the inland districts of British Guiana. What sensitive white-skinned people have suffered from mosquitoes alone may be judged from this. At the season when the mosquitoes were at their worst, Mr. Brett's Indian crew, after a long and hard day's pull up the river, would sometimes paddle through the night for many a weary mile to the river's mouth and out to the open sea, in the hope of escaping for two or three hours from the stings of these excruciating pests.

Of the Indian tribes described by Mr. Brett, the Waraoons are in some respects the most interesting, precisely because they are the most primitive. When Sir Walter Raleigh was passing through the channels of the Orinoco delta in search of his imaginary El Dorado, he and his men were astonished to see fires burning high up in the air under the leafy crowns of palm trees. These were the hearth fires of the Orinoco Waraoons, who become tree dwellers for several months of the year when their country is turned into a vast sheet of muddy water. Building a platform far up the stem of a palm tree, under the shelter of its overarching fronds, they plaster a part of the platform

A TITANIC COMBAT

Hearing a noise outside during service, Mr. Brett's congregation without ceremony
went out to find a battle between an alligator and an enormous anaconda in progress.
They had a long and terrific struggle, but at last the anaconda got into a position which
enabled it to use its powers of compression to the utmost, and it literally crushed the
life out of its opponent, only to be shot itself by a native.

with clay to serve as a hearth, and sit smoking contentedly in their airy habitations, except at such times as they feel disposed to slip down into a canoe so as to visit a friend in a neighboring tree or go out fishing with a view to supper.

The Waraoons of Guiana are not tree-dwellers, for the floods on their rivers are not so severe as to make this necessary. But they are just as simple and unsophisticated and pagan as their brethren of the Orinoco. Except when Europeans come into their neighborhood and set up a standard and a rule of social decency, both men and women go absolutely naked. They are predominantly gentle and unwarlike, even as their forefathers were four or five centuries ago when the Caribs swept down upon them and drove them into the swamps. While skillful in their own arts of canoe-hollowing and hammock weaving, they are extremely easy going in their way of life, and combine a good-natured disposition with a vein of humor, which is somewhat rare among the Indian peoples. Like all other Indians, they have a genuine belief in the Great Spirit, and they have many legends of their own about him and his dealings with men. The account they give of their origin is striking—though with a touch of the grotesque humor which characterizes them. The Waraoons, they say, originally dwelt in a country above the sky. The arrow of a bold hunter, falling by chance through a hole, revealed to this hunter the existence of the lower world. Making a rope of cotton, he descended by it to the earth, and when he climbed up again brought such a glowing report of the game that swarmed in earthly forests that the whole race was tempted to come sliding down the cotton rope out of the Paradise above. The last to make the attempt was a woman, and she, being fat, stuck in the hole and could neither squeeze herself through nor yet struggle back again. There she remains to this day; and that is the reason why the human race cannot even peep through the hole in the sky into the world above. A curious version, we may think, of the story of Paradise Lost, and an equally curious version of woman's responsibility for the absolute closing of the gates of Eden.

Among all the Indian tribes of Guiana piai men, or sorcerers, are the priests of religion. The piai man corresponds to the "medicine man" of the North American Indians and the "obeah man" of Africa. No one dares to oppose him in anything, for he is an expert in poison, and his enemies have a way of dying suddenly. In sickness, the most implicit confidence is placed in his powers, which to some extent are medicinal no doubt, for he generally has a real acquaintance with the healing virtues of the plants of the forest, but to a much greater degree are supposed to be supernatural. His special function is to drive away the evil spirit that has taken possession of the sick man. This he does by rattling a hollow calabash containing some fragments of rock crystal—an instrument of magical efficacy and the peculiar symbol of the piai man's office, by chanting a round of monotonous incantations, and by fumigating the patient plentifully with tobacco smoke, the incense of this "Indian weed" being firmly believed to exert a potent if mysterious influence.

It was naturally from these piai men that the strongest resistance came to the introduction of Christianity among the Indians of Guiana. One of them, as has been mentioned

already, poisoned an English missionary and his family; and
Mr. Brett himself was frequently warned that the sorcerers
were going to piai him also. Instead of this, a strange thing
happened. Saccibarra ("Beautiful Hair"), the chief of the
Arawaks and their leading sorcerer, became disgusted
with the tricks and hypocrisies of his profession, broke
his marakka or magical calabash rattle, and came to Mr.
Brett's hut, asking to be taught about "the Great Our Father,
Who dwelleth in heaven." By and by he was baptized,
receiving, instead of his heathen name, the Christian name
of Cornelius. Cornelius the Arawak was a man of great
intelligence, and it was with the aid of this converted Indian
and his family that Mr. Brett was able to carry through his
first efforts at translation. Still better things ensued, for
five other sorcerers followed the example of Cornelius,
gave up their marakkas to Mr. Brett in token that they had
renounced the practice of magic, and became faithful and
useful members of the Christian Church. Evangelists arose
among the Indians themselves. Chapels sprang up here and
there in the depths of the forest—two of them, as it was
accidentally discovered at a later stage, having been built
on ancient cannibal mounds. Struck by the appearance
of these mounds, Mr. Brett was led to undertake a little
excavation; and his researches speedily proved that the
very spots where the House of God now stood and Christ's
Gospel was preached from Sunday to Sunday had once
been the kitchen middens of large cannibal villages.

We spoke of the adventure of missions; and even from
the most external point of view they are often full of the
excitement that belongs to all heroism and adventure.

But to those who look deeper the spiritual romance is the most wonderful—the transformation of character and life, the turning of a savage into a Christian. In the Pomeroon district of Guiana, the center of Mr. Brett's labors, more than five thousand persons had been brought into the Church through baptism. As for the moral and spiritual effect of his patient and heroic exertions, we may cite the testimony of the Pomeroon civil magistrate, who at first did not encourage Christian work among the Indians:

"A more disorderly people than the Arawaks," he wrote, "could not be found in any part of Guiana. Murders and violent cases of assault were of frequent occurrence. Now the case is reversed. No outrages of any description ever happen. They attend regularly divine service, their children are educated, they themselves dress neatly, are lawfully married, and as a body there are no people in point of general good conduct to surpass them. This change, which has caused peace and contentment to prevail, was brought about solely by missionary labor."

NOTES AND AUTHORITIES: The chief authority for this chapter is Mr. Brett's *Mission Work in Guiana* (London, S.P.C.K.). Reference has also been made, however, for some points to *Ten Years of Mission Life in British Guiana*, by the Rev. W.T. Veness (S.P.C.K.), and *Protestant Missions in South America*, by Canon F.P.L. Josa and others (New York, Student Volunteer Movement).

THE SAILOR MISSIONARY OF TIERRA DEL FUEGO: PART I

CHAPTER FIFTEEN

FROM THE EDITORS: "Hope deferred, not lost," the words of Captain Allen Gardiner and later the slogan of his mission society, is the most fitting phrase to describe this chapter, Part I in the history of Christian evangelization on Tierra del Fuego — the Land of Fire. From the time of its discovery by Magellan as he rounded the tip of South America, this group of islands came to be a terror to sailors. The Straits of Magellan were known for their fierce and sudden storms — the death knell for many a ship. For any sailors who happened to survive a storm and swim ashore, the cannibalistic natives ensured certain death. So fierce and seemingly debased were the inhabitants, that Charles Darwin at one point considered them as a clue to the "missing link" for his false evolutionary theories.

Such a dark, bleak land and ferocious people could only be changed by the power of the Gospel, and as such they would be, but only through a most remarkable story of martyrs for the cause of Christ. The change would begin through the heroic efforts of Captain Allen Gardiner. Born in Berkshire, England in 1794 he entered the naval academy in Portsmouth at thirteen years of age and went to sea two years later. He was not a believer, scoffing at the Christian principles with which he was raised. However, on his numerous voyages around the world, he studied various faiths and pondered the question of God. After many years, the prayers of his faithful mother (then deceased), were answered. God brought about a true spiritual conversion. After rising to the position of Commander through distinguished service in the British Royal Navy, he finally retired at age forty, so as to devote the rest of his life to worldwide evangelism. About the same time, his first wife Julia died. His first mission work to the South African Zulu tribesmen ended due to wars with the Dutch. He married again to Elizabeth, and moved his family to South America, where they served among the Araucanian tribes of the Pampas and Cordilleras. It was hard work, as his efforts were in a great part hampered by the Catholic priests who poisoned the natives' minds against his message of the Gospel.

It was at this point that Tierra del Fuego seemed to beckon him, a desolate series of islands absorbed in thick spiritual darkness. The intensity of this call, the sacrifices involved, and the perseverance demonstrated in this story make for one of the most outstanding stories of missionary work in all of Christian history. This is the story of Captain Allen Gardiner.

Captain Allen Gardiner (1794—1851)

If from the point of view of Christian evangelization South America has been called by some, "The Neglected Continent," there is no part of it to which until the twentieth century the description more fitly applied than that southern portion of the mainland called Patagonia, together with the large archipelago of closely huddled islands which projects still farther towards the Antarctic Ocean, and is known by the rather inappropriate name of Tierra del Fuego, or "Land of Fire." (The name was given to the group by Magellan, who discovered the islands in 1520. It is supposed to have been suggested to him either by volcanic flames which are now extinct, or by the numerous fires kindled by natives which he saw along the coasts).

The inaccessibility and desolation of the whole region, and the ferocious and almost inhuman character of the tribes encountered by vessels passing through the Straits of Magellan, which divide Fuegia from the mainland, for long made any thoughts of carrying the Christian Gospel to this part of the heathen world seem absolutely visionary. The Fuegians in particular were looked upon as degraded almost beyond the hope of recovery. Travelers dwelt on their stunted figures, their repulsive faces, their low grade of intelligence, their apparent lack of natural affection, as shown by the readiness of parents to throw their children overboard in a storm in order to lighten a canoe, or of children to eat their own parents when they had grown old and useless. Their speech was hardly articulate. Captain Cook has compared it to a man clearing his throat, but certainly no European ever cleared his throat with so many hoarse, guttural, and clicking sounds."

And yet, through the enterprise begun and inspired by that heroic man of whom we have now to tell, the almost unpronounceable sounds of the Fuegian speech have been reduced to writing and made to convey the story of the Gospels, while the Fuegians themselves have been changed from murderous cannibals and thieves into peaceful, honest, and industrious members of a Christian community. When Charles Darwin learned, on the unimpeachable authority of a British admiral, of the extraordinary difference which a few years had made in the habits of these people, whom he had once been inclined to regard as possibly furnishing a missing link between the monkey and the man, he confessed his astonishment. "I could not have believed," he wrote, "that all the missionaries in the world could ever have made the Fuegians honest," and he went on to speak of this transformation as one of the wonders of history. Of course, the praise alone must go to the power of Almighty God, the Creator of all men, including the Fuegians, for the transformation of lives through His saving Grace. Though not by any means a professing Christian, nor an advocate in general of Christian missions, Darwin became from that time a regular subscriber to the funds of the society with whose founder we are at present to study in this chapter — "about as emphatic an answer to the detractors of missions," *The Spectator* once remarked, "as can well be imagined."

Allen Gardiner was an ex-captain of the British Navy. As a midshipman he had distinguished himself during a fierce engagement in 1814 between his ship, the *Phoebe*, and an American man-of-war, in which the British vessel was victorious; and he had risen step by step to the position of commander. When about forty years of age, however, he determined to abandon his chosen profession and devote the rest of his life to work among the heathen, by whose wretched condition he had been deeply impressed in the course of his many voyages in all parts of the world.

He turned first of all to South Africa, and had some interesting experiences among the subjects of Dingaan, the redoubtable Zulu chief. But war broke out between the Zulus and the Boers, and he was forced to leave the country. Several years thereafter were spent in the search for a suitable field of operations among the most neglected peoples of the world. We find him for a time on the coast of New Guinea, where, if he had not been thwarted by the Dutch officials, who had not the slightest sympathy with his aims, and declared that "he might as well try to instruct monkeys as the natives of Papua," he might have largely anticipated the splendid work which was afterwards accomplished by the heroic "Tamate."

But it was in the Western, not in the Eastern, Hemisphere that the great work of his life was to lie, and it was towards South America in particular that his steps were now guided. He was not drawn, however, in the first instance towards the Straits of Magellan, but to the brave Araucanian tribes of the Pampas and the Cordilleras. Two or three years were spent in toilsome and dangerous journeys through bristling forests and swampy jungles, and over well-nigh impassable mountains, where precipices yawned on one hand, while on the other avalanches of snow or rock threatened to hurl the traveler to destruction. But though he met with many kindnesses from the natives, he found wherever he went that the Romish friars and priests poisoned the minds of the ignorant people against him and prevented him from being allowed to settle down among them. And so, he had to go forth again in search of his proper sphere.

It was at this stage that he began to think of that dreary and desolate region in the neighborhood of Cape Horn, that as a sailor he had more than once visited, and with which in the history of modern missions his name will forever be associated. How to get there was his first difficulty, and it was a one which only an experienced and skilful seaman could have overcome. He chartered a crazy old schooner, the owners of which regarded her as no longer fit to go to sea, and though still further hampered by a drunken and troublesome crew, succeeded in reaching the Straits of Magellan in March, 1842. He had provided himself with a few stores, and his plan was to settle on one or other of the islands and try to win the confidence of the inhabitants. How difficult this task would be he soon discovered. Wherever he landed, whether on the islands or on the Patagonian coast, the Indians showed themselves so unfriendly that he realized the impossibility of making any headway without some help and some more adequate equipment. He resolved accordingly to return to England without delay, and try to persuade one or other of the great missionary societies to take Patagonia and Tierra del Fuego under its care.

Unfortunately, not one of the existing societies was in a position at that time to undertake any fresh responsibilities. But Gardiner, nothing daunted, next made his appeal to the Christian public, and succeeded at last in originating on a very humble scale what is now known as the South American Missionary Society. He undertook to labor, as he had always done before, at his own expense, but the Society furnished him with an assistant in the shape of a catechist named Mr. Hunt.

Embarking in a brig called the *Rosalie*, which was to pass through the Magellan Straits, these two devoted men were landed with their stores about three months after on the south coast of Patagonia, and there left to their own devices. For a time they could see nothing of any natives, though they lighted fires in the hope of attracting notice. Meanwhile they set to work to build huts in which to shelter themselves; and shortly after they had completed this task received some troublesome visitors in the person of a chief whose name was Wissale, his wives and children, and a party of followers. Wissale, who had picked up a few words of English from passing ships, combined unbounded greed with a good deal of slyness. He soon began to make matters exceedingly uncomfortable for the two Englishmen. His intentions apparently were to force his company upon them, especially at meal times, and compel them to put their scanty stores at his disposal. He came into the hut attended by his patriarchal family, and placing one child in Captain Gardiner's arms said, "This your son Hontechi;" while he handed another to Mr. Hunt with the remark, "Mitter Hunt, this your son Lux." From

greed and impudence he gradually passed to threats of
violence, and it was speedily evident to the two unfortunate
philanthropists, not only that their provisions would soon
be eaten up, but that in the mood of Wissale and his men
their lives were hanging by a very slender thread. In this
state of matters a passing ship bound for Valparaiso seemed
to be providentially sent. Captain Gardiner felt that he had
no alternative but to confess himself defeated, and once
more to return to England.

The members of the Patagonian Society, as the South
American Society was originally called, were much
discouraged. The leader of their forlorn hope, however,
never for a moment lost heart. "Hope deferred, not lost,"
is now the Society's motto: and the faith embodied in
these words was the faith by which Gardiner lived. In the
meantime he volunteered to see whether anything could be
done among the Indians of Bolivia, and flung himself into
this new departure with characteristic energy, until one
of those domestic revolutions, which are so common in
the history of South American republics, drove him out of
the country, and made him feel once again that Tierra del
Fuego was his Macedonia which was calling to him for help.

On this occasion, having raised the necessary funds by
his own exertions, he persuaded the Society to allow him
to take out a party of four sailors and a ship's carpenter.
He intended the expedition to be in a measure one of
exploration, the special purpose being to see whether a
suitable base of operations could not be secured, and what
would be the best method of reaching the scattered tribes
of the archipelago. Owing to his former connection with

the Navy he had some influence at headquarters, and by this means one of Her Majesty's ships, the *Clymene*, which was about to sail for Peru, was placed at his disposal.

The *Clymene* reached Magellan Straits at a time when a hurricane of wind was blowing, accompanied by violent storms of sleet and hail; but after suffering severely from exposure to the inclement weather, Captain Gardiner was able to select a spot for his proposed station in a cove to which he gave the name of "Banner Cove" (with reference to Psalm 60:4). The friendly warship, however, had not yet proceeded to her voyage when a band of natives came down on the little party encamped on the shore in so hostile and threatening an attitude that Gardiner felt that he must decide immediately whether it would be right to remain in this situation without any possible means of escape in the event of an attack. He had only a few hours in which to make up his mind, and the conclusion he came to was that he had no right to run the risk of sacrificing the lives of his five companions. He now began to realize that the only way in which he could hope to evangelize Fuegia was by having a vessel of his own, on board of which he might live when necessary, and be free at the same time to move about among the islands. Accordingly, he re-embarked with his party on the *Clymene*, and continued his voyage to Peru, from which he made his way homeward via Panama and the West Indies.

Though his new idea filled him with fresh enthusiasm, his enthusiasm was not widely shared. At this we can hardly wonder. There are not many persons who possess a hero's indomitable courage together with the perseverance of

Bruce's spider. Some of the Captain's best friends advised him to give the whole thing up. "Only with my life," was his reply. Finding so little prospect of help in England, he went over to Germany and tried to enlist the sympathies of the Moravian Brethren; but though deeply impressed by the man and his story, and very anxious to do what they could, they were obliged to abandon the thought of giving him any practical aid. He next visited Scotland, and laid his plans before the mission boards of the three great Presbyterian Churches, but none of them felt free to plunge into a new and difficult undertaking. At this juncture, just when the prospects were most unpromising, a lady in Cheltenham came forward with a munificent donation, while at the same time several exceedingly suitable offers of personal service were received by the Society. The result was that a party of seven was made up which included, besides Captain Gardiner himself, Mr. Williams, a surgeon; Mr. Maidment, a Sunday-school teacher; three Cornish fishermen, and the ship's carpenter who had taken part in the previous expedition. Further, in accordance with the leader's plans, two strong double-decked launches were provided, either of which could furnish sleeping accommodation for the whole party.

Having taken passage from Liverpool in the *Ocean Queen*, Captain Gardiner and his companions with their stores and boats were landed in Banner Cove on December 17th, 1850. Writing by the *Ocean Queen*, which left next day for California, Gardiner says, in the last letter which his friends in England were ever to receive: "Nothing can exceed the cheerful endurance and unanimity of the whole party. I

TYPES OF PATAGONIAN WOMEN

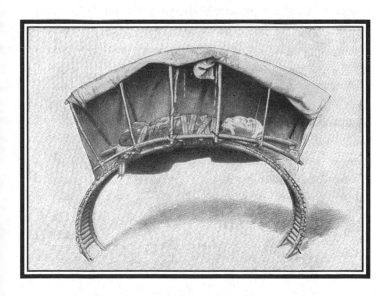

A NATIVE CRADLE IN PATAGONIA

feel that the Lord is with us, and cannot doubt that He will own and bless the work which He has permitted us to begin."

From that point all communication with the outer world absolutely ceased. From the hour when they stood in their two launches, the *Pioneer* and *Speedwell*, waving their last farewells to the departing ship, those seven brave men were never seen by friendly eyes in life again. It was in the awful loneliness and desolation of those barren islands and bleak southern seas that the tragedy was enacted of which we now have to tell.

When the party landed they were provided with necessaries for only half a year, the arrangement being that early in 1851 supplies for the other six months should be dispatched from England. Early in January, the Society began to make inquiries about a vessel, but to their dismay not one could be got to undertake the commission. From every quarter to which they applied the answer came, "No vessel would risk her insurance by attempting to land so small a freight as your stores in such a place as Tierra del Fuego." Matters were growing very serious, for ocean telegraphs were still things of the future, and those were the slow days of sailing ships. Application was made to the Admiralty in the hope of getting the goods conveyed by one of their vessels. At the time, however, no Government ship was commissioned to that quarter of the world, and it was not till the last day of October 1851, more than a year after the departure of the *Ocean Queen* from Liverpool, that *H.M.S. Dido* left Devonport with the belated stores on board. By that time Captain Gardiner and every member of his party had already been starved to death, and their unburied corpses were lying here and there along a wild and rocky shore.

But we must now return to Banner Cove and follow the story, as it lies revealed in Gardiner's own diary. Having landed with some difficulty owing to a sudden gale that sprang up before the *Ocean Queen* was out of sight, the seven pioneers succeeded in making a cache among the rocks without being observed by the natives. Here they deposited a reserve stock of provisions, thinking it safer to do this than to keep everything stored in the launches. Not long after the Fuegians made their appearance. Several war-canoes gathered in the bay, the men on board being all armed with spears, and it was clear from their demeanor that nothing but their dread of guns kept them from attacking instantly, and that they were only waiting for a suitable opportunity to make a sudden and overwhelming rush. The Captain accordingly resolved, though with great reluctance, to leave Banner Cove, and sailed to another inlet known as Spaniard Harbor. A few days after their arrival in that place, one of those violent hurricanes sprang up for which the region all around Cape Horn is so notorious. The boats were torn from their anchorage and dashed ashore. The stores and bedding were much damaged, but were secured and transferred to a damp cave. Here the whole party slept for two nights, with the result that every one of them was attacked by severe rheumatism. Meanwhile, the *Pioneer* had been driven high up on the beach in so disabled a condition as to be past repairing, and it was decided to let her lie where she was and use her cabin as a sleeping place.

Troubles now began to thicken. Scurvy broke out—a

deadly disease for men in such a situation, and not long after provisions began to run short. Now and then a few fish were caught, or an occasional wild fowl was knocked over on the beach, but no reliance could be put upon these sources of support. An expedition was accordingly made in the *Speedwell* to Banner Cove, in the hope of securing the provisions left in the cache, but two casks of biscuits were all that could now be found, and these were hardly got when the natives again gathered in force and compelled a hasty retreat.

The remaining months were months of dreadful suffering. It had now become evident that food might utterly fail before any relief came. The outlook was dark indeed. Not only was starvation staring them in the face, but disease had laid its innervating hand upon every one of them. We can picture those weary men with each returning morning standing on the shore and scanning the horizon with anxious eyes, "waiting for the ship that never came, while the waves beat monotonously on the beach and the sea-birds screamed ominously overhead." And yet they seem never to have lost their courage or their faith. When the hope of life was gone they waited patiently for death, and when it came at last met it with cheerful resignation.

And now something must be said of the search for Gardiner and its results. *H.M.S. Dido* was not the first vessel to reach Banner Cove. The schooner *John Davidson*, under Captain W.H. Smyley, which had been hastily commissioned for the purpose in a South American port, arrived there on October 21, 1851. No one was to be seen, but on the rocks at the entrance to the cove the words were painted:

CAPTAIN GARDINER IN PERIL

Several war canoes full of armed Fuegians approached, and it was evident that nothing but dread of guns kept them from attacking instantly.

"DIG BELOW—GO TO SPANIARD HARBOUR—
MARCH 1851"

Digging they found a note written by Captain Gardiner
in which he said, "The Indians being so hostile, we have
gone to Spaniard Harbour." Following these directions,
Captain Smyley sailed to the place indicated, where, in his
own words, he saw a sight that was "awful in the extreme."
In a stranded boat on the beach a dead body was lying; not
far off was another washed to pieces by the waves; while
yet a third lay half-buried in a shallow grave. One of the
three was the surgeon, Mr. Williams; the other two were
fishermen. No traces of Captain Gardiner and the rest were
to be seen, and a heavy gale which sprang up all at once
made it impossible to linger. Captain Smyley and his men
had barely time to bury the dead on the beach in the teeth
of a blinding snowstorm, and, as it was, experienced great
difficulty in getting back to the schooner. They sailed at
once for Monte Video with their dreadful news.

Next came the *Dido* from England. She too was guided
from Banner Cove to Spaniard Harbour by the notice on
the rocks, and her commander, setting to work with the
energy and thoroughness characteristic of a British naval
officer, succeeded in clearing up all that remained of the
painful mystery. The body of Mr. Maidment was found
in a cave to which direction was given by a hand painted
on the rocks, with Psalm 62:5-8 painted underneath. The
remains of Captain Gardiner himself were discovered by
the side of a boat from which he seemed to have climbed
out and been unable to get in again. For protection against

the cold he had put on three suits of clothes and drawn woolen stockings over his arms above the outer clothing. Below the waistcoat the seagulls had been at work, and had lessened the effects of corruption. His Bible was at hand, containing numberless underlined passages, many of which seemed to have been marked during the time of his suffering as peculiarly suited to his circumstances. Gardiner's journal was also found, carefully written up to the last, and giving many touching details of those dreadful months of starvation, disease, and slowly approaching death. Throughout all that period of anxiety and pain the strong faith of this heroic man appears to have burned like a lamp, while a spirit of affectionate brotherhood and quiet acceptance of the Divine will was displayed by every member of the doomed band. The Captain's last words seem to have been written when death was very near, and when his mind had begun to wander a little. He addresses himself to Mr. Williams—apparently forgetful of the fact (which is proved by his own journal) that the surgeon was already gone. The note is in pencil, written very indistinctly, and obliterated here and there.

"MY DEAR MR. WILLIAMS, - The Lord has seen fit to call home another of our little company. Our dear departed brother left the boat on Tuesday afternoon, and has not since returned. Doubtless he is in the presence of the Redeemer, Whom he served faithfully. Yet a little while, and though ...the Almighty to sing the praises...throne. I neither hunger nor thirst, though five days without food... Maidment's kindness to me...heaven.

"Your affectionate brother in...

"Allen F. Gardiner. . .September 6th, 1851."

Captain Morshead, of the *Dido*, gathered the remains together and buried them close to the cave in which the body of Mr. Maidment was found. The ship's flags hung at half-mast, one of the officers read the service for the dead, and three volleys of musketry were fired over the solitary grave.

Allen Gardiner's life is apt to strike us at first as one that was no less tragic in the fruitlessness of its great purpose than in the misery of its end. But it was not in vain that he strove, and, above all, it was not in vain that he and his brave comrades laid down their lives for Tierra del Fuego. The story of Captain Gardiner's death stirred England as he had never been able to stir her during his strenuous life. It gave a new impulse to the ideals which had led to the formation of the South American Missionary Society. It helped to bring about in due course, through the heroic labors of other noble men who took up the unfinished task, that complete transformation of the Fuegians to which reference was made in the beginning of this chapter. The people of Tierra del Fuego are no longer a degraded and cruel race, the terror of the sailor wrecked up on their dreary coasts. In every part of the archipelago to which the message of the Gospel has penetrated they are humane and civilized folks, ready to give a kindly Christian welcome to any poor shipless mariner who has struggled to their shores out of the devouring waves. The story of this transformation is detailed in the next chapter.

NOTES AND AUTHORITIES: *Hope Deferred, Not Lost*, by the Rev. G.P. Despard, B.A. (South American Missionary Society); *From Cape Horn to Panama*, by Robert Young, F.R.S.G.S. (Simpkin,

Marshall, Hamilton, Kent, and Co.); *Captain Allan Gardiner: Sailor and Saint*, by Jesse Page (S. W. Partridge and Co.); *Journal of Researches during the Voyage of H.M.S Beagle*, by Charles Darwin (John Murray).

THE SCHOONER OF KEPPEL ISLAND: PART II

CHAPTER SIXTEEN

Not long before the death of the heroic sailor who forms the subject of the preceding chapter, he drew up a plan for the future prosecution of the work to which he had devoted his life. He had learned by painful familiarity the difficulties and dangers which beset any attempt to settle at that time among a savage and unfriendly people in a barren and inhospitable land. Experience had shown him that there was a better way of attacking the problem of how to reach the inhabitants of Tierra del Fuego. And though he was not spared to make trial of that way himself, those who took up the task which death compelled him to lay down reaped the benefit of his hard-earned wisdom.

His plan in brief was this. The headquarters of the Mission should be transferred to one of the Falkland Islands, a lonely British group lying in the South Atlantic, some four or five hundred miles to the northeast of Cape Horn. To this station a few of the Fuegian natives should be taken in successive parties, so that the missionaries might have the double opportunity of acquiring their language and instructing them in Christian truth and elements of a Christian civilization. As soon as sufficient progress had been made in both directions, a little vessel of about one hundred tons was to be built for the purpose of cruising about in the Straits of Magellan. It must be perfectly seaworthy, so as to face the fierce storms that rage around Cape Horn from the icy waters of the Antarctic Ocean. But it must also be fitted up internally in keeping with its character as a floating mission-house. In this way Captain Gardiner hoped that the problem that had baffled him so long would at last be resolved.

When the news reached England of the dreadful calamity which had overtaken the founder of the South American Missionary Society and his whole party, the general feeling was that the brave seaman's hopes and plans were now buried with him forever in his lonely grave. But it was not so. At a time when most of the supporters of the Society were crushed and dispirited, the honorary secretary, the Rev. G. P. Despard, uttered the noble words, "With God's help, the Mission shall be maintained." He aroused in many others a spirit of prayerful determination like his own, and before long Captain Gardiner's schemes began to be literally fulfilled. A stout little schooner, fitly called the *Allen Gardiner*, was launched at Dartmouth, and sailed from Bristol in 1855 with a fresh staff of missionaries. Keppel Island, one of the West Falklands, was secured from the British Government as a mission station. To crown the brightening prospects, Mr. Despard himself offered his services as superintendent of the Mission, and sailed for the Falklands with his own family and several additional helpers. Among these, it is interesting to note, was Mr. Allen W. Gardiner, demy of Magdalen College, Oxford, the only son of the departed hero.

The first work that faced the missionaries, on reaching the dreary uninhabited island which was to be their home, was the building of houses, the digging of peat for winter fuel, and the endeavor to contribute to their own maintenance by catching fish and birds for food and spearing seal for oil. It was a toilsome life they had to live, but not without variety. Every morning the men turned out at 6:30 to dig in the peat moss till breakfast time. Each following hour of the day brought its appointed tasks. But when evening fell they gathered round their seal-oil lamps to study those languages which seemed most likely to fit them for the greater work to which they eagerly looked forward.

The first voyage which Mr. Despard made to Tierra del Fuego in the *Allen Gardiner* was chiefly important because it enabled the members of the new staff to see among the wild rocks of Spaniard Harbor the last resting place of their seven predecessors. An interesting feature of the cruise was the fact that Mr. Allen W. Gardiner was one of those on board. He kept a careful diary; some of the entries in which are particularly touching. Thus we find him, when the schooner is about to leave Spaniard Harbor, asking the captain for the gig and rowing himself ashore alone to take a last look, with what feelings we can imagine, at Pioneer Cavern and his father's grave.

There was comparatively little intercourse with the natives on this first expedition to the islands, but better success attended a voyage in the following year. There was a well-known native at that period who had once been take to England by a ship captain, and had picked up a little English which he was always pleased to air before the sailors of any passing vessel. He had also acquired an English name, for he called himself Jemmy Button; while the little island on which he lived, and which lay off Woollya in the large island of Navarin, was known as Button Island.

In the hope of coming across Jemmy Button, the *Allen Gardiner* bore up for Woollya. It was a regular winter morning when they arrived, "snow lying on the deck and drifting into the sails and rigging, the wind fitful, howling, and gusty." Running for a cove abreast of Button Island, they found two canoes lying in shelter. One of the natives shouted out as the schooner approached, "Hillo, hoy, hoy!" which suggested that he might be the celebrated Button in person. But when the name "Jemmy Button" was shouted back, he only pointed to the island.

It was two days after, a lovely winter morning, with the sun shining brightly on the frosty ground and the high peaks of the mountains all dazzling white with snow, when four canoes were seen rounding the point of Button Island and coming across the sound. As soon as they were within hailing distance Mr. Gardiner sang out, "Jemmy Button," whereupon a man stood up in the foremost canoe and answered, "Yes, sir." In a few minutes Jemmy came up the ladder and shook hands, and was soon down in the cabin enjoying a breakfast of bread and butter with coffee. He seemed very frank, and gave his own people a good character, but mentioned that an English ship had fallen shortly before into the hands of an adjoining tribe, by whom every one of the crew was killed.

As Jemmy's command of a little English promised to be useful he was asked if he would like to come with his wife and children to Keppel Island for several months. He was perfectly willing to do so, perhaps thinking that a course of English breakfasts would be a pleasant change from an unvarying diet of fish and seaweed. His family and he were accordingly given a passage to Keppel, the history of which as a mission station may now be said properly to begin.

The Buttons made themselves both agreeable and useful during their stay. Mrs. Despard speaks of Jemmy's great politeness, and tells how for any little trifle she might give him he would go and pick her a beautiful bouquet of wild flowers, or spear her a basket of fish. His eldest child also, to whom he had given the curious and inexplicable name of Threeboys, became a general favorite. But the family were of less service as instructors in the Fuegian language than had been expected. They did not like to speak their own tongue before the white strangers, and when they conversed with one another always did so in a whisper.

On his next voyage to Tierra del Fuego Mr. Despard took Jemmy Button, according to promise, back to the familiar life of the wigwam and the canoe. He had no difficulty, however, in persuading three other natives with their wives and children to return with them to the Falklands. These families stayed, as the Buttons had done, through the winter and spring, and delighted everyone by their progress. Two lads named Okokko and Lucca seemed to be especially promising. They not only learned with ease to do a little carpentry, but appeared to understand all that was told them about God and Christ, and even began to give thanks at their meals and to pray at their bedtimes.

Forming his judgment of the Fuegian character from what he had seen of the native at Keppel during months of close observation, Mr. Despard believed that the ferocity of the people must have been overstated, and that they could not be so bloodthirsty as they were commonly represented. He thought therefore that the first steps should now be taken towards establishing a missionary station in Tierra del Fuego itself, and he resolved to make a start at Woollya, the neighborhood from which all his visitors had come. The enterprise was put into the hands of Mr. Phillips, one of the most trusted of the staff, and the *Allen Gardiner* sailed from Keppel Island for Woollya in the month of October, 1859.

Week after week passed away, and there was no sign of the returning vessel. At length Mr. Despard grew so anxious that he made his way to Stanley, the chief port of the Falklands, and engaged Captain Smyley, of the schooner *Nancy*, to sail at once on a voyage of inquiry.

It was not long before Captain Smyley returned with news not less terrible than that which he had been the first to bring eight years before regarding the fate of Captain Gardiner and his party. The natives at Woollya had massacred Mr. Phillips, Captain Fell of the *Allen Gardiner*, and six others. Of the whole company on board the schooner only one had escaped. From this man, who had been the ship's cook, the following narrative was obtained.

When the *Allen Gardiner* had reached Woollya, the people appeared perfectly friendly, and for several days a good deal of intercourse went freely on between the vessel and the shore. Sunday coming round, a landing was made on the island with the view of conducting Christian worship in the presence of the natives, only the cook being left on board in charge.

For a time everything seemed to go well. But suddenly a concerted rush was made up on the white men and all were barbarously murdered. Not a hand or a voice was raised in their defense, though the cook saw the lad Okokko running up and down the beach in evident distress. We can imagine the feelings of that solitary watcher on the schooner's deck as he gazed with horror-stricken eyes on the dreadful scene which was enacted on the shore a few hundred yards from where he stood. With a sense of absolute helplessness to assist them, he saw all his companions brutally put to death, and he knew that his own turn would come unless he could make his escape before the savages, now drunk with blood, attacked the vessel.

Realizing that now or never was his chance, he slid down into a boat, and rowing with all his haste to the shore, disappeared in the depths of the dense forest before his red-handed pursuers could overtake him. In these forest depths he lay hid for several days, till at length hunger and cold drove him out among the natives. By this time their passion for blood seemed to have been sated, and though he got rough treatment from some of them, others supplied him with food and showed him a little kindness until the arrival of the *Nancy* placed him once more in the midst of friends.

Meanwhile the *Allen Gardiner* had been completely ransacked and plundered, but not burnt or otherwise destroyed, and Captain Smyley was able to convey her back to the Falkland Islands in safety. He brought along with him the lad Okokko and his wife Camilenna, who were very earnest in their entreaties to be removed from their barbarous surroundings and be taken back once more to their Christian friends at Keppel Island.

Thus, what may be called the first chapter in the strange adventures of a missionary schooner closed in a scene of tragedy and blood. It was more than three years before the *Allen Gardiner* sailed to Tierra del Fuego again.

The next voyage of the schooner was to England, to which Mr. Despard now returned, leaving two missionaries to hold the fort in Keppel Island until better days should come. One of these was William Bartlett, who had care of the Mission farm. The other was Mr. Bridges, Mr. Despard's adopted son, a young man of very fine spirit and possessed of a rare faculty for language. To him more than to any other the missionaries owed their eventual mastery of the difficult Fuegian tongue—an acquirement which smoothed away many obstacles and misunderstandings. In the care of the Mission property, in the further instruction of Okokko and Camilenna, and in the task of learning not only to speak Fuegian, but how to reduce it to a grammar, these two brave men whiled away the lonely months and years of waiting.

After two such crushing blows as had now fallen upon the South American Mission Society within the space of eight years, it might almost be supposed that any idea of converting the Fuegians would be finally abandoned. But the patient heroism of the founder had become part of the Society's inheritance, and there was no slackening in the determination to go on. The story of some Missions is inspiring because of the vast and striking results that are achieved. There was no possibility of vast results among the scanty and dwindling tribes of a desolate archipelago. But this only makes us admire the more the undaunted courage and unfaltering perseverance of those who, in the face of one terrible disaster after another, still took for their motto, "With God's help, the Mission shall be maintained."

With a view to increasing both her seaworthiness and her accommodation, the *Allen Gardiner* was now lengthened, and thereafter this historic schooner sailed from Bristol once again, with a fresh missionary party, to resume her work in the icy Southern seas. The leader of the enterprise on this occasion was the well-known Mr. Stirling, who seven years afterwards was consecrated as the first Bishop of the Falkland Islands.

The plans of the Society as well as its schooner had now been enlarged. Its operations were about to be extended northwards along the South American coast until they should reach from Cape Horn to Panama. Tierra del Fuego, however, still remained the special objective of the *Allen Gardiner*, and one of Mr. Stirling's earliest duties was to reopen that communication with the natives which had ceased after the massacre of 1859. He was greatly assisted in this task by both Mr. Bridges and Okokko, for the former had now become quite an expert in Fuegian, while the latter could speak English very well. As the schooner sailed about among the island, the missionaries by means of these two highly competent interpreters made their friendly intentions everywhere known. At Woollya they were received with some suspicion, for the people there, recognizing the vessel, thought not unnaturally that it had come back now on a mission of vengeance. But when persuaded that their crime had been forgiven, and that Mr. Stirling and his companions had no thoughts towards them but thoughts of peace, they became quite enthusiastic, and far more of them volunteered to come to Keppel Island than could possibly be accommodated there. The chief difficulty now was to select from among the applicants those who were most likely to be of use in furthering the aims of the Mission.

The change for the natives from Tierra del Fuego to the Falklands was, no doubt, great. At home their time was largely spent in paddling about in their frail canoes. They lived mainly on fish, which they speared with great dexterity, their only vegetable diet being seaweed from the rocks, or fungi, which grew plentifully on the rugged hills. One of the occasional excitements of existence came from the arrival of a shoal of whales. They did not venture to attack those monsters of the deep in the open sounds, but they were frequently indebted to the fierce swordfish, which would so harass the clumsy creatures that they floundered into the shallows and got stranded; and then the hungry and watchful Indians had their chance.

At Keppel Island the Fuegians had to live a life that was much more civilized. They were expected to attend at Christian worship every day, and the younger members of the community were taught the elements of an ordinary education; but they were not asked to live after a fashion which would have been quite unnatural for them, as it was recognized that allowance and provision must be made for their hereditary instincts. And so, while they were trained to habits of industry in the Mission gardens and the peat valley, they still enjoyed the pleasures of spearing fish, as well as the novel and to them most exhilarating excitement of chasing the cattle, which were bred on the Mission farm, but allowed to run in a wild state over the island. It shows the deep-seated impulses of the natural man that even those who had stayed for a period at the station, and had learned to appreciate the comforts of a settled life and the blessings of Christianity, were generally quite glad by and by to go back to their own people. Their minds were now uplifted and enlarged, but they still loved the old, familiar, adventurous canoe life among the creeks and sounds of the Magellan Straits.

Sometime after the arrival of Mr. Stirling, the growing confidence inspired by the missionaries received a striking illustration. On one of the cruises of the *Allen Gardiner* the natives of Woollya of their own accord pointed out the spot where they had laid the bodies of the eight men whom they had murdered in November, 1859. They had carefully carried them to a quiet place among the rocks and covered them with large stones to keep them from being eaten by the foxes: and here ever since in their rocky sepulchers they had been lying undisturbed. Two of the bodies—those of Mr. Phillips and Captain Fell— could still be identified quite unmistakably. All were reverently lifted and buried in a Christian grave, the collect for St. Stephen's Day was most appropriately read, with its reference to the first Christian martyr and his prayer for those who murdered him. The schooner's flag meanwhile hung half-mast high, and at the close of the service two signal guns, booming across the water and echoing from rock to rock, announced to the company of Christian mourners and awestruck natives that all was over.

Year after year the *Allen Gardiner* continued to go forth on her blessed work, bringing successive batches of natives to Keppel, and taking them back again after a while to their wild homes to act the part of the leaven in the midst of the meal. And at last in 1869 a mission station was opened by Mr. Stirling in person at Ushuaia, some distance to the west of Spaniard Harbor, sacred to the memory of Captain Gardiner, and on the south coast of the main island of Tierra del Fuego. Here for seven months Mr. Stirling lived in a little hut, before which he often paced up and down as the shadows of evening were falling upon the sea and mountain, feeling, he tells us, as if he were "a sentinel stationed at the southern most outpost of God's great army."

From this remotest outpost of the Body of Christ he was summoned suddenly to England to become consecrated Bishop of the Falkland Islands, with a diocese which included practically the whole of the South American continent. The work he had begun in Ushuaia was taken up by Mr. Bridges and others, and when Bishop Sterling next saw the place in 1872, it was a little Christian settlement that lay before him. Stirling House, the iron house of the Mission, occupied a conspicuous position, while around it were the wigwams and cultivated gardens of a native colony. A little chapel showed the consecration of the whole to God, and in that chapel on the Lord's Day the Bishop joined with Mr. Bridges—now an ordained clergyman—in administering the sacrament of Baptism to thirty-six Fuegians and in joining seven couples in Christian marriage.

A genuine reformation in the Fuegian character had now begun. That for which, first, Captain Gardiner and his whole party, and at a later date Mr. Phillips and Captain Fell, with six other gallant men, had laid down their lives was already in process of accomplishment. The brutal natives of the Archipelago were being transformed into the likeness of peaceable Christian men and women. The best proof of this, because the most disinterested, is found in a British Admiralty chart of 1871. In this chart the attention of mariners passing through the Straits of Magellan is directed to the existence of the mission station of Ushuaia; and they are assured that within a radius of thirty miles no shipwrecked crew need expect other than kindly treatment from any native into whose hands they may fall.

NOTES AND AUTHORITIES: For the foregoing narrative the author is indebted to *The Story of Commander Allen Gardiner*, R.N., by the Rev. John W. Marsh, M.A., and the Rev. W. H. Stirling, D.D., Bishop of the Falkland Islands (James Nisbit and Co.), and also to Mr. Marsh's *First Fruits of the South American Mission*, which was kindly lent him by the Secretaries of the Society.

PART IV

SOUTH
PACIFIC

THE MARTYR OF MELANESIA

CHAPTER   SEVENTEEN

FROM THE EDITORS: Fiji, Hawaii, Guadalcanal, New Zealand, Tahiti, the New Hebrides, Samoa, the Solomon Islands — all are names of South Pacific island groups that bring to mind stirring stories of adventure, shipwrecks, tropical beaches, and savage natives. While many adventure stories and sailor tales exist about trips to these exotic locations, the following narratives of mission work in the South Pacific contain every aspect of heroism and bravery imaginable for the sake of the Gospel of Jesus Christ.

Born to a well-to-do noble family in England, the son of Sir John Patteson and Lady Frances Coleridge Patteson, young John Coleridge Patteson was given every advantage in early life. Trained at the finest schools and college institutions, "Coley" as his friends called him, was destined for the Church. After three years at Oxford, he toured in Europe for a time before returning home to take a local parish position in Ottery St. Mary, England. However, in 1854 he received the call to leave England and travel as a missionary to assist his friend and mentor, Bishop Selwyn of the Church of England, who had labored for years in the Melanesian Islands. Patteson was to spend the rest of his life ministering to the natives of the South Pacific, furthering the work started by Selwyn, and ultimately laying down his life for this calling.

In May of 1856, Patteson began his first of many journeys on the missionary schooner, the *Southern Cross*, cruising throughout the islands preaching the Gospel and recruiting young native boys for a missionary training school. The Melanesian Island chain is located off the northwest coast of Australia and is comprised today of New Guinea, Fiji, the Solomon Islands, the Maluku Islands, and New Caledonia. From island to island he went, facing sometimes hostile reception, at times barely escaping with his life. Over time he visited Aneityum, Erromanga, Mota, Guadalcanal, the Solomon Islands, and the New Hebrides.

Throughout his travels he faced the anger and fear of the natives stirred up by Roman Catholic priests, not to mention the bane of slave traders, shipwrecks, sicknesses, and violent attacks from the islanders.

Today, the work begun by Selwyn, Patteson, and others has taken root and the Gospel has flourished in many island regions, and Christianity remains the predominant religion in most of Melanesia. Numerous missionary opportunities still remain, and some people groups still have not read the Bible in their own language nor heard the Gospel.

John Coleridge Patteson (1827—1871)

The Duke of Wellington used to be credited with the striking remark, "The battle of Waterloo was won in the playing fields of Eton." Like many other memorable sayings which have been attributed to great men, this one is now generally believed to be apocryphal. Nevertheless, in its own paradoxical and exaggerated way, it embodies the truth, being that the boy is "the father of the man," and that the victories of after years find their explanation in the qualities of strength and courage and manly endurance which have been worked into the character when life was young. The hero of the following story happens to have been an Eton schoolboy, and one who greatly distinguished himself among his companions in the Eton playing fields. And no one who reads the story of his life can fail to see that the schoolboy was the father of the missionary, that it was the same qualities of athletic vigor, of enthusiasm, of moral strength by which Coley Patteson was marked out at Eton College that gained him his place of renown in the history of missions as the apostle and martyr of Melanesia.

John Coleridge Patteson, Coley Patteson, as he was familiarly called, was the son of Mr. Justice Patteson, a distinguished lawyer in his time, and the grandnephew of the poet Coleridge. As a boy he was especially distinguished for his physical prowess, which raised him ultimately to the coveted position of captain of the Eton Eleven cricket team. Once, in the annual match with Harrow at Lord's, it was Patteson who won the game for his school by putting on fifty runs and completely breaking the neck of the Harrow bowling. On another occasion, in a game at Eton, he so persistently defied the bowling of Lillywhite, the famous professional, that the latter became quite irritated and said, "Mr. Patteson, I should like to bowl to you on Lord's ground, and it would be different." It was characteristic of young Patteson's modesty to reply at once, "Oh, of course; I know you would have me out directly there."

But this brilliant Eton cricketer had other qualities that do not always accompany athletic distinction. He was a quick and diligent scholar, especially strong in languages, a fact which stood him in good stead when he came to move about in a scattered archipelago, almost every island of which had its own separate dialect. Better still, he was a lad of fearless moral courage. While up to any amount of fun, ready to sing his song at a cricket or football supper as mirthfully as the most lighthearted of the party, he could not tolerate any kind of coarseness or indecency. At the annual dinner of the Eton Eleven the custom had grown up of allowing rather objectionable songs to be given. After Coley Patteson had passed into the Eleven he was present at a dinner when one of the boys began to sing a ditty of a decidedly questionable character. At once Coley called out, "If that does not stop, I shall leave the room;" and as the singer went on, he jumped up and went out. His next step was to intimate to the captain that unless an apology was made he would leave the Eleven. Knowing that he could not dispense with so brilliant a bat, the captain compelled the offender to apologize; and during the rest of Coley Patteson's time at Eton no more songs of that kind were sung at the annual dinner.

It was while Coley was at Eton, and when he was about fourteen years of age, that a vision of what was to be the great work of his life first dawned upon him. In the parish church of Windsor, one Sunday afternoon, he heard a missionary sermon from Bishop Selwyn of New Zealand (of the Church of England), a diocese which at that time included the Melanesian Islands, and he was deeply touched by the Bishop's appeal for help. Not long afterwards in his father's house he met Bishop Selwyn face to face. The Bishop, who was just about to leave England for the South Seas, turned to the boy's mother and said, half in playfulness, half in earnest, "Lady Patteson, will you give me Coley?" From that day forward, deep down in the heart of the lad, there lived the thought of some day joining the heroic Bishop of New Zealand in his pioneer work among the islanders of the Pacific.

But something must now be said about Melanesia and Bishop Selwyn. When the see of New Zealand was first formed the Bishop was entrusted with the care of the innumerable islands dispersed in various groups over the South Pacific. The interests of the Church of England in the islanders, however, had been anticipated by the zeal of other Churches, or missionary societies. The Wesleyans were at work in the Fiji Islands...the Presbyterians to the New Hebrides, the London Missionary Society, ever since the time of John Williams, in Polynesia. There still remained farther to the west, and forming a far off fringe along the southeastern coast of New Guinea and the northeastern coast of Australia, the Melanesian or Black Island group, so called because the inhabitants are darker skinned than the other Pacific races and appear to have a good deal of the Negro in their composition.

Bishop Selwyn very wisely resolved that, to prevent overlapping of missionary effort and consequent confusion of the native mind, he would confine his attentions to these Melanesians, and he entered into his labors among them with all the ardor and heroism of the true pioneer. Like his future colleague, Coleridge Patteson, he was a distinguished athlete. He had rode in the first Inter-University Boat Race in 1829, and was further a splendid pedestrian and magnificent swimmer. In his work in Melanesia all these powers came into full play. There was nothing of the conventional bishop about his outward appearance or manner of life. His usual way of landing on an island was to take a header from a boat which lay off at a safe distance, and swim ashore through the surf. When hard manual work had to be done, he was the first to set the example. If dangers had to be met, he did not hesitate to face them. If hardships had to be borne, he bore them cheerfully. Once, for instance, when an inhospitable chief refused him the shelter of a hut, he retired to a pig-stye and spent the night there in patience and content. How versatile he was may be judged from an instance like the following. On one occasion he had undertaken by request to convey to New Zealand in his missionary schooner a Melanesian chief's daughter and her attendant native girl. The pair were dressed according to the ideas of propriety which prevailed in the islands, but were hardly presentable in a British colony. The Bishop spent much of his time on the voyage in manufacturing to the best of his ability out of his own counterpane two petticoats for the dark maidens. And so attractive did he make the garments, with their trimmings of scarlet ribbon, that the girls were as delighted to put them on, as the Bishop was anxious that they should do so.

One of the great difficulties of the work in Melanesia sprang from the endless varieties of dialects that were employed. Bishop Selwyn conceived the plan of persuading native youths from the different islands to come with him to New Zealand to undergo there a course of instruction and training which would fit them for Christian work among their own people when they returned. But if this plan was to be carried out efficiently there was need of assistance, and such assistance as was required was by no means easy to find. The man wanted must be possessed of physical hardihood, ready and fit to "rough it," as the Bishop himself did while cruising among the islands. But he must also be a man of culture and character, to whom the difficult task of educating the native youths could be safely entrusted.

In search of such a helper as this Bishop Selwyn eventually paid a visit to England. Thirteen years had passed since he had stirred the missionary instinct in young Patteson's soul by saying to his mother in his hearing, "Will you give me Coley?" Neither the Bishop nor the boy had forgotten the incident. But Coley meanwhile had passed through Oxford and become curate of Alfington, in the parish of Ottery St. Mary. His mother was dead, his father now an old man in poor health. A strong sense of filial love and duty had hitherto kept him from the thought of leaving home so long as his father was alive. But Bishop Selwyn came to see Sir John Patteson and Coley, and set the claims of Melanesia before them in such a way that both father and son realized that they must not hesitate to make the needful sacrifice of affection. That sacrifice was soon made. When the Bishop sailed again for his far off Pacific see, Coleridge Patteson stood beside him on the deck as his devoted follower and brother missionary.

As Patteson knew that his work would largely consist of sailing about among the islands, he applied himself busily throughout the long ocean voyage not only to the task of mastering the native languages under the Bishop's tutelage, but to a careful study under the captain of the art of navigation. He soon became an expert shipmaster, so that he was able by and by to navigate the *Southern Cross*, the little missionary schooner, on her various voyages through dangerous seas.

Arriving in New Zealand, he speedily had a taste of the kind of life that was in store for him. His immediate work lay in the College which had been established for the native youths, but he had to be ready, just as Bishop Selwyn himself was, to turn his hand to any kind of duty. In one of his letters he tells how, as the two were superintending the landing of their goods from a vessel by means of carts, the tide being very low, three of the horses got into water which was rather deep for them, and were in danger of being drowned. In a moment the two missionaries had their coats off and their trousers rolled up, and had plunged into the rescue, splashing about in the muddy water in full view of the crowd on the beach. "This is your first lesson in mud-larking Coley," remarked the Bishop, as they emerged at length wet and dirty, and laughing at each other's appearance.

But Patteson's special task was, as he put it himself, "to rove about the Melanesian department," and for several years he spent half of his time at sea. Fortunately he was a good sailor, and in every way worthy to be the skipper of the *Southern Cross*. He took thorough delight in his work, enjoying its adventurous aspects, but still more feeling the privilege of carrying the Gospel of Christ to men and women who had never heard it before, and who needed it very sadly. On his early cruises he was accompanied by the Bishop, and their most frequent method of landing at any island to which they came was to plunge into the sea in light suits which they wore for the purpose, and make for the crowd of armed natives who were sure to be standing by on the beach. Sometimes they were in danger, but firmness, kindness, and tact carried them through, and in not a few cases they were able to persuade a chief to allow his son, or some other promising youth, to return with them to New Zealand to join the other young men who were receiving at the College the elements of a Christian education.

So friendly was their reception for the most part, that Patteson was inclined to scoff at the notion of describing these gentle-looking people as savages at all. "Savages are all Fridays," (from "Robinson Crusoe") he wrote, "if you know how to treat them." But at times he was inclined to carry his confidence in them too far, and it was well for him in those early days that he had the Bishop at hand, who had learned by experience the need for perpetual caution. For there were plenty of real savages in Melanesia, and now and then came sharp reminders of the fact. At one island, where they were received with every sign of friendliness and conducted to the chief's long hut, they saw hanging from the roof a row of human skulls, some of them black with soot, others so white that it was evident they had been quite lately added to the collection. And in another place, while passing through some bush, they came upon remains of human bodies, relics of a recent cannibal feast. Occasionally, too, as they swam away from what had seemed to be a friendly crowd, an arrow or two whizzed past their heads, showing that they had left some ill-disposed persons behind them. One island that they visited in safety they knew to have been the scene sometime before of a deed of blood of which the crew of a British vessel were the victims. Their ship had struck upon the reef, and when they got ashore the natives killed the whole ship's company of them, nineteen in all. Ten of these the cannibals ate on the spot; the remaining nine they sent away as presents to their friends.

A voyage over, and the chief fruits of the cruise gathered together in the persons of a number of bright lads who had been persuaded to become scholars, Patteson would settle down for some months to play another role, that of a college tutor, but under circumstances very different from any that the name is apt to suggest. He had to teach his pupils everything, not only reading, writing, arithmetic, and the elements of Christian truth, but how to sweep their rooms and make their beds, how to print and weave and saw and build. Lessons in school over, his old proficiency in cricket became useful once more, and the former captain of the Eton Eleven might be seen patiently coaching his young barbarians, until they caught something of the English skill and enthusiasm for the great English game.

At length after six years of strenuous apprenticeship to the work of a pioneer missionary in the Pacific, there came a great change in Coleridge Patteson's position. Bishop Selwyn had long been convinced of the necessity of forming Melanesia into a separate diocese, and had come to recognize not less clearly the preeminent fitness of Mr. Patteson to occupy the new see. The representation he made to the home authorities on this subject was successful, and in 1861 Coley Patteson became Bishop of Melanesia for the Church of England, at the early age of thirty-three.

His elevation made little difference, however, either in the general character of his work or in his manner of doing it. He cruised among the islands as before—dressed commonly in an old flannel shirt, and trousers somewhat the worse for wear—a handy costume for one who had constantly to do a good deal of swimming and wading. His voyages as Bishop, at the same time, were on a wider scale than any he had attempted formerly, for he felt his larger responsibilities, and tried to reach even those islands which had hitherto been regarded as inaccessible.

Several times he had very narrow escapes. Once in particular, when he had gone ashore to a place where the natives made a show of friendship, he discovered from their conversation and gestures as soon as they had him in their power that it was their deliberate intention to kill him. The reason, he found afterwards, was that one of their friends had been murdered by a white trader, and with the savage sense of justice they felt that they were entitled to take this white man's life. The Bishop knew that humanly speaking he had no chance of mercy, but he begged permission to be allowed to pray, and kneeling down he committed his soul to God. The natives did not understand a single word that he uttered, but the look they saw in his face as he knelt so impressed and overawed them that they said to one another, "He does not look like a murderer." And as soon as he was done, with many signs of courtesy they conducted him back to the beach again and bade him farewell.

On another occasion, in connection with a later cruise, a sad incident took place at the island of Santa Cruise. The natives here showed no signs of opposition when he landed, but after he had returned to his boat and pushed off, a shower of arrows was discharged from the beach. The Bishop, who was at the stern, unshipped the rudder and held it up as a shield to try to ward off the deadly shafts. In spite of his efforts, three of the party, all of them Christian young men, were transfixed. Fortunately the arrows were not poisoned, as Melanesian arrows often were, but Patteson had great difficulty in extracting them. In one case he found it quite impossible to draw out the arrowhead from a man's wrist and was obliged to pull it from the other side right through his arm. This poor fellow took lockjaw, and died in a few days, after dreadful agonies of pain.

For ten strenuous years after his consecration as Bishop, Patteson sailed to and fro among the Melanesian Islands. Sometimes, through illness and weakness, brought on by the constant strain, he was in great suffering; but he never ceased to rejoice in his work. At last, however, a dark shadow fell across his path, a shadow which deepened to the awful tragedy of his death.

BISHOP PATTESON DEFENDING HIMSELF AND
HIS MEN WITH A RUDDER

They were attacked by the natives of Santa Cruz just after they had pushed
off from the shore. Fortunately the arrows were not poisonous, but one of
the natives died of his wounds.

The traders of the Pacific had discovered that it was more remunerative to kidnap natives, clap them under hatches, and sail with them as virtual slaves to the plantations of Queensland or Fiji, than to busy themselves in collecting sandalwood or copra for the legitimate market. Not a few of them had entered into this unscrupulous and vile traffic, which soon produced an unpleasant change all over the islands in the attitude of the natives to white men.

Worst still, some of these kidnappers used Patteson's name as a decoy. Coming to an island where he was known and trusted, they would tell the people that the Bishop was on board and wanted to see them. In some cases they even went the length of making an effigy of him, dressed in a black coat and holding a Bible in his hands; and this they placed in a position where it could be seen by those ashore. When the unsuspecting blacks came off in their canoes and climbed on board, they were quickly tumbled down into the hold among the other miserable wretches who were imprisoned there.

These were the malign influences that led to the murder of Bishop Patteson. He is the Martyr of Melanesia, but it was the kidnapping traders more than the ill-used natives who were responsible for his death.

It was on a day of September 1871, that the *Southern Cross* stood off the coral reef on the island of Nukapu. Several canoes were seen cruising about apparently in a state of some excitement. The Bishop entered the schooner's boat and pulled towards the reef, but the tide was too low for the boat to get across. At this juncture two natives approached, and proposed to take the Bishop into their light canoe and paddle him over the reef to the shore.

He at once consented. The boat's crew saw him land safely on the beach, but after that lost sight of him. For about half an hour the boat had been lying to and waiting, when from several canoes, which had been gradually drawing near, a shower of arrows fell upon the crew. They pulled back immediately in great haste and were soon out of range, but not until three persons had been struck with poisoned arrows, two of whom, the Rev. Joseph Adkins and a Christian native, subsequently died.

When the tide rose high enough to make it possible for the boat to cross the barrier reef, it was dispatched from the schooner, in hope of getting some intelligence about the Bishop. As the men pulled across the lagoon towards the shore two canoes put off to meet them. One cast off the other and went back, the one which was left drifting towards them as they approached.

As it came near they noticed what looked like a bundle lying in the bottom, and when they drew along side they saw this was the dead Bishop, lying there with a calm smile on his upturned face. His body was wrapped in a native mat, and over his breast there lay a leaf of the cocoanut palm, with five knots tied in the long sprays. What those mysterious knots meant was partly explained when the mat was unwrapped and five deadly wounds, inflicted with club, spear, and arrows, were discovered on the body.

It was afterwards learned that five Nukapu natives had been stolen by the kidnappers. The islanders doubtless looked upon them as having been murdered, and so their nearest relatives, exercising the old tribal right of exacting "blood for blood," had stained their weapons one by one in the blood of the white Bishop, who was thus called upon to lay down his life for the sins of his own unworthy fellow-countrymen.

The people of Nukapu have long since repented of their crime. On the spot where the Bishop fell there now stands, by their own desire, a simple, impressive cross with this inscription upon it:

In Memory of
John Coleridge Patteson, D.D.,
Missionary Bishop,
Whose life was here taken by men for whom he would
gladly have given it.

NOTES AND AUTHORITIES: The authoritative source for Bishop Selwyn's life is the biography by Rev. H.W. Tucker, and for Bishop Patteson's, *The Life of John Coleridge Patteson*, by Miss C.M. Yonge (Macmillan and Co.). Mention should also be made of *Bishop Patteson*, by J. Page (S.W. Partridge and Co.), which is an excellent popular narrative.

ONE OF THE UNRETURNING BRAVE

CHAPTER EIGHTEEN

FROM THE EDITORS: From dangers in the surf, to dangers in the forest, from encounters with wild beasts to constant threatenings from savage cannibals, James Chalmers was equal to the occasion. A man whose heart loved adventure and burned with a passion for sharing the Gospel, he was every bit a man's man. At times facing down angry savages, at other times surviving shipwrecks in wild storms, Chalmers, nicknamed "Tamate" by the natives, became a beloved friend of the Papuans in New Guinea, as they came to recognize his sincere love for them and his Lord. He was cast out of the same mold as David Livingstone or Frederick Stanley Arnot, as explorer and missionary, who looked to acknowledge and realize the Lordship of Jesus Christ over every square inch of this earth's surface.

Chalmers was born in Scotland August 4, 1841, during a time when that country produced a great number of missionary heroes for the cause of Christ. He lived in a fishing community on Loch Fyne, and quickly came to love the water, happiest when sailing, swimming, or paddling some raft. Three times he was spared from drowning, at which point his father offered a prophetic statement over the lad: "You will never die by drowning." As a youth he loved danger and excitement, and his love of the ocean would serve him in good stead later in life when braving the pounding surf on the shores of New Guinea or navigating the mission schooner through storms. In November 1859, while leading a group of delinquent young lads to break up a revival meeting, Chalmers overheard the words of the preacher and there he was convicted of his sin. He was converted shortly after at the age of eighteen, never to turn back again to the sinful ways of his youth.

The same fervor with which he lived his life outdoors, now carried him into his studies as he prepared for missionary work in the South Pacific. In 1865 he married Miss Jane Hercus. Together, they departed in the service of the London Missionary Society, bound for Rarotonga. After surviving a shipwreck en route, they finally arrived in May 1867, sixteen months later. Ten years of faithful service in the Cook Islands was rewarding for the young family, but Chalmers wanted to go where no missionary had gone before. He wanted to reach a people who had never heard the Gospel, and so he and his wife sailed for New Guinea in September 1877. Rev. Lawes, who had spent a few years of discouraging labor in New Guinea previously, had reported that, "Cannibalism in all its hideousness flourishes on many parts of the coast. Every man is a thief and a liar. The thing of which the men are most proud is the tattooing marks, which mean that the man who is tattooed has shed human blood."

To a man like James Chalmers, such reports serve as a clarion call to service. He was convinced that he must minister to as many natives as God had ordained for him, and he could work in faith and enjoy God's protection all the days of his life. And so he did for twenty-five years. Chalmers, accompanied by his brave wife, first settled on Stacey Island, where savages wearing necklaces of human bones would surround them to hear the good news of Christ. The Chalmers were invited to cannibal feasts, and James was presented with a chief's daughter in marriage (an offer which he turned down). Mrs. Chalmers died two years after they arrived in New Guinea. James continued serving alone until 1886 when he returned to England to encourage church support for missions in New Guinea. He married Sarah Eliza Harrison in 1888, who settled with him in New Guinea, as they continued the work. After taking ill, she was forced to sail for England in 1892, rejoining him again in 1897 on the field where she remained until her death in 1900. In April 1901, James Chalmers set out on his last expedition, to visit a tribe of fierce cannibals up the Fly River. This would be his last missionary journey.

James Chalmers (1841—1901)

Papua, or New Guinea, lies to the northeast of the Australian continent, separated from it by the Torres Straits, and only eighteen miles across. In size it measures 1,490 miles in length, while it is 430 miles in breadth across the thickest part. Covering as it does an area of considerably more than 300,000 square miles, it is quite six times the size of England. Its chief river, the Fly, is tidal at a distance of 130 miles from the sea, and has been navigated by large vessels for over 600 miles of its course. The island can boast of a mighty range of mountains quite worth to be compared to the Alps, the loftiest peak, indeed, rising nearer to the sky than the white dome of Mont Blanc.

Of the people of this great island, however, hardly anything was known until about 1875, except that they were warlike cannibals, whose only regular trade was to barter sago for earthenware pots in which to cook man. To Port Moresby, on the southeast coast of this mysterious and dreaded land, there came in 1876 James Chalmers, or "Tamate," an agent of the London Missionary Society. Combining, as he did in a very unusual degree, the qualities of missionary and explorer, he soon greatly increased our knowledge of the geography of New Guinea and of the superstitions, habits, and social customs of its various and widely differing tribes.

Chalmers was no inexperienced explorer of the South Seas when he first arrived at Port Moresby to enter upon that career of constant adventure by land and sea, on the rivers and in the forests, with Papuan savages or with the Papuan surf, in which the next twenty-five years of his life were to be spent. He had already been shipwrecked on a coral-reef in the *John Williams*, the London Missionary Society's vessel, named after that splendid hero of Polynesia whose true successor Chalmers himself became. He had gone with his young wife on a voyage of 2,000 miles in the brig of "Bully Hayes," the notorious pirate of the Pacific, and had so fascinated that ferocious nineteenth-century buccaneer that he behaved to his unwonted passengers like a perfect gentleman. He had spent ten years on Rarotonga, among the former cannibals of that beautiful coral island. It was from the Rarotongans that he got the name "Tamate," which stuck to him for the rest of his life, though it was nothing else than the result of an ineffectual native attempt to pronounce the Scottish name of "Chalmers." In Rarotonga, Tamate had gained much valuable experience; but the restless spirit of the pioneer was in his blood, and it was a joyful day for him when word came from London that he was to proceed to New Guinea to enter upon what he felt from the first to be the true work of his life.

The people of New Guinea are sprung from various original stocks, and are broken up besides into numerous isolated tribes which differ greatly from one another in color, feature, and language. But Chalmers found that, in addition to this, every village formed a community by itself, living at enmity with its neighbors and in constant suspicion of them. The best proof of this was afforded by the construction of the houses, built as they invariably were with a view to protection against sudden attack. Along the coast marine villages were common, Port Moresby itself being an example. The houses were erected on tall piles driven into the sea-bottom at such a distance from the shore that a small steamer was able to thread its way between the houses, and even to anchor safely in the main street. Inland villages, similarly, were built on poles, which projected not less than ten feet above the ground, access to the platform on which a house stood being obtained by means of a ladder. Among the hill-tribes, again, tree-dwellings were most common, these being particularly inaccessible and thus most easy to defend. On his first arrival at Port Moresby, Chalmers took a long walk inland till he was about 1,100 feet above sea-level, and found houses built not only on the summit of a mountain ridge, but on the tops of the very highest trees that were growing there.

Tamate at once set himself to acquire some knowledge of his vast diocese and to win the confidence of the natives. He had all the qualities for the work that lay before him. He could navigate a whaleboat through the heavy surf which crashes along the level coasts, as if bred to the job. And at tramping through the forests or climbing the mountains no one could beat him; though he confesses to sometimes having sore feet, and expresses the wicked wish that shoemakers could be compelled to wear the boots they send out to missionaries. As for the natives, he won them by a kind of personal fascination he had which was felt by every one who met him—man-eating savage or missionary-loving old lady, a piratical outlaw like "Bully Hayes," or a literary dreamer and critic like Robert Louis Stevenson. Unarmed but fearless, Tamate never hesitated to walk right into the midst of a crowd of armed and threatening cannibals. For the most part he won their friendship at the first meeting without difficulty, though every now and then he came across some troublesome customers and had a narrow escape with his life.

One of Chalmers's earliest expeditions was a cruise along the south coast from east to west, in the course of which he visited 105 villages, 90 of which had never seen a white man before. Being new to the country, he met with much to surprise or amuse him. The Papuans are passionately fond of pigs, especially when roasted; but it astonished their visitor to find that they preserved the skulls of dead pigs in their houses along with those of their departed relatives, and still more to see a woman nursing her baby and a young pig. One day when he had taken his seat in the middle of a native house, right in front of the fire, and was busy tracing his course on a chart, he looked up and saw a recently deceased person had been made up into a bulky parcel and hung from the roof right above the fire, with a view to being thoroughly smoked and dried. Tamate's shout of disgust brought in the owner of the house, who hastily took down the bundle and walked off with it on his shoulder, to deposit it elsewhere until the departure of this too fastidious traveler.

But if Chalmers was sometimes astonished at first by the Papuans and their ways, the astonishment was by no means altogether upon his side. His white skin was a source of perpetual wonder, especially if he had occasion to roll up his sleeves or change his shirt, and so exposed the white parts of his body that were not so bronzed as his cheeks by the sea air and the burning sun. Great, too, was the perplexity caused by his combination of a white face with black and toeless feet—perplexity which suddenly turned to horror if he lifted his legs and pulled off his boots.

These, however, were among the lighter phases of his experiences as a pioneer. Until he became known, along many a league of coast and in the deep recesses of the forest, as the best friend of the Papuan people, Tamate had constantly to face death in the grimmest forms, and with a vision of the cannibal cooking-pot lying ever in the background. Here is a hairbreadth escape which looks thrilling enough as we read it in his *Adventures in New Guinea*, though it does not seem half so dramatic on the printed page as it did when the present writer heard Tamate relate it himself—"a big, stout, wildish—looking man," as R.L. Stevenson described him, "with big bold black eyes," which glowed and flashed as he told his story and suited the action to the word.

On one of his coasting voyages in the *Ellengowan*, a little steamer that belonged to the Mission, he came to a bay in which he had never been before. He put off for the shore as soon as possible, but the moment his boat touched the beach, he was surrounded by a threatening crowd of natives, every one of them armed with club or spear. The savages absolutely forbade him to land, but he sprang ashore notwithstanding, followed by the mate of the *Ellengowan*, a fine, daring fellow with something of Tamate's own power of feeling least fear where most danger seemed to be. Up the long sea-beach the two men walked, accompanied by the hostile crowd till they came to what was evidently the house of the village chief. The old man sat in solemn dignity on the raised platform in front of his house, and did not condescend to take the least notice of his visitors. Climbing up to the platform, Tamate laid down some presents he had brought, but the surly magnate flung them back in his face. It now became apparent that a row was brewing, for the crowd took its cue from the chief, and was

A NATIVE VILLIAGE IN NEW GUINEA

The Houses are all built on piles driven into the ground.

beginning to jostle rudely and indulge in bursts of brutal laughter. Turning to the mate, who stood a little way behind, Tamate asked him in English how things looked. "Bad, sir," he replied; "the bush is full of natives, and there are arms everywhere. They have stolen all my beads and hoop-iron. It looks like mischief." Even Chalmers now felt that it was time to retire. "Gould," said he to the mate, "I think we had better get away from here; keep eyes all around, and let us make quietly for the beach." Chalmers used to describe the next quarter of an hour as one of the most uncomfortable in his life. The crowd followed, growling savagely, and one man with a large stone-headed club kept walking just behind the missionary and most unpleasantly near. "Had I that club in my hand," thought Tamate, "I should feel a little more comfortable." A few steps more and he said to himself: "I must have that club, or that club will have me." Wheeling suddenly around, he drew out of his satchel a large piece of hoop-iron, a perfect treasure to a native, and presented it to the savage. The man's eyes glistened as if he had seen a bar of gold, and he stretched out his hand to grasp the prize. In a moment Tamate seized the man's club, wrenched it out of his hands, and brandishing it in the air as if he meant to use it, headed the procession and marched safely down to the boat. Long afterwards, when these natives became his friends, they told him that he "looked bad" at the moment when he took possession of the club; and Chalmers confesses that was just how he felt.

As we have indicated already, the traveler in New Guinea soon finds that the dangers of the Pacific surf are hardly less than those of the shore or the forest. From the time when as a boy he had learned to swim and row and steer through the often stormy waters of the Highland loch beside which he was born, Tamate had been passionately fond of the sea; and it was his constant habit to make trips of exploration along the New Guinea coast in a whaleboat, acting as his own skipper. On the southern coast at certain seasons of the year huge rollers sweep in continually from the Papuan Gulf and burst upon the beach with a noise like thunder. A strong nerve and a cool judgment, as well as a stout arm at the steering-oar, are required if a landing is to be effected in safety; and even to the finest swimmer, to be overturned in the midst of the surf may mean a death either from drowning or by the teeth of swarming crocodiles, or by being pounded to jelly on the rocks. In the "riding of the surges" Tamate was a master, but though he performed the feat successfully hundreds of times, he once or twice came to grief and had the narrowest escape with his life.

In one of his letters he tells of an exciting experience that he had in company with a Mr. Romilly, a Government agent, whom he had taken with him in his whaleboat:

"We were very deeply laden. On nearing the bar it did not seem to me as very dangerous, so we stood on. The first sea bar sped us on, the second one caught us, we shipped water, the steer-oar got jammed, the boat swung and went over. It was deep and the seas heavy, and for a short time it seemed some of us must go. It is a terrible place for crocodiles, but I suppose so many of us frightened them. The smashing in the surf was enough to kill. The boat's crew of native students did nobly. We got ashore. I feared at one time Romilly was drowning. I felt somewhat exhausted myself. I fancy Romilly must have been struck with an oar. The boys got the boat in after a good hour's hard work. I got three times onto the boat's keel, and each time was swept away. At last got an oar, and assisted by a native I got to a sandbank—resting a little, then ashore. A fire was lighted, around which we all gathered, when one of the students engaged in prayer, and with full hearts we all joined him with thanksgiving. During the night things were washed ashore, and amongst them my swag."

They spent all that night on the beach, gathered round a fire. Sunday followed. It is not strange to find Chalmers remarking, "We all felt sore and unfit for much exertion." But it is characteristic that he adds that he had two services that day.

The reference which Chalmers makes in the foregoing passage to his having the company of a Government agent on this unlucky trip makes it suitable to mention at this point that in 1884 the British flag was formally hoisted at Port Moresby, and that the whole of Southeastern New Guinea declared to be a British Protectorate; while in 1886 the step was followed by the proclamation of Queen Victoria's sovereignty. Of these actions of his Government Chalmers fully approved, and his service to the British officials then and afterwards were of the most valuable kind. No one else knew the country as he did; no one was so familiar with the habits of the people, their languages, and their modes of thought. His work for the Empire has received the most appreciative notice from various quarters. In a letter to the London Times, written just after the news of Chalmers's death had reached England,

A CRITICAL MOMENT

Chalmers was followed by a big and angry crowd. One savage with a large club walked immediately behind him. Chalmers felt that he must have that club or it would have him, so taking a piece of much-appreciated hoop-iron from his satchel he wheeled suddenly round, held it to the man's dazzled eyes, and at the same moment wrenched the club from his hand. Chalmers then walked on, feeling considerably relieved, and succeeded in escaping on this occasion.

Admiral Bridge says, speaking of the assistance rendered him by Chalmers in 1884-5, "His vigilance, cheeriness, readiness of resource, and extraordinary influence over native savages, made his help quite invaluable. I can honestly say that I do not know how I should have got on without him. He had an equal power of winning the confidence of savages quite unused to strangers, and the respect, and even love, of white seamen...It is difficult to do justice in writing to the character of this really great Englishman. One had only to know and live with him in out of the way lands to be convinced that he was endowed with the splendid characteristics which distinguished our most eminent explorers and pioneers."

Admiral Bridge was right in describing Chalmers as essentially an explorer and pioneer. In many respects he was a man cast in Livingstone's mold, and he was never happier than when pushing his way into regions where the foot of a white man had never trod before. Not only did he explore by whaleboat or steam launch all the coasts and bays of Southern Papua, but he was the first white man to walk right across New Guinea to its eastern end, and he penetrated farther up the difficult Fly River than the most adventurous travelers had ever been before.

And yet he never forgot that his work was primarily that of a Christian teacher, and he never shrank from the little monotonies that were involved. Even when his position became virtually that of a missionary overseer, with duties of superintendence not only over the great Fly River delta, but also over the scattered islands of the Torres Straits, he cheerfully undertook day by day the duties of an elementary schoolmaster. He taught the A, B, C's to young and old—though it should be added he had the shrewdness to take advantage of the Papuan love of song and music by teaching the people to sing it to the tune of "Auld Lang Syne." One who visited him when he had made his home in the midst of the mangrove swamps of the Fly River found him at daybreak in a rudely constructed schoolhouse that he had built on the sand just above the high water mark. He had a class which was learning English, and with a small bamboo stick for a baton was leading his scholars as they sang, first "God Save the Queen," and then "All Hail the Power of Jesus' Name." "I don't think," his friend writes, "that Chalmers ever appeared quite so great a man as when I saw him thus teaching that group of Fly River children."

Thus for five and twenty years Tamate of the big warm heart went out and among the tribes of New Guinea, until his Polynesian name had become a household word alike in the sea dwellings of the shore, the tree houses of the hills, and the great dubus or barracks in which in the larger communities the people herd together by the hundred. But the day came when Tamate was to go out no more. Writing from the Vailima to his mother in November, 1890, Robert Louis Stevenson said of the friend whom he loved and admired so greatly: "I have a cultus for Tamate; he is a man nobody can see and not love...He has plenty of faults like the rest of us; but he is as big as church." And he expressed the hope that he "shall meet Tamate once more before he disappears up the Fly River, perhaps to be one of the 'unreturning brave.' " The words were almost prophetic. Possibly they gave voice to a dim presentiment of which

Chalmers himself was sometimes conscious, and of which he may have spoken of to his friend.

It was only a few months after, in the beginning of April 1901, that Tamate set out to visit the district around Cape Blackwood, on the eastern side of the Fly River delta, which was inhabited by a ferocious tribe of savages. He knew that these people were both skull hunters and cannibals, and for that very reason he had long been eager to get a footing among them. He was accompanied on this occasion by the Rev. Oliver Tomkins, a young and promising colleague lately arrived from England. At a place called Risk Point a swarm of natives, armed with bows and arrows, clubs, knives, and spears, came off in their canoes and took forcible possession of the *Niue*, the Mission vessel. With the view of inducing them to leave, Tamate decided to go ashore. He did everything he could to persuade Mr. Tomkins to remain on board, probably because he anticipated trouble. Mr. Tomkins, however, refused to allow his leader to go alone; and so the two went off together. Those on board never saw them again.

The captain of the *Niue* waited for two days, sailing about the coast and keeping a sharp lookout, but no trace could be seen either of the Mission party or their boat. Seeing now that a tragedy must have taken place, he sailed with all speed to Daru and reported the matter to the British Governor. At once the Governor started in person, accompanied by a sufficient force, in order find out exactly what had taken place and to inflict punishment if necessary. From a native who was captured he secured the following tale, which was afterwards corroborated in all particulars.

NEW GUINEA LAKATOIS PREPARING TO SAIL

When the two white men got ashore they entered the long dubu of the village, their native boys being induced to enter also by the promise of something to eat. No sooner was the whole party within than the signal was given for a general massacre. The first to be killed were the two missionaries, who were knocked simultaneously on the head from behind with stone clubs. Both fell senseless at the first blow, and their heads were immediately cut off. Their followers were then similarly killed and then beheaded, though one of them, a powerful man, managed to snatch a club from one of his assailants and kill another at a blow before being himself felled. The heads were distributed as trophies among the murderers. The bodies were cut up and handed over to the women to cook. They were cooked at once, the flesh being mixed with sago, and were eaten the same day.

It was a painful and tragic end to the life of one who, by the testimony of Sir William MacGregor, Governor of New Guinea for seven years, has justly been called "The Apostle of the Papuan Gulf." And yet how much truth there is in the Governor's words in his official report of the massacre and of the steps he felt obliged to take for the punishment of the perpetrators: "I am not alone in the opinion that Mr. Chalmers has won the death he would have wished for of all others—in New Guinea and for New Guinea."

NOTES AND AUTHORITIES: The authorities for the life of Chalmers are *Adventures in New Guinea* and *Pioneering in New Guinea*, both by Mr. Chalmers himself; *James Chalmers* and *Tamate*, both by Richard Lovett, M.A. all published by the Religious Tract Society.

AMONG THE CANNIBAL ISLANDS

CHAPTER NINETEEN

FROM THE EDITORS: Of all the South Pacific islands, none has a more barbarous and bloodstained history than that of the Fiji Islands. Evil in the extreme, the hold that Satan and his evil hordes maintained over the natives was worse than the most vivid imagination could envision. But, where darkness and evil reign supreme, so much so that many people would altogether abandon hope, the light of the Gospel and power of the resurrected Christ shines all the more clearly. The story you are about to read is utterly fascinating, and it is at points difficult to read due to the descriptions of the degraded state of paganism. Yet, such records are important to better understand the power of the Gospel of Christ unto Salvation, and to recognize the faith, courage, and commitment to Christ retained by these missionaries.

Sent out by the Wesleyan Church from England, Rev. James Calvert and his wife Mary served in Fiji for seventeen years. James was born in Pickering, Yorkshire in 1813, and was a printer/bookbinder by trade. After receiving the call to the mission field, he completed his studies at the Wesleyan Theological Institution. Mary, his wife, was born in 1814 and they were married in 1837, just prior to their departure for Fiji.

On the voyage to the islands, the ship's captain tried to dissuade the Calverts from their mission when he told them, "You will lose your life and the lives of those with you if you go among such savages." To this, James responded, "Sir, we died before we came here." Such was their mindset knowing with the apostle Paul that "it is no longer I who live, but Christ who lives in me." Such was the testimony of James and Mary Calvert. Through their lives and ministry work, the love of God broke through and the Fiji Islands were forever changed.

James Calvert (1813—1892) and Mary Calvert (1814—1882)

Almost due north of New Zealand, but at a distance of nearly 1,200 miles, there lies embosomed in the midst of the Pacific Ocean a British group of islands of surpassing loveliness. They are about two hundred and fifty in number, ranging from the size of a large English county to barren rocks, which disappear altogether at the highest tides. To the invariable beauty of all volcanic islands in the tropics this group adds the peculiar charms of the coral formations of the Pacific. Mountains clothed in the most luxuriant vegetation toss their fretted peaks high into the air. Great green breakers dash perpetually on the barrier reefs, sending their snowy foam up to the very roots of the coconut trees that fringe the long shining beaches. Inside of the reefs again, the lagoon lies sleeping, indigo-blue where its waters are deepest, emerald-green nearer to the shore; but always of such crystal clearness that the idle occupant of a canoe can see far down at the bottom the white sands, the richly tinted seaweeds, the exquisite coral growths— branching into innumerable varieties of form, and blossoming with all the colors of the rainbow. These are the Fiji Islands, ceded by King Thakombau to Queen Victoria in 1874. But if it had not been for the splendid labors of a band of Wesleyan missionaries, of whom the Rev. James Calvert was the most notable, the possession of Fiji would have brought the British monarchs the questionable honor of being a "King of the Cannibal Islands."

It was not of Fiji that Bishop Heber wrote, "Though every prospect pleases, only man is vile." But to these islands in 1850 the words might very fitly have been applied. Even among the savage peoples of the South Seas the Fijians were notorious for every kind of brutal abomination. Man-eating was not only practiced, but gloried in and gloated over. It had become a lust so overmastering that men were known to murder their nearest relatives in order to gratify the craving for human flesh. To such an extent was it carried on that there were some who could boast of having eaten hundreds of their fellow creatures. Miss Gordon Cumming, in her most interesting book, *At Home in Fiji*, tells of a row of stones she saw, extending to a distance of 200 yards, which was nothing else than a cannibal register formerly kept by two chiefs to represent the number of persons they had themselves eaten—each stone standing for a human body. Woe betide the unfortunate crew whose ship drifted on to the reefs of a Fiji island! If they escaped from the cruel breakers, it was only to be dispatched by a club as soon as they reached the shore, and cooked forthwith in a huge cannibal oven.

But cannibalism was only one of the many forms of Fijian cruelty. In these fair islands, one might say, the air was always tainted with the smell of blood, for without the sacrifice of human blood nothing of importance could be undertaken. If a war canoe was to be launched, it was dragged down to the water over the prostrate bodies of living men and women, who were always mangled, and often crushed to death in the process. When a chief's house was being built, deep holes were dug for the wooden pillars on which the house was to rest. A man was thrown into each hole, and he was compelled to stand clasping the pillar with his arms while the earth was filled in right over his head. At the death of a Fijian of any consequence all his wives were strangled and buried beside him to furnish what was called "lining for his grave." His mother also, if still alive, suffered the same fate. The lives of more distant female relatives and connections were spared, but they had to express their grief by sawing off one of their fingers with a sharp shell, joint by joint, so that it was hardly possible to see a woman in the islands who had not suffered mutilation in both her hands. In short it was a land where Satan reigned supreme.

In spite of their cruelty, however, the Fijians were a race much superior, both in physique and intelligence, to the majority of the South Sea islanders. Unusually tall and muscular, both men and women sometimes displayed proportions that were quite magnificent. Their social laws were elaborate, and they possessed some of the arts of civilization. As manufacturers of cloth, and especially of pottery, they were famous far and wide in the Pacific, and canoes came hundreds of miles from other island groups to purchase their ware. They also enjoyed a unique reputation as wig-makers and hairdressers. Every chief had his own private hair artist, who spent hours each day over his master's head. With all kinds of fantastic variations in the particular style, the general idea was to get the hair to stick out as far as possible from the skull; and especially skillful operators were able to produce a coiffure five feet in circumference. Like everything else in this world, however, this elaborate top-dressing had to be paid for, and the payment came at bedtime. It was impossible to lay such a head upon a pillow, much more upon the ground. The Fijian had to rest his neck all night long on a bar of bamboo raised above the floor by two short legs.

It was between the 1830's and 40's that the first pioneers of Christianity came to Fiji. About 250 miles to the east lay the Friendly Islands, inhabited by a race called Tongans. These Tongans were much bolder sailors than most of the South Sea races, and were in the habit of visiting Fiji periodically for purposes of trade. Eventually some of them settled in the most easterly islands of the group, a fact which led to still closer intercourse. In the Friendly Islands the Wesleyan missionaries had met with remarkable success. The Tongans nearly all became Christians, including their king, King George, as he was called after his baptism. In his heathen days this man had been a famous fighter, leading out his war canoes, like some Viking of the Pacific, and spreading death and devastation far and near. Now that he was a Christian he was no less zealous in seeking to spread the Gospel of peace. Both he and his people were especially anxious that Christianity should be carried to Fiji, and they persuaded the Wesleyans to make the attempt. The Rev. James Calvert was among the pioneers in this dangerous enterprise; the only one who was spared to see the marvelous transformation which passed over the archipelago within the course of a single generation, and can only be compared to the transition that takes place within a single hour in those same tropical regions from the darkness of the night to the glory of the morning.

It was in Lakemba, one of the eastern or Windward Islands, as they are called, that Mr. and Mrs. Calvert first landed. It was a suitable place in which to begin, for here they were in the neighborhood of the Tongan colonies where King George's influence was felt. All the same, they were subjected to a great deal of unkindness, and had to face constant dangers and hardships, especially as Mr. Calvert's district covered not Lakemba only, but twenty-four surrounding islands. Many days and nights had to be spent on the ocean in frail canoes. Many an anxious hour Mrs. Calvert had in Lakemba, alone in the midst of fierce savages, thinking too, of her absent husband, who might be battling with the storm in a sea full of coral reefs, or standing unarmed in the midst of a throng of excited cannibals.

After some years of labor in their first sphere, it was

decided that the Calverts should leave the eastern outskirts of the archipelago and make for the very citadel of Fijian heathenism and savagery. In the island of Bau, which lies near the heart of the whole group, there lived at that time an old king called Tanoa, one of the most ferocious of man-eaters, and his son Thakombau, a prince of almost gigantic size and at the same time of unusual intelligence and character. Both the king of Bau and his son were celebrated warriors. In case of need they could summon to their banner many scores of war canoes, and their power to strike was felt all over Fiji. Thakombau was capable of mildness, but with Tanoa bloodthirstiness had become a kind of mania of the most horrific sort.

With characteristic courage the Wesleyan missionaries determined to strike at the very center of Fijian cruelty, for they knew that if heathenism could be cast down in Bau, the effects of its downfall would be felt in every island of the archipelago. On Bau itself Tanoa would by no means permit them to settle, nor would he allow any Christian services to be held in that island. He made no objections, however, to Mr. Calvert's building a house on an islet called Viwa, which is separated from Bau by only two miles of water, and he was quite willing to receive personal visits. Mr. Calvert had many a conversation with the old king and his son. On Tanoa he made not the slightest impression; but over Thakombau he gradually gained an influence which was to lead in due course both to the Christianization of the Fiji Islands and to their incorporation in Britain's world-wide empire.

But it was Mrs. Calvert, not her husband, who gained the first victory in the fight. Hospitality was a thing on which King Tanoa prided himself, and he never failed to entertain important guests with a banquet of human flesh. If enemies could be secured for the table, so much the better, but if not, he had no hesitation in sacrificing his own subjects. On one occasion a party of envoys from a piratical tribe had come to Bau to offer the king a share of their spoil by way of tribute. At once a hunting party was sent out under the leadership of Ngavindi, a notable chief, which soon returned with fourteen captures, all women—women being considered an even greater delicacy than man. In those days the fishing in Fiji was nearly all done by the gentler sex, and these unfortunates were wading in the sea with their nets when the hunters sighted them. Creeping up with his men under the cover of a fringe of mangrove bushes which ran along the shore, Ngavindi dashed suddenly into the water and seized the screaming women, who knew only too well what sort of fate awaited them. Word of the occurrence came to Viwa almost immediately. Mr. Calvert was absent at the time on one of his numerous expeditions, but his wife and another lady who was with her resolved to do what they could to save the doomed wretches. They jumped into a canoe and paddled hastily across the strait. Before they reached the shore the din of death-drums told them that the work of butchery had already begun. Every moment was precious now, and when they got to land they took to their heels and ran towards the king's house. By the laws of Bau no woman was at liberty to cross Tanoa's threshold on pain of her life, unless he sent for her; but these two ladies thought nothing of their own danger. They rushed headlong into the king's presence, and with arms outstretched besought him to spare the remaining victims. The very boldness of their action made it successful. Tanoa seemed quite dumbfounded by their audacity, but he at once ordered the work of slaughter to cease. Nine of the poor women had already been killed and carried off to the ovens, but the remaining five were immediately set at liberty.

There was another custom not less cruel than cannibalism, and even more difficult to uproot, since it was deeply intertwined with the religious ideas of the people and especially with their thoughts about the future life. This was the practice of strangling a man's wives and even his mother on the occasion of his funeral, so that their spirits might accompany him into the invisible world. As King Tanoa was an old man whose end seemed to be drawing near, the prospect of his death and what might happen in connection with it gave Mr. Calvert the deepest concern. He knew that if Fijian usage was adhered to, the departure of so great a chieftain from the world was sure to be attended by a wholesale immolation of his women-folk. He also saw that if the practice could be broken down at Tanoa's obsequies, a deadly blow would be struck at such abominations. He therefore visited Thakombau, the heir-apparent, again and again, and urged him by every consideration in his power to abandon the idea of slaughtering his father's wives. He tried to appeal to his better feelings; he promised to give him a very handsome present if he would refrain from blood; he even went so far as to offer to cut off his own finger, after the Fijian fashion of mourning, if the women might be spared. But though Thakombau was evidently impressed by Mr. Calvert's pleadings, he would give no assurance, and Mr. Calvert learned afterwards that all the while Tanoa himself had been privately instructing his son that his wives must on no account be kept from accompanying him on his journey into the unseen.

The old king's death took place rather suddenly in the end, and on this occasion too Mr. Calvert happened to be absent on duty in a distant island, so that it fell to a younger missionary, Mr. Watsford, to take action. As soon as he heard of the death, he made for Bau with all possible haste. Within Tanoa's house and in the very presence of the corpse the work of massacre had begun, two wives were lying dead, and a third had been summoned, when the missionary burst in. When Thakombau saw him enter he became greatly excited, and trembling from head to foot he cried out, "What about it, Mr. Watsford?" "Refrain, sir!" Mr. Watsford exclaimed, speaking with great difficulty, for his emotions almost overpowered him. "Refrain! That is plenty; two are dead." But though Thakombau was moved, he would not yield. "They are not many," he said, "only five. But for you missionaries, many more would have accompanied my father." And so the other three victims were brought in—newly bathed, anointed with oil, and dressed in their best as if going to a joyous feast. And there, in the very presence of the white man as he kept pleading for their lives, they were put to death in the usual way.

But though King Thakombau had not the courage at the time to defy the ancient traditions of his people, the influence of a higher teaching had been slowly telling upon him, and the day-dawn in Fiji was about to begin. Soon after Tanoa's funeral a Bau chief died, and Mr. Calvert was able in this case to persuade Thakombau to forbid any sacrifice of the women of the house. The usual preparations for murder had already been made, and the royal command gave great offense to many. The chief executioner flung down his strangling-cord and exclaimed, "Then I suppose we are to die like anybody now!" But a great victory had been won for humanity and Christianity. A precedent against a brutal custom had been established, which made it much easier for all time coming to rescue the proposed victims of superstition and cruelty.

But the greatest triumph of all came when Thakombau resolved to renounce heathenism altogether and take his stand on the Christian side. In the presence of a vast crowd, summoned by the beating of the very death-drums which had formerly rolled out their invitation to the islanders to be present at a cannibal feast, the king of Bau renounced his past, proclaimed his faith, and declared his intention to live henceforth as a follower of Christ. That day of 1857 was not only a day of gratitude and thanksgiving in the experience of Mr. Calvert and his colleagues, but one of the most important days in the history of Fiji. It was the precursor, indeed, of another day some seventeen years later when Thakombau, having applied to be taken under the protection of the British Crown, formally ceded the Fiji Islands to Queen Victoria, handing over at the same time to the British Envoy his old war-club, in token of the fact that his people were now "abandoning club law and adopting the forms and principles of civilized society." Thakombau's magnificent club, together with his drinking-bowl, of which he made a present to Britain's Queen, may now be seen by interested visitors in the British Museum. Innocent as they now look in their Museum case, it requires some exercise of the imagination to picture forth the awful scenes of massacre and the loathsome cannibal orgies in which that same club and drinking-bowl once had their share.

This book is called *Adventures of Missionary Heroism*. To those who read his story afterwards, the heroism and excitement of a missionary's life often lies in the faith, courage, and tenacity with which he faced toils and dangers, even though his endeavors did not result in great outward achievements. But there are other cases in which the romance of the missionary adventurer's life appears not only in the trials and difficulties he faces, but in the wonderful victories he wins. Now and then there comes a fortunate knight of Christ before whom embattled hosts go down, and who wins his way into the City of Jerusalem and claims it in the Lord's name. James Calvert was such a happy knight. When he and his young wife reached Fiji, one of his first tasks was to gather up and bury the skulls, hands, and feet of eighty men and women who had been sacrificed at a single feast. All around them day-by-day deeds of horror went on which might well have frozen the blood of any one who was not sustained by faith in God. Men and women bound with ropes were dragged past their door, going literally like oxen to the slaughter. Yet they hardly dared to express their disgust and loathing. A brother missionary and his wife narrowly escaped from being themselves burnt alive because the lady had ventured to close the window and draw down the blind in order to shut out the sight and smell of what was going on in front

of their house. On his visits to strange islands, too, Mr.
Calvert always went with his life in his hand, and more
than once had marvelous escapes from a death that seemed
certain. But this same missionary, who had seen Fiji in its
midnight gloom, was spared to see it in the light of the
sun rising. He was spared to see the islands provided with
1,300 Christian churches, crowded Sunday after Sunday
by devout congregations. And where once the stillness of
the night had been often broken by the death-shriek of the
victim or the cannibal's exultant death-song, he was spared
to hear, as he passed along the village paths after dark had
fallen, the voices of fathers, mothers, and little children
rising together from many a home in sweet evening hymns.

NOTES AND AUTHORITIES: *Cannibals and Saints*, by James
Calvert; *At Home in Fiji*, by Miss C. F. Gordon Cummings
(William Blackwood and Sons); *James Calvert*, by R. Vernon
(S.W. Partridge and Co.).

SOUTH   PACIFIC

THE APOSTLE OF THE NEW HEBRIDES

CHAPTER   TWENTY

FROM THE EDITORS: Discovered in 1606 by the Spanish explorer Fernandez de Quiros, the chain of eighty islands in the South Pacific known as the New Hebrides were inhabited by warring tribes and vicious cannibals. The first Christian influence on the island came when John Williams and James Harris landed on Erromanga in 1839. The two men were summarily killed and eaten by the natives. In 1842 the natives drove off another group of missionaries, and then two more arrived in 1848 and 1852. With the arrival of John G. Paton in 1858, the work of evangelism on the islands began in earnest.

Born near Dumfries, Scotland in 1824, from early in his life Paton was profoundly influenced by his humble father's vision for missions. When the time came for young Paton to leave his family and set forth on his preparations for the mission field, the following unforgettable scene is described by Paton himself:

"My dear father walked with me the first six miles of the way. His counsel and tears and heavenly conversation on that parting journey are fresh in my heart as if it had been but yesterday; and tears are on my cheeks as freely now as then, whenever memory steals me away to the scene. His tears fell fast when our eyes met each other in looks for which all speech was vain! He grasped my hand firmly for a minute in silence, and then solemnly said: 'God bless you, my son! Your father's God prosper you, and keep you from all evil!'... Hastening on my way, I vowed deeply and oft, by the help of God, to live and act so as never to grieve or dishonor such a father and mother as He had given me."

Sent out by the Reformed Presbyterian Church of Scotland, Paton's was not a glamorous mission field, but one that required hard work, courageous efforts, and great persistence. Shortly after his arrival, several missionaries were murdered. Within a year of his arrival, Paton's wife Mary and his newborn son died of fever. Alone on the island of Tanna, he labored for four years under constant threat of death, until he was driven off the island in February of 1862. He would spend the following four years in Australia and Great Britain galvanizing support for the mission work.

In 1864 Paton married again to Margaret, and together they returned to a smaller island in the chain, called Aniwa. After fifteen years of service on Aniwa, practically the entire population had turned to Christ. Eventually, other men joined him in the work, and Paton had the joy of seeing his own son, Rev. Frank Paton resume his efforts on the island of Tanna. Amazing conversions came about, chapels were built, Christian schools were organized, and gradually these islands once populated by cannibals gave way to a Christian way of life.

John and Margaret served together in missionary efforts for forty-one years until Margaret's death in 1905. John followed her two years later, dying on January 28, 1907. They lived to see the fruits of their labors, and by 1907 over 12,000 former cannibals of the New Hebrides had been converted and 133 native teachers had been trained and sent out as preachers and teachers of the Gospel to their own people. To this day, the majority of the population consider themselves Christian.

John G. Paton (1824—1907)

Of all the many island clusters of the South Pacific there is none, perhaps, which has so good a claim as the New Hebrides to be regarded as classic ground in the history of Christian missions. It was on Erromanga, one of this group, that John Williams, the greatest of all the missionaries of Oceania, the "Apostle of the South Seas," as he has justly been called, fell in death under the club of a fierce cannibal. And it was on Tanna, an adjacent island, that the veteran Dr. John G. Paton, a man not less apostolic than John Williams, began a career so full of intrepid action and hairbreadth escape and of thrilling adventure, mingled at times with dreadful tragedy, that more almost than any other in the missionary annals of modern times it serves to illustrate the saying, "Truth is stranger than fiction."

In 1858 Dr. Paton was sent out by the Reformed

Presbyterian Church of Scotland to begin his life work among the cannibals of the New Hebrides. Tanna was the island chosen for his sphere, an island hitherto untouched by Christianity; and the Tannese were among the most ferocious savages of those southern seas.

When he landed, war was afoot between an inland tribe and a tribe of the shore. He tells how, on the very first night that he spent on Tanna, five or six men who had been killed in the fighting were cooked and eaten at a neighboring spring, so that the next morning, when he wanted some water to make tea for his breakfast, the spring was so polluted with blood that it could not be used. On the second evening the quiet of the night was broken by a sound more blood curdling even than the howls of infuriated warriors—" a wild, wailing cry from the villages around, long-continued and unearthly." It told of the strangling of the widow, that she might accompany her dead husband into the other world and be his servant there as she had been here.

At first Mr. Paton had the companionship of his brave young wife amidst the trials and perils, which had daily to be faced. But in a few months she was cut off by fever, together with the little son who had just been born to them. The lonely man had to dig a grave with his own hands, and lay the bodies of his beloved ones in the dust. At this time, when he was almost distracted with grief, a providential visit from Bishop Selwyn and Mr. Coleridge Patteson in their Mission ship brought him the consolation of true Christian sympathy. "Standing with me," he writes, "beside the grave of mother and child, I weeping aloud on his one hand, and Patteson—afterwards the Martyr of Melanesia—sobbing silently on the other, the godly Bishop Selwyn poured out his heart to God amidst the sobs and tears, during which he laid his hands on my head, and invoked Heaven's richest consolations and blessings on me and my trying labors."

Strengthened by this angel visit from the noble pair of Church of England missionaries, Mr. Paton set to work once more, though day by day he was made to feel that his life hung by a single thread. Constantly the savages threatened him with death; sometimes during the night they made cowardly attempts upon his life. But in some way or other—the stumbling of an assailant, the barking of his trusty dog, the working of superstitious fear in the heathen heart—the danger was always turned aside.

One morning before daybreak Mr. Paton was wakened by the noise of shots being fired along the beach. He had brought a few native teachers from the Christian island of Aneityum to help him in his work, and one of these men rushed in breathlessly to say that six or seven natives had been shot dead to make provision for a great cannibal feast, and that the murderers were coming to kill Mr. Paton and the Aneityumese for the same purpose.

At once he called all the teachers into the house, locked the door, and barred the window. By and by the tramp of many approaching feet was heard. And all through the morning and the long forenoon the cannibals kept running round the house, whispering to one another, and hovering about the window and the door. But the expected attack was never made. The Tannese knew that Mr. Paton had a fowling piece and a revolver in the house; they did not know that he had vowed never to use them to destroy human lives. And the fear of these weapons in a white man's hands must have held them back, for towards noon they stole silently away, and held their gruesome feast without the additions of Christian victims.

Amidst scenes like this Mr. Paton went on steadily with his work, teaching all whom he could get to listen, mastering the language, translating parts of the Bible into Tannese, and printing them with a little printing-press that he had got from Scotland. He was greatly cheered at last by the arrival of another missionary, Mr. Johnston, who was accompanied by his wife. But not long after their arrival a painful tragedy befell.

It was New Year's night, and the Johnstons had joined Mr. Paton at family worship. Worship over, they retired to their own cabin, which was only a few yards off; but Mr. Johnston came back immediately to inform Mr. Paton that two men with painted faces were standing just outside his window armed with huge clubs.

Going out, Mr. Paton at once confronted these nocturnal visitors, and asked them what they wanted. "Medicine for a sick boy," they replied. He told them to come in and get it, but the agitation they showed, and their evident unwillingness to come into the light of the room, made him suspect that they had some murderous design. He allowed no sign of his thoughts to appear, however, but stepped, along with Mr. Johnston, into the house, followed by the two men; and, keeping a watchful eye on them all the while, quietly prepared the medicine.

When he came forward with it the men, instead of

taking it, tightened their grasp upon their killing-stones. But his steady gaze seemed to cow them, and when he sternly ordered them to leave the house they turned away.

At that moment Mr. Johnston stooped down to lift a little kitten of Mr. Paton's that was running out at the door, and instantly one of the savages leaped forward and aimed a blow at the stooping man. Mr. Johnston saw it coming, and in trying to avoid it rolled over and fell prostrate on the floor.

Quick as thought, Mr. Paton sprang in between his friend and the savages, upon which the two men turned on him and raised their stone clubs in the air to strike him down. He was saved by the courage and fidelity of his two dogs. One of them in particular, a little crossbred retriever with terrier's blood in him, showed the utmost boldness, and sprang furiously at the faces of the cannibals. The dog was badly hurt, but the savages were foiled, and at last they took to their heels through the door.

Accustomed to such scenes, Mr. Paton retired to rest, and slept soundly. With the newly arrived missionary it was otherwise. He had received a nervous shock, from which he never recovered; and in three weeks he was dead. Again Mr. Paton had to make a coffin and dig a grave. And then, he says, referring to the heart-broken young widow and himself, "We two alone at sunset laid him to rest close by the Mission House, beside my own dear wife and child."

Shortly after this a dreadful deed of blood was wrought on Erromanga, where John Williams had been murdered fully twenty years before. The Rev. Mr. Gordon and his wife, Presbyterian missionaries from Nova Scotia, had been settled on the island, and were making some inroads on its heathendom. But the sandalwood traders of the New Hebrides, a very debased set of men in those days, hated Mr. Gordon because he denounced their atrocities and warned the natives against their vices. In revenge they excited the superstitions of the Erromangans by persuading them that a plague of measles and a hurricane, both of which had recently visited the island, were brought about by Mr. Gordon. Thus the sandalwooders were responsible for a calamity which made Erromanga once more a martyr isle, and all but led to a scene of martyrdom on Tanna also.

One day, when Mr. Gordon was hard at work thatching a printing shed, in which he hoped to provide the Erromangans with the Word of God in their own tongue, two men came to him and begged for medicine. At once he left his work and started with them towards the Mission House. As he was stepping over a streamlet that ran across the path his foot slipped, and at that moment the two men were upon him with their tomahawks. A terrible blow on the spine laid him on the ground; a second on the neck almost parted his head from his body. Immediately a band of natives, who had been hiding in the surrounding bush, rushed out and danced in frantic joy round the dead missionary.

Meanwhile Mrs. Gordon, hearing the noise, came out of the house, wondering what had happened. The spot where her murdered husband lay was fortunately concealed from her eyes by a clump of trees. One of the natives approached her, and when she asked him what the noise meant, told her that it was only the boys amusing themselves. Then, as she turned to gaze once more in the direction of the shouting, he crept stealthily behind her, drove his tomahawk into her back, and severed her neck with his next blow.

Just after this double murder a sandalwood trader brought a party of Erromangans over to Tanna in his boat. These Erromangans urged the Tannese to kill Mr. Paton as they themselves had killed the Gordons; and though some of the Tanna chiefs refused to have anything to do with the business, the great majority of them began to cry aloud for the missionary's death. Crowds came flocking to the Mission House and shouting in Mr. Paton's hearing, "The men of Erromanga killed Missi Williams long ago, and now they have killed Missi Gordon. Let us kill Missi Paton too, and drive the worship of Jehovah from our land." Another favorite cry of the time, and one that boded ill for this "much-enduring" man, whose constant perils, adventures, and escapes recall the story of old Ulysses—was "Our love to the Erromangans! Our love to the Erromangans!"

At this juncture, just when Mr. Paton's life from day to day seemed to be hanging by a single hair, two British warships sailed into the harbor. Seeing the state of matters, the Commodore urged Mr. Paton to leave Tanna at once, and offered to convey him either to New Zealand, or to the island of Aneityum, where Christianity had obtained a firm footing. But though grateful for the Commodore's kindness, he firmly declined to leave his post. He knew that if he did so his station would immediately be broken up, and all the labors of the past three or four years would go for nothing. Moreover, in spite of all that had happened, in spite of the fact that so many of the people would willingly have put him to death, he loved those cruel savages with

DR. PATON'S LIFE SAVED BY HIS
FAITHFUL DOGS

that Christian love which sees the latent possibilities of goodness in the very worst of men. To him a troop of howling cannibals, literally thirsting for his blood, were his "dear benighted Tannese" after all.

It takes a hero to understand a hero. And it may help us to appreciate Mr. Paton's heroism in standing fast at what he felt to be the post of duty, when we find what Bishop Selwyn thought of it after hearing the whole story of the incident from Commodore Seymour's own lips. Describing to a friend how the brave Scotchman had declined to leave Tanna by *H.M.S Pelorus*, he added, "And I like him all the better for so doing." The following words in one of his letters show how high he rated Mr. Paton's conduct:-

"Talk of bravery! Talk of heroism! The man who leads a forlorn hope is a coward in comparison with him, who, on Tanna, thus alone, without a sustaining look or cheering word from one of his own race, regards it as his duty to hold on in the face of such dangers. We read of the soldier, found after the lapse of ages among the ruins of Herculaneum, who stood firm at his post amid the fiery rain destroying all around him, thus manifesting the rigidity of the discipline amongst those armies of ancient Rome which conquered the world. Mr. Paton was subjected to no such iron law. He might, with honor, when offered to him, have sought a temporary asylum in Auckland, where he would have been heartily received. But he was moved by higher considerations. He chose to remain, and God knows whether at this moment he is in the land of the living."

After the departure of the men-of-war, constant attempts were made on Mr. Paton's life. Sometimes

"YOU MUST KILL ME FIRST"

These were the brave words of a chief who, when many of the natives were intent on
killing Dr. Paton, sided with him and saved his life.

his empty revolver drove away his cowardly assailants. Frequently he was delivered by his perfect faith in the Divine protection and the confidence with which he asserted that faith. Once, for example, as he was going along a path in the bush, a man sprang suddenly from behind a bread-fruit tree, and swinging his tomahawk on high with a fiendish look, aimed it straight for Mr. Paton's brow. Springing aside, the missionary avoided the blow. And before the ruffian could raise his weapon a second time, he turned upon him and said in a voice in which there was no fear, "If you dare to strike me, my Jehovah God will punish you. He is here to defend me now." At once the man trembled from head to foot, and looked all around to see if this Jehovah God might not be standing near among the shadows.

Another time it seemed that the end had surely come. A conch shell was heard pealing out a warlike summons. Evidently it was a preconcerted signal, for the ominous notes had not died away before there was seen an immense multitude of armed savages advancing at the double down the slopes of a hill some distance off. Abandoning the Mission House, Mr. Paton along with his native teachers escaped through the bush to the village of a half-friendly chief some miles away; but it was not long till the savages were hot-foot on their trail.

The fugitives saw them coming, and knew that God alone could save them. "We prayed," says Dr. Paton, "as one can only pray when in the jaws of death." And then a strange thing happened. When about 300 yards off, the pursuers suddenly stood stock-still. The chief with whom he had taken refuge touched Mr. Paton's knee and said, "Missi, Jehovah is hearing!" and to this day Dr. Paton can give no other explanation of what took place. That host of warriors, to whom no opposition could possibly have been offered, hesitated, turned back, and disappeared into the forest.

At length there came what Dr. Paton's brother and editor describes as "the last awful night." Driven from his own station, Mr. Paton had succeeded, after encountering dreadful risks and hardships by sea and land, in joining Mr. and Mrs. Mathieson, who occupied another post of the Mission at the opposite end of Tanna. But soon the cannibals were on his track again, and the crisis came which led to the breaking up for a time of all Christian work on Tanna.

The Mission House was in a state of siege, and Mr. Paton, worn out with fatigue and constant watching, had fallen into a deep sleep. He was wakened by his faithful dog Clutha pulling at his clothes. Feeling sure that the instincts of the animal had not deceived it, and that even in the dead silence of the night it must have scented some danger, Mr. Paton wakened his companions.

Hardly had he done so when a glare of red light fell into the room. Then dark figures were seen flitting to and fro with blazing torches and making for the adjoining church, which was speedily in flames. Next the savages applied their torches to the reed fence by which the Mission House was connected with the church. And now the inmates knew that in a very few minutes the house also would be on fire, and that outside in the night armed savages would be waiting to strike them down with coward blows if they tried to make their escape.

Then it was that Mr. Paton performed a deed which, if done by a soldier on the field of battle, would be thought worthy of the Victoria Cross. Seizing the little American tomahawk with his right hand, and taking his empty revolver in the left, he issued suddenly from the door before the savages had closed in upon the house. Running towards the burning fence, he attacked that part of it which was still untouched by the fire, cutting it down with his tomahawk in a frenzy of haste, and hurling it back into the flames so that it might no longer serve as a conductor between the church and the house. At first the savages were spellbound by his boldness, but soon several of them leaped forward with clubs uplifted. Leveling his revolver at them, Mr. Paton dared them to strike him; and though they all urged one another to give the first blow, not one of them had the courage to do it.

So they stood facing each other in the lurid glow of the burning church, now flaring up through the midnight like a great torch—the intrepid white man and that band of bloodthirsty cannibals. And then there occurred something which the chief actor in this most dramatic scene never ceased to attribute to the direct interposition of God. A rushing, roaring sound came out of the south, like the muttering of approaching thunder. Every head was turned instinctively in that direction, for the natives knew by experience that a tornado was about to burst upon them.

In another moment it fell. Had it come from the north, no power on earth could have saved the Mission House and its inmates; but coming from the quarter exactly opposite, it swept the flames backwards and destroyed every chance of the house taking fire. And on the heels of the loud hurricane there came a lashing torrent of tropical rain, which before long extinguished the fire altogether. With this furious onset of the elements a panic seized the savages. "This is Jehovah's rain," they cried. And in a few moments every one of them had disappeared into the darkness, leaving Mr. Paton free to rejoin Mr. Mathieson and his wife in perfect safety.

That was Mr. Paton's last night on Tanna. The next morning the *Blue Bell*, a trading vessel, came sailing into the bay, and by it the missionaries were rescued from their now desperate situation and taken to Aneityum. Both Mr. and Mrs. Mathieson died soon after. The strain of their experiences on Tanna had been too great. But in Mr. Paton's case those years of trial and apparent defeat proved but his apprenticeship for the extraordinary work he has accomplished since.

His labors were first rewarded on the island of Aniwa, which lies between Tanna and Erromanga. The natives there, though cannibals too, were less violent and brutal than the Tannese. Dr. Paton tells how, in clearing ground to build himself a house on Aniwa, he gathered off that little spot of earth two large baskets of human bones. Pointing to them, he said to an Aniwan chief: "How do these bones come to be here?" "Ah," replied the native, with a shrug worthy of a cynical Frenchman, "we are not Tanna men! We do not eat the bones!" The tale of Mr. Patton's life in Aniwa is as thrilling as any in the annals of the Missionary Church. But that, as Mr. Kipling would say, is another story, and cannot be told here.

Nor can we do more than allude to the adventures of Mr. Paton's wanderings through the Australian bush and over the cities of England and Scotland in connection with the building of the *Dayspring*, or rather of a succession of *Daysprings*, for shipwreck was a common thing in those coral-studded seas, and the time came besides when for mission work, as for other work, the ship of sails had to give place to the ship of steam.

And to come back to Tanna again, it can only be said that fruit appeared at length in "that hardest field in Heathendom." Dr. Paton had the joy of seeing other men enter into his labors, and the peculiar joy of giving his own son, the Rev. Frank Paton, to that same island where he toiled in loneliness and tears till driven from its shores by the savages themselves. His patient sufferings no less than his unselfish work helped to bring about at last a relenting of the Tannese heart. His early ploughshare, we might say, driven through the hard soil, opened the way for the hopeful sowers and glad reapers who came in due season.

NOTES AND AUTHORITIES: The author desires to acknowledge his special obligations to the Rev. James Paton, D.D., minister of St. Paul's Church, Glasgow, who is Dr. John G. Paton's brother and the editor of his works, for allowing him to make use of both the *Autobiography* and *The Story of John G. Paton*.

KAPIOLANI AND THE GODDESS OF THE VOLCANO

CHAPTER TWENTY-ONE

FROM THE EDITORS: How wondrous are the works of God in governing the course of nations and of men, to accomplish his plan, whether for judgment or for redemption! The history of missions in Hawaii began in such an amazing way that there could be no doubt but that God, in his providence, saw fit to show mercy to those island peoples.

In 1820, seventeen missionaries sailed for the Hawaiian Islands, sent by the American Board of Foreign Missions. On arrival, one of the missionaries named Mr. Bishop, undertook evangelism around the main island of Hawaii. One of his early converts was Kapiolani, the high chieftainess of Kaavaroa.

While not a missionary in the traditional sense, Kapiolani devoted herself to Jehovah God, and may have than anyone else done more to bring Hawaiians to Christ. She was born the daughter of Keawe-mau-hili, high chief of the Hilo region. In time, she married Na-ihe, high chief of the Kona region on the western side of Hawaii. After hearing the preaching of Mr. Bishop and other missionaries in 1822, both Na-ihe and Kapiolani were among the first Hawaiian tribal leaders to convert. This is the story of the Queen who demonstrated remarkable faith and turned her people to the true and living God.

Kapiolani (dates unknown)

One morning in the second decade of the nineteenth century, as some Yale students passed up the college steps on their way to their classrooms, they found sitting at the entrance door a dark-skinned lad who was crying silently. When they asked who he was and what was wrong, he told them in his broken English a story at once strange and sad.

He was a native of the Hawaiian Islands. In one of the constant and barbarous inter-tribal fights, his home had been destroyed by the victors and his father and mother cut down before his eyes. Taking his infant brother on his back, he had tried to escape, but was soon noticed, pursued, and overtaken. A ruthless spear was thrust through the body of the child he bore, while he himself was seized and dragged away into slavery.

He had gained his liberty by hiding himself on board an American ship which had called at Hawaii and was homeward bound for New Haven, Connecticut. On the long voyage round Cape Horn he was treated kindly enough, but when the vessel reached its destination he was of no use to anyone, and was turned adrift to follow his own devices.

Unlike Neesima of Japan, of whom at some points his story reminds us, Opukahaia, for that was the name of this Hawaiian lad, had no Mr. Hardy waiting for him in the strange port. But as he roamed about the town, wondering what was to become of him, he came to Yale College, and saw the bands of students passing in and out. In the few words of English which he had picked up from the sailors he asked a passer-by what that great building was, and why those young men kept coming and going. He was told that this was a school of learning, and that those who entered its walls did so that wise men might teach them all that it was best to know.

Now though a Pacific islander and half a savage, Opukahaia had that same thirst for knowledge which delighted Dr. Samuel Johnson so greatly when he discovered it one day in a young waterman who was rowing him across the Thames, and which frequently appears in persons who would hardly be suspected of having any intellectual tastes at all. In this youth from Hawaii, with his dark skin and restless eyes and broken speech, there burned an eager longing to know much more than he did, and especially to learn the secret of the white man's wisdom. It seemed natural to him to turn his feet towards the College, since there, it seemed, the fountain of truth and knowledge was to be found.

But when he climbed the steps and reached the portal his heart had failed him utterly; and that was why the students found him crouching there that morning with the tears rolling down his cheeks.

His questioners were half-amused by this curious tale. But there were kind men among them, and many kind and Christian hearts among the good folk of the old Puritan town. An interest was awakened in Opukahaia, which led to his being provided for, and taught not only something of the wisdom of the white men, but the great saving truths of the Christian faith.

After some years had passed, Opukahaia felt that he must go back to his own islands and tell his people the good news that he had learned himself. But meanwhile the story of this Hawaiian youth had become widely known, and an interest in him and his country had grown up among the American Churches. The American Board of Foreign Missions took up the matter, and decided to begin missionary work in the Hawaiian Islands. The scheme was entered into with a great deal of popular enthusiasm. And when at length in 1820 the pioneers set sail on their long voyage round the South American continent, the party included no fewer than seventeen persons besides Opukahaia himself.

In a very real sense Opukahaia may be looked upon as the founder of the American mission in Hawaii. If he had not sat weeping some years before on the doorstep of Yale College, that band of missionaries would never have sailed in the *Thaddeus* for those far-off heathen islands. But here his share in the enterprise comes to an end. He was not destined to carry the Gospel to his countrymen. The harsh New England winters had been too much for one born amidst the soft, warm breezes of the Pacific Ocean. He died of a decline, and it was left to others to carry out that idea, which his mind had been the first to conceive, of giving to the Hawaiian people the blessings of a Christian civilization.

Beginning so romantically, the story of this American

expedition grew even more wonderful as time went on. Perhaps there has never been in the whole history of Protestant missions another record of such rapid and wholesale transformation of a degraded heathen race as took place in connection with this enterprise which had been inspired by the strange vision of a Sandwich Islander knocking at the gates of a Christian college. The Rev. Titus Coan, for example, one of the leading figures of that stirring period, baptized more than 1,700 persons on a single Sunday, and in one year received considerably more than 5,000 men and women into the full communion of the Church. Persons who up to the time of their conversion had lived the lawless life of the savage—robbers, murderers, drunkards, the former high priests of a cruel idolatry, "their hands but recently washed from the blood of human victims"—all assembled together in Christian peace and love to partake of the sacrament of the Lord's Supper. As Dr. A.T. Pierson remarks in his *New Acts of the Apostles*, the transforming energies which swept through the islands in the early years of the Mission "find no adequate symbols but those volcanic upheavals with which the Kanakas are familiar." And yet, sudden as it was, this was no transient emotional result. It was a reconstruction of the community from its very base, "the permanent creation of an orderly, decorous, peaceful Christian State."

Of all the arresting incidents of this great religious revolution, the most dramatic is one which took place within the very crater of Kilauea, the largest and most awful of the active volcanoes of the world. In this dread amphitheatre, on the very brink of the eternal "Fire Fountains of Hawaii,"

Kapiolani, the high chieftainess of Kaavaroa, openly challenged and defied Pélé, the indwelling goddess of the volcano, as every Hawaiian believed. Her act has been likened to that of Boniface at Geismar, when with his axe he hewed down the venerable oak which had been sacred for centuries to Thor the Thunderer, while those around looked on with the fascination of horror, expecting every moment to see him struck dead by a bolt from heaven. Still more aptly the incident is compared by Miss Gordon Cumming to the great scene on Carmel, when Elijah challenged the idolatrous priests of Baal in the name of Israel's God.

In 1825 one of the missionaries, the Rev. Mr. Bishop, made a preaching tour right round the main island of Hawaii. An adventurous tour it was, for he constantly had to clamber on hands and knees up the face of precipitous cliffs, and to make his way over rugged lava beds or across deep gullies and swollen mountain torrents. At other times it was necessary to skirt the frowning rocky coast in a frail canoe, so as to circumvent those inland barriers that could not be crossed.

The native villages were often difficult to find, hidden as they were in almost inaccessible glens. But whenever this brave, adventurous preacher stood face to face with the people, the most wonderful results followed, and he was amply repaid for all his danger and toils.

Among the converts of that time was Kapiolani, the most noted of all the female chiefs of Hawaii, who ruled over large possessions in the southern part of the main island. Previous to this, she had been intensely superstitious, and like most of the natives, had lived a reckless and intemperate life. Now she was utterly changed. First she set herself to reform her own life, dismissing all her husbands but one, who like herself professed Christianity, and adopting strictly sober habits. Next she did her utmost to uproot idolatrous notions and customs among her people, putting down infanticide, murder, drunkenness, and robbery with a firm hand, and without counting the possible cost to herself.

She soon realized that the great obstacle to the progress of the Gospel among the Hawaiians was their superstitious faith in the divinities of Kilauea, and above all in Pélé herself, the grim and terrible goddess who was supposed to have her dwelling-place within the crater of the burning mountain. Pélé had her retinue of priests and prophets, both male and female, whose hold upon the popular imaginations was nothing short of tremendous. Their false teaching seemed to be reinforced by the great volcano with its smoking summit—an ever-present reality in the eyes of all. Its frequent eruptions revealed the might of the unseen goddess. The deep thunders of Kilauea were Pélé's own voice. The long filaments spun by the wind from the liquid lava and tossed over the edge of the crater were Pélé's dusky, streaming hair. And those priests and priestesses who offered daily sacrifice to her divinity were the living oracles of her will. Upon their most cruel and licentious dictates and practices there rested the sanctions of the invisible world.

Kapiolani saw quite clearly that the power of the fire goddess must be broken before Christianity could spread in Hawaii. She accordingly resolved to challenge that power in its innermost stronghold and sanctuary, by defying Pélé to her face on the very floor of the crater of Kilauea.

When she announced her intentions to her followers, they did everything they could to hold her back from such a project. Even her husband, though himself a professing Christian, begged her to abstain from a deed so rash and dangerous. But to all expostulations she had one reply. "All *tabus*," she said, "are done away. We are safe in the keeping of the Almighty God, and no power on earth or hell can harm His servants." When her people saw how determined she was they gave up trying to dissuade her, and about eighty of them were even so bold as to volunteer to accompany her to the summit of the fiery mountain.

From Kapiolani's home Kilauea was distant about one hundred miles in a straight line. To reach it was a toilsome journey—a journey which took her and her companions over jagged mountain peaks and rough lava-beds. But no detour would she make. She pressed straight on towards the volcano, over which there ever hung a dark pall of smoke by day, a lurid cloud of fire by night.

As she advanced, the people came in crowds out of the valleys to watch the progress of this strange pilgrimage. Many of them implored her to turn back ere it was too late, and not to draw down upon herself and others the vengeance of the fire-gods. But this was her invariable reply: "If I am destroyed, you may all believe in Pélé; but if I am not destroyed, you must all turn to the only true God."

At length, after a most fatiguing march, this bold champion of the new faith reached the base of Kilauea and began the upward ascent. As she approached the cone, one of Pélé's weird prophetesses appeared and warned her back in the name of the goddess. In her hand this Hawaiian pythoness held a piece of white bark-cloth, and as she waved it above her head she declared it to be a message from Pélé herself. "Read the message!" exclaimed Kapiolani. Upon which the woman held the pretended oracle before her, and poured out a flood of gibberish, which she declared to be an ancient sacred dialect. Kapiolani smiled. "You have delivered a message from your god," she said, "which none of us can understand. I too have a *pala pala*, and I will read you a message from *my* God, which every one will understand." Whereupon she opened her Hawaiian Bible and read several passages that told of Jehovah's almighty power and of the heavenly Father's saving love in Jesus Christ.

Still pressing on, Kapiolani came at length to the very edge of the vast crater, which lies one thousand feet below the summits of the enclosing cone, and led the way down the precipitous descent towards the black lava-bed. On the crater's brink there grew, like the grapes of Vesuvius, clusters of the refreshing *ohelo* berry, sacred to Pélé herself, which no Hawaiian of those days would taste till he had first cast a laden branch down the precipice towards the fiery lake, saying as he did so, "Pélé, here are your *ohelos*. I offer some to you; some I also eat"—a formula which was supposed to render the eating safe, but without which an awful *tabu* would be infringed.

Seeing the berries hanging all around her, Kapiolani stopped and ate of them freely without making any acknowledgment to the goddess. She then made her way slowly down into the bowl of the crater, and when she reached the bottom, walked across the undulating crust of

THE QUEEN DEFIES THE
GODDESS OF THE VOLCANO

The natives of Hawaii held the goddess of the volcanic mountain of Pele in the greatest
dread. The Queen, when she became a Christian, saw that the superstition must
be broken down. This she achieved by flaunting the authority of the goddess in the
volcano itself, and in the presence of some of her terrified people.

lava till she came to the *Halemaumau* itself, the "House of Everlasting Burning." Standing there, she picked up broken fragments of lava and flung them defiantly towards the seething cauldron, which writhed and moaned and flung out long hissing tongues of red and purple flame.

Having thus desecrated Pélé's holy of holies in the most dreadful manner of which a Hawaiian imagination could conceive, she now turned to her trembling followers, who stood at some distance behind, and in a loud clear voice, distinctly heard above all the deep whispers and mutterings of the volcano, she spoke these words, which were engraved forever afterwards on the memories of all who heard them: "My God is Jehovah. He it was who kindled these fires. I do not fear Pélé. Should I perish by her wrath, then you may fear her power. But if Jehovah saves me while I am breaking her *tabus*, then you must fear and love Him. The gods of Hawaii are vain."

Kapiolani then called upon her people to kneel down on that heaving floor and offer a solemn act of adoration to the One Almighty God, and thereafter to join their voices with hers in a hymn of joyful praise. And so by Christian praise and prayer the very crater of Kilauea, formerly the supposed abode of a cruel goddess, was consecrated as a temple to the God of holiness and love.

The news of Kapiolani's bold deed soon ran from end to end of Hawaii. It sent a shiver of despair through the hearts of Pélé's priests and votaries. Every one felt that the old dominion of the fire-gods must be tottering to its fall. Ere long the people began to turn in crowds from their idolatries. Even the heathen priests and priestesses renounced their allegiance to dark and bloody alters, and made professions of their faith in Christ.

One day a sinister figure presented itself before one of the missionaries, among a number of people who were waiting to receive some Christian instruction. It was a man whose gruesome office it had been, in the service of Pélé's alter, to hunt and catch victims that were needed for the human sacrifices demanded by the goddess. This dreadful being had acquired the skill of a wild beast in lurking in the by-paths of the forests to leap upon the passers-by, and was possessed of such enormous strength besides that he could break the bones of his victims by simply enfolding them in his iron embrace. No wonder that on seeing him the people shrank back in terror as if from some monster of the jungle. But even this man was conquered by the Gospel of love and peace, and turned from serving Pélé to follow Jesus Christ.

In the larger centers of population the natives gathered in vast multitudes to listen to the missionaries. More than once Mr. Bishop preached to assemblages that numbered upwards of ten thousand persons. Other chiefs and chieftainesses followed Kapiolani's example by openly professing their Christian faith. One chief showed his earnestness and zeal by building a church large enough to accommodate four thousand people. For weeks his whole tribe flung themselves joyously into the task—hewing timber in the forests, dragging it to the appointed place, cutting reeds for the thatch, and binding it carefully to the roof.

If ever there were romantic days in the history of a Christian mission, such days were experienced by those who witnessed the sudden glory of the Christian dawn that rose upon the Hawaiian Islands, flushing mountain, shore, and ocean with the radiance of the skies. There were giants and heroes, moreover, in those days; for pioneers like Mr. Bishop and Titus Coan deserve to be described by no lesser words. But so long as men tell the wonderful story of the spread of Christianity over the islands of Oceania and recall the heroes and heroines of the past, the figure of Kapiolani will stand out bravely, as she is seen in the strength of her new-born faith defying Pélé's wrath in the dark crater of Kilauea.

NOTES AND AUTHORITIES: The story of the American Mission to Hawaii, and in particular the incident of Kapiolani's challenge to the fire-goddess, are drawn almost entirely from Miss C.F. Gordon Cumming's *Fire Fountains: The Kingdom of Hawaii* (William Blackwood and Sons), which she has generously permitted the author to make free use of for the purposes of this book.

HISTORY OF THE WORLD

The Transforming Influence of Jesus Christ

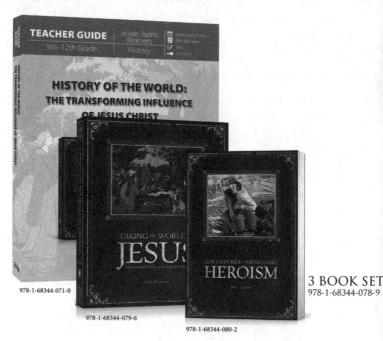

978-1-68344-071-0

978-1-68344-079-6

978-1-68344-080-2

3 BOOK SET
978-1-68344-078-9

A study of world history that examines the spread of the Gospel and the growth of the Church.

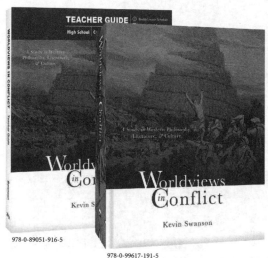